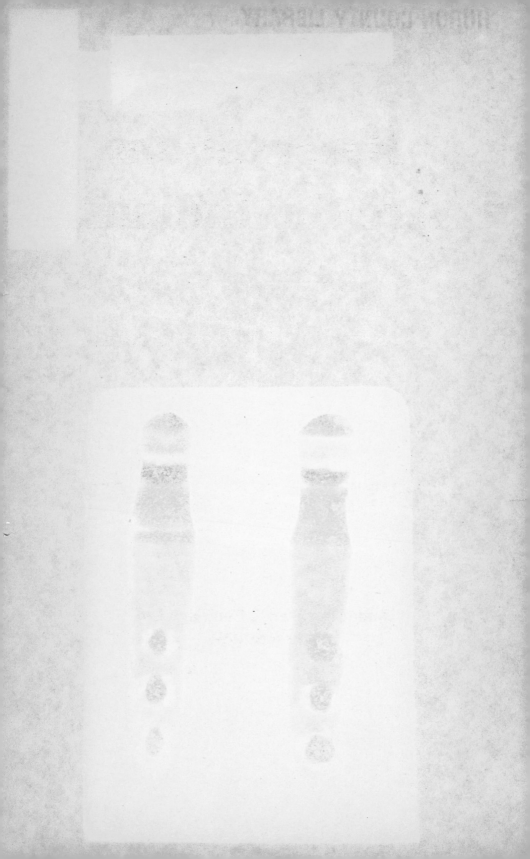

Reservations
Are for Indians

Second Edition

Heather Robertson

James Lorimer & Company Ltd.
Toronto 1991

Canadian Cataloguing in Publication Data

    Robertson, Heather, 1942-
       Reservations are for Indians
    2nd ed.
    ISBN 1-55028-367-7 (bound)   ISBN 1-55028-365-0 (pbk.)
    1. Indians of North America - Canada. I Title.

578.02R6 1991 971'.00497 C91-095274-4

Cover art: Patricia Deadman

James Lorimer & Company, Publishers
Egerton Ryerson Memorial Building
35 Britain Street
Toronto, Ontario
M5A 1R7

Printed and bound in Canada

Contents

Preface

The idea for this book came to me in the late winter of 1965 when an anxious but determined band of Indians marched through the streets of Kenora, Ontario. Their demonstration was peaceful, their demands for jobs and justice were reasonable, but for Indians to behave in such an organized and politically sophisticated way was revolutionary. The civil rights movement in the United States was clearly having an impact in Canada, and we were entering a new era of confrontation.

I was 23, a recent university graduate steeped in the academic social analysis of the New Left and a rookie reporter with *The Winnipeg Tribune*. I was not assigned to the Kenora story, but the photographs of the demonstration in the press made an indelible impression on my mind. I had never seen photographs of Indians before. I had seen Indians in Kenora and in Minaki to the north, and I had watched them posing for tourists in front of the Hudson's Bay Company store, picturesque in their plaid shawls and calico skirts, but I had not seen them in the context of my own expectations and experience. My experience was white, middle class, conventional and constricted; Indians were beyond the pale, dark and invisible people, my shadow caught in the glare of a flashbulb.

Who were they, and who was I? Finding out became my Centennial project. In 1966 I entered a competition sponsored by Imperial Tobacco to write a book about Canada in the year 2000. Approaching this theme in terms of the status of Canada's Indians seemed very tenuous at the time, although prescient now, and my proposal was one of 10 accepted. I received $3,000 and a deadline of September 1, 1967; the winning writer would get a prize of $30,000 and a publisher.

It was hard to know where to begin. There was very little literature on Canada's Indians, and almost nothing written by Indians themselves. The literature focused on crafts and folklore, and much of it was written by priests, who depicted their native flocks as simple, childlike folk who had to be sheltered from the evil world of the white man. The standard book, *The Indians of Canada* by sociologist Diamond Jenness, had been published in 1932. Jenness confidently predicted that Indians would become extinct by the time I was writing. They were not.

Finding Indians was difficult. Indian reserves were not marked on road maps, and in the north many were virtually inaccessible. The Department of Indian Affairs provided me with maps and advice. I was told that there were "good" Indians and "bad" Indians. The Six Nations Indians were considered to be "good"; the Ojibwa "bad." I quickly understood that Indians were evaluated according to the degree of white "civilization" they had acquired. I decided to stick with the bad guys.

I was terrified. I was warned that I would be raped, assaulted or murdered if I set foot on an Indian reserve. The Indians on Winnipeg's Main Street were frightening enough—drunk, raucous and violent— and in Kenora many of the Indians I had seen on the street were crippled or scarred from knife wounds. My friends thought I was crazy: I should go to Yorkville and smoke pot, a much more dangerous adventure as it turned out.

The first reserves I visited produced paralyzing culture shock: I had never seen such heartbreaking poverty or been among people with whom I could not communicate. The language barrier was formidable: the old people spoke no English, the young spoke obliquely, drawing from a life experience so opposite to my own I could not comprehend it.

Yet everywhere I was met with courtesy, honesty and a wry sense of humor. Most Indians had never met a white woman who wasn't a teacher or a nurse, and I was an object of intense curiosity. I felt like Alice down the rabbit hole, but I was a reporter, and I tried to behave like one. Unlike the sociologists and anthropologists who stampeded after me, I did not invite myself to live in people's homes or presume to become "part of the community," an assumption I considered as intrusive as a stranger inviting herself into my house to study me. I stayed in hotels or with other members of the "outside" power structure, an option that gave me a privileged insight into the colonial bureaucracy that ran the reservation system.

The reservation system is what this book is about. Canada's reservation system was established at gunpoint more than 100 years ago, justified by fraudulent treaties and enforced by the law. Deprived of their traditional lands in the interests of agriculture or electricity, Indians were confined to small parcels of communal territory. For generations they were not allowed to leave their reserves, to drink liquor, own property or vote. Thousands died of smallpox, tuberculosis, influenza and venereal disease, all plagues introduced by white conquistadors, and thousands more died of hunger and despair. Corrupt Indian agents sold Indian land without permission; Indians were forbidden to establish businesses, run their own local councils or teach their children in their own language. Missionaries substituted Christianity for Indian pantheism; residential schools deprived Indian children of their homes, their culture and their dignity and abused them emotionally and sexually in return.

Most Indians fled the reserve. Many were bribed to give up their Indian status; others wanted to make their own way. They are part of our society, our next-door neighbors: some very famous Canadians have Indian ancestry, although it is not something they mention in *Who's Who*. This book is about those Indians who remained on the reserves, the hard-core Indians, and it is about survival.

Surviving against all odds, against all the genocidal ideology and practice of the British Empire, is at once their miracle and their nemesis. When I arrived on the scene in the late sixties, it was obvious that most Indian reserves could not support their exploding populations: they had no economy, no tax base and hundreds of hungry mouths to feed. All income came from the federal government or from casual labor outside the reserve; the family allowance cheque was the highlight of the month, and the family allowance, small as it was, encouraged women to bear more children. The reservation system is a Darwinian experiment where only the fittest survive. The survivors are very fit, but the casualty rate is appalling.

Reservations Are for Indians was the first book by a white writer to confront Indian drunkenness, dependency, violence and suicide. Drunkenness was obvious, so ubiquitous it was a puzzle to judges and police officers as well as everyone else, and sociologists developed whole schools of thought on the reasons for it. I said it was political, a form of aggressive behavior the American writer Tom Wolfe called "Mau-Mauing," and I still think so. As a woman, I could understand dependency, and I found violence in Indian communities to be largely domestic, although because of the lack of privacy much more public than in white suburbia. When I discovered that many accidents involving Indians were suicide, I had difficulty believing my own evidence, yet in the subsequent 20 years, suicide has been revealed as epidemic on many Indian reserves, especially among teenagers and young women. At the same time, more Indian children are finishing high school and university, band councils are running their own businesses, the standard of living has increased and Indians are organizing their own community services.

I have not gone back to the communities I visited in 1966 and 1967. By the time this book was first published in the spring of 1970, I knew that Indians would write their own stories, and this book is really about my personal confrontation with the corrupt and racist society that was my own. It reflects my anger, innocence and cultural bias: I didn't win the $30,000, but I did come out with double vision. I will never know what it feels like to be an Indian because I'm not, but I can grasp what that feeling is.

When I began my research, I approached a Canadian publisher who stated that Indians were "boring" and I should not bother with the idea. Later, my finished manuscript sat in various of his editors' basements for more than a year, possibly because it was approximately 1,000 pages long. In December, 1969 *The Unjust Society* by Alberta native leader Harold Cardinal created a sensation, and *Reservations,* cut by two-thirds, was published in April, 1970 by James Lorimer under the imprint James Lewis & Samuel.

It wasn't boring at all. The book sold more than 10,000 copies in the first few months. It was praised as revelation and denounced as racist. I am told that a group of Indians from Alberta traveled to The

Pas, Manitoba to denounce my portrayal of Indian prostitution, only to discover the same pitiful crowd of teenage girls in the bars that I had seen; one Indian girl in The Pas, Helen Betty Osborne, was stabbed to death by a gang of white boys in 1968, a year after I was there.

I did not anticipate that the Indian political movement that emerged in 1965 would today be a major force in Canadian society. In retrospect, I see that I was too pessimistic. I failed to recognize the endurance, common sense and basic morality that have enabled Indians to surmount persecution and deprivation. In the spring of 1990, an Indian armed with an eagle feather, Elijah Harper, rose in the Manitoba Legislature to say no to an accord between Canada and Quebec that would have left the First Nations in limbo, and the accord failed. That summer, Indians of the Kahnawake reserve in Quebec barricaded the bridge to Montreal in a dispute over Indian land; a Quebec police officer was killed and the stand-off created a crisis that is still unresolved. Indians are rediscovering their religion and their history and their identity. An immense literature on Indian affairs, by Indians, has sprung to life in the past 25 years, and Indian artists are creating a native renaissance in Canadian drama and poetry.

But the casualty rate is still appalling. Indian politicians are all male, and Indian politics is financed by the Department of Indian Affairs. Government support seems to be predicated on a belief that all Indians must be represented by one leader, a stratagem as absurd and destructive as the suggestion that all women could be represented by one matriarch. Although we spend billions of dollars supporting Indian communities, most reserves remain without an economic base, and while the income level is higher, the employment level is not. Some bands are now surviving on compensation payments for having had their lives destroyed by hydro projects and mercury pollution. What will be next?

Indian self-government appears to be next, but since Indians, because of their special treaty status, do not pay property taxes, how is this going to work? The concentration camp was invented in Canada and transplanted to South Africa, where it flourished and grew into apartheid. Will Canadian Indians be prepared to work "outside" for wages and live in a self-governing Indian "homeland"? In South Africa, blacks have no choice; in Canada, Indians do, and in the past they have voted with their feet.

The trick will be to become an Indian and a Canadian at the same time, a trick we immigrants are still learning how to do in our own racial and cultural terms. It ain't easy, but we all have the same balls in the air. The most dramatic and unexpected change since I wrote this book more than 20 years ago has been the complete turn-around in the attitudes of white Canadians towards Indians: racism has been supplanted by guilt, bigotry by sympathy. This transformation has a great deal to do with Indian respect for the land and our common survival.

Heather Robertson
June, 1991

We are different than we used to be.

The government has us in a little box, with a lid on it. Every now and then they open the lid and do something to us and close it again.

We are a dying race. Not this generation but the next, will die.

— Willie Denechoan, medicine man,
Hay Lake

A little while and I will be gone from among you, whither I cannot tell. From nowhere we come and into nowhere we go. What is life? It is a flash of a firefly in the night. It is a breath of the buffalo in the wintertime. It is the little shadow that runs across the grass and loses itself in the sunset.

— Chief Crowfoot,
just before his death,
1890

Chapter 1
Blueberries

I don't remember the first time I saw Indians, but I must have been very young. In my youth, riding the C.N.R. main line, I saw them many times, staring from the train window while the men loaded baskets of blueberries onto the baggage cars. I passed that scene so many times that it is fixed in my mind like a picture, and is always exactly the same.

"Look at the Indians! The Indians are here." The phrase, with the magic word, passes from family to family down the crowded day coaches. People rush to push their faces against the windows on the side of the train where you can see best, and the kids poke to the front to get a good view. Three white canvas tents are pitched in a clump in the trees on the top of the granite rocks sloping up from the railway embankment, only a few yards from the tracks, on eye-level with the train windows. The tents are not teepee style, but more like big pup tents with the door flaps drawn back on either side. They are surprisingly white in the sun except where they are blotched with mildew or flickering shadows from the poplar leaves. They are pitched in a rough semi-circle, the doors all facing towards the tracks. The earth in front has been trampled black. A fire burns in the middle, and something stews over the flames in a big blackened pot which looks like an old lard tin with parts of the red label not burned off yet. Beyond the smoke and steam, bright pieces of clothing hang on lines strung between the tents.

A woman, standing to the left of the fire, turns her face toward the train, her body still half-facing the flames. She has a long-handled spoon or ladle in her hand, as if, still stooped, we had surprised her in the act of stirring. Her face is blank, abstracted, far-away. She doesn't straighten up; her expression doesn't change; she doesn't assume the expected posture of curiosity, interest, indifference or annoyance. She is looking at the train and at the faces peering out at her, but she does not see us. She doesn't go back to her cooking either. She just stands there, suspended, a mark on the landscape. Maybe she can't straighten up. Her back is bony, hunched, her shoulders rounded and stooped. She is hollow-chested. Her full red and blue flower-patterned skirt makes strange lumps over her hips and hangs, draggle-tailed, past her ankles. Her feet are encased in something shapeless. Strange bits and ends of cloth hang out past her hem and under her royal blue cardigan sweater. There is nothing to relate her clothes to her and they could belong to anyone of indiscriminate shape, or to no one. Her breasts have sunk to her waist. She is twisted out of kilter, jumbled, her dark face all wrinkles, like smoked leather, all one color, lips, eyes, everything. Even at this distance, it is plain how large and gnarled her hands are. Some half-naked small children stand motionless and stare. A man, in plaid shirt and blue, stained trousers sagging from wide suspenders, sits in the shade near the tent door, smoking and gazing at us.

A chubby little girl in a striped T-shirt, an egg salad sandwich stuffed in my mouth, I watch them with impassive, indifferent curiosity from the musty train coach, much as I look at those illuminated boxes in the museum which display sad stuffed prairie dogs in a painted bright green illuminated setting. The glass keeps out the noise of voices and the smell of burning wood.

I didn't wonder about what was in the blackened lard pail over the fire or how much the family was in debt to the Hudson's Bay store for the tent and their clothes, or what the price for blueberries was that year and how much welfare money they got when the profits were gone. They looked very strange but that was fine—they were Indians.

I belong to the place where the blueberries go and the trains come from.

Blueberries we had in common. I had picked enough blueberries to know how long it took in sweaty, backbreaking, hunched-over, mosquito-bitten, scorching heat to pick one quart jug full of berries. Imagine picking berries all day every day for weeks! And then not being able to eat them. I was appalled.

"How can the Indians pick so many berries? " I asked my mother, contemplating the heaps of three-quart baskets on the station platform.

"They don't pick clean," she said. "Indians use scrapers

which take off all the leaves and green berries at the same time. It's fast, but they pick dirty."

In the summer of 1966, when I started driving through Western Canada in search of Indians, it appeared that a civil rights movement was underway among Canada's Indians. There had been two important demonstrations in 1965: the Indians of Hay Lake, Alberta, marched on the Legislature in Edmonton, and the Kenora Indians marched on the city council. These actions by Indians were unprecedented in western Canada and to many they were astonishing. Although both marches failed when the Indians were bought off with welfare and token concessions, many people, especially those in government, were jolted and the stereotype of the lazy, apathetic Indian was broken. Bureaucrats in the Department of Indian Affairs, accustomed to speak of Indians as helpless, naive and politically inept, were seriously embarrassed. Indians from the most isolated areas of the country were suddenly showing initiative, intelligence and political sophistication. And as a result of these demonstrations, although Indian Affairs officials continue to speak of Indians as helpless and inept, now fewer people believe them. Most important, the Indians no longer believe them.

I spent eight months, off and on, from May, 1966 to April, 1967, travelling in western and northern Canada before starting to write. I am not sure yet exactly why I did it. It was mostly a need for adventure, but also, like many of my friends, I had a lot of romantic ideas. The motives of those of us who went west to the Indians in 1965 and 1966 were similar to the impulses which sent many American college students to the South a few years earlier. I believed vaguely in liberty, democracy and the North American way of life. I believed that people were basically good, honest and well-meaning, and that skin color made no difference. I identified with the poor and oppressed, but nevertheless, I was prejudiced. I had the typical, unconscious middle class liberal inhibitions, basically a fear of losing caste. I was afraid of Indians, afraid of physical assault, of being insulted or put down, of being made a fool of, of misunderstanding.

My inhibition was mainly the result of recent mythologies about Indians, reports that Indians beat up white people on impulse, that they are a silent, uncommunicative race, that they are intrinsically different. These ideas came mainly from conversations with Indian Affairs people and other Indian experts before I visited reserves. It is common for these people to say "you have to get to know Indians." This process, it is revealed, takes from 10 to 40 years, and is usually directly related to the length of the expert's own tenure in the Indian industry. The experts, of course, "know Indians," and frequently suggest that one has to live with Indians over an extended period of time. Many Indian agents crow loudly about their intimate knowledge of the Indian character after five years spent in government houses in the vicinity of a reserve.

The experts also like to range various Indian tribes and reserves on the scale of humanity. I heard many times that the Saulteaux or Ojibwa are the "lowest" kind of Indian and the Iroquois the "most civilized". Similarly, I was told that certain reserves were "bad places", containing a "very poor type" of Indian, and that other reserves were "more advanced, a higher type." The experts described Indians, often in hushed tones, as peculiar, irrational, violent, immoral, and in spite of their professed knowledge, confessed themselves baffled by Indian actions. They could see no reasons for what Indians did, no connection between their actions. Although many were critical of Indian Affairs, they could see no relation between government policies and the behavior of the Indians themselves.

So utterly fallacious, misleading and mischievous is the information given out by white people about Indians, that it is impossible for Canadians not to be racist in their attitudes. The surprise caused by my intention to visit reserves indicates the gulf between Indians and other Canadians. My visits were regarded, by Indian experts as well as others, as completely stupid and wasteful of time. Reserves were places where do-gooders and social workers went. I began to feel self-conscious about it, suspecting my own motives. I was amazed too at the sheer physical difficulty of finding reserves to visit. They are not marked on most road maps, and you can drive past without knowing one is near. It was a time-consuming job, locating reserves via Indian Affairs maps or by word of mouth, and nothing else made me so aware of the invisible limbo in which Indians exist.

I was shocked by the reserves and Metis communities, shocked by the destitution, the squalor, the chaos, the brutality, the apathy. Worse, however, was the people's fear, servility and hatred, and the knowledge that these feelings were based on the color of my skin, as my fear was based on the color of theirs. I was from the outside, the other side, a stranger and a threat, irrevocably on the side of Indian Affairs, the oppressors. I realized when I became aware of the relationships between Indians and Canadian society, that I could no longer believe that society to be benevolent, nor could I believe the government to be just. Once you have stepped outside your society to look at it, you can never really get comfortably in again. You begin to understand what Indians feel like.

As I drove my car across the unmarked boundary of a reserve, I drove into a world without normal orientation, a world in which time, order, money were irrelevant. Repeated, peculiar, and different confrontations confused my responses to the situations I was experiencing: A toothless, gnome-like old man in rags and a floppy tweed hat shuffles up, plucks at my sleeve and babbles out some hilarious but incomprehensible gibberish which seems, to him, of terrible significance. A middle-aged man sits beside me on a broken kitchen chair; suddenly he turns and fixes me with a stare that goes right through. "We are human too," he says knowingly, with no connection with anything that has gone before.

Even outside reserves, the Indian industry has an air of unreality and pretense. At the annual Indian-Metis conference in Winnipeg, Indian chiefs shuffle around in rusty blue postman's suits they have been given for uniforms looking helpless and embarrassed. One after another they rise to make impassioned pleas to the government on trivial housekeeping issues while the Indian Affairs personnel, yawning behind their hands, glance at their watches and say that nothing can be done. Everyone talks in the monosyllabic language of western movies—"White man and Indian heap good friends now, eh? " Bureaucrats with university degrees talk about the nice pow-wow they're having; the Indians sometimes talk about going on the warpath or smoking the peace pipe.

I found there was no civil rights movement among the Indians, certainly not the coherent mass uprising my imagination anticipated. Only a handful of chiefs have ever seen a text of the Indian Act, and few of them have been able to interpret its jargon. All feel oppressed, but do not know the extent of the oppression or its causes. Old people are obsessed with treaties they have never read; and they stridently proclaim rights they have never been granted. Circumscribed by isolation, poor education and a language barrier, with pathetically scanty knowledge of Canada's political system, their blunders amuse the bureaucrats who keep them in ignorance and confuse them with half-truths. Most Indians are, like all people, too preoccupied with the daily chore of getting food to care much about examining their position.

Indian spokesmen come forward only to vanish in months, while Indian organizations spring up and die. Some, such as the defunct National Indian Council, exist only to acquire money from the government for their own entertainment. Indians appear to be speaking out more, but 40 years ago strong Indian spokesmen were making representations to Ottawa to no avail. Even though exhaustive Senate-Commons hearings into the status of Indians were held in the late 1940s and again 10 years later, the Indians' cries of poverty, injustice and discrimination are as loud now as then.

I was depressed when I saw the disorder, apathy and psychological paralysis of most reserves. There seemed no evidence of political activity besides the pursuit of handouts from the government, and it was several months before I realized that here, right before everyone's eyes, in all the chaos and withdrawal, was the *real* Indian resistance. Indian lives are a study in passive resistance. Other forms of political activity, like band councils, are tokens to throw people off the track. Reserve society is instinctively geared to alienating white people, whether by frightening them by drunkenness, begging and threats, intimidating them by silence, or retreating from them through feigned stupidity and fake psychosis. Indians have instinctively patterned their lives to prevent whites from really knowing what is going on among the Indians.

They have succeeded. As late as 1938, experts were predicting the Indians' extinction. The Indians have confounded

everyone by continuing to exist. There is no need for a civil
rights movement along the lines of the abortive Martin Luther
King demonstrations. So appalled is the Trudeau government by
the moral and economic morass of Indian reserves that it wants
simply to sweep them away. It proposes to remove the legal
restrictions, phase out the Department of Indian Affairs, and
grant Indians equal status with other Canadians. The Indians
have won their war with the government simply by being
unpleasant and unmanageable. The heroes of that war were the
men who spat at policemen and went to jail, the women who
abandoned their children to the mercy of the government, the
youths who were incorrigible delinquents, the families who
existed for generations on welfare. The middle class Indians in
white shirts who smiled through endless meetings with condescending civil servants accomplished nothing.

The government's intention to abandon the Indians has
opened the possibility for real discussion and negotiation. The
opening stages of these negotiations are well described in Harold
Cardinal's *The Unjust Society*, and Mr. Cardinal makes a
convincing argument that the Trudeau government is trying
once more to do away with the Indians. There is, of course,
always the chance that this time the passive resistance of the
Indians will not be enough, that this time the government will
succeed. But the real struggle is not with the government, but
with Canadian society, and it is just beginning. By removing
legal handicaps, the government cannot remove Indian poverty;
it cannot make white people erase their prejudices; it cannot
wipe away the Indians' fear, anger, hatred, despair and dependency which have accumulated for so many generations. The
confrontation for which the Indians are preparing themselves
and from which they want to protect themselves by new
treaties and compensation payments could be vicious and
destructive.

It is customary for Canadians to see Indian poverty,
segregation and psychological dependency as an unfortunate
accident, an aberration, an omission which people of good will
can, with a little effort, put right. But it is apparent that, after
100 years of intensive civilizing, Indians still are not "civilized".
The Canadian response to this fact is usually a call for a

stepping-up of the civilizing process, with more education, more indoctrination, relocation, electricity and bathtubs. It is fashionable to say that Indians have been "neglected"; the warm, encompassing arm of the Canadian way of life has in some way omitted them.

But Indian poverty is neither a mistake nor an omission. It is a deliberate and inevitable product of Canadian attitudes and social structures. The Indian has become the negative image of the white Canadian, the living expression of attitudes and emotions which Canadians find it necessary to repress. He is a reverse image, a reflection, a dark twin, a creation of the white imagination. Onto him, the respectable Canadian can project those emotions, impulses and fears which Canadian society does not find acceptable. The Indian is joined as closely to the white man as his shadow; he is an integral part of the Canadian experience.

It is these shadow communities I visit in this book. Every Indian community has its adjoining white community, even if just the Indian Affairs office, and many white communities have Indian twins. Every community has a life of its own, governed by its own history, patterns and laws. Indian behavior is not inexplicable and not accidental. There are reasons for everything Indians do or believe, and those reasons can usually be found in the white counterpart. The Indian situation today is the product of a tight, closely supervised economic system, a system which produces not only the wealth of many Canadians, but also the destitution of the Indians.

Chapter 2
Hay Lake

Monday morning, February 22, 1965 was cold, grey and windy. In Edmonton, Alberta the thermometer stood at -20 degrees. Snow had fallen recently and crunched underfoot. People ran, heads down, into the warmth of the office buildings, and cars puffed a thick fog of fumes into the air. The morning rush traffic had thinned by 10:30 a.m. when three big yellow school buses pulled up to the Indian-Metis Friendship Centre, and discharged one hundred and eleven men in front of the Friendship Centre. They were all Indians, Slaveys from Hay Lake, a community of about 600 people in the northwestern corner of Alberta near the boundary of the Northwest Territories, and they were the entire population of able-bodied men on the reserve.

Two white men, Father P.E. Plouffe, the parish priest, and Hector Boissoneault, community development officer employed by Indian Affairs, came with them, crammed into the school buses for sixteen and one-half hours, driving 600 miles to Edmonton from Hay Lake. No proper road goes to Hay Lake, so for the first 60 miles they had bumped over a winter road, used by bombardiers bringing in supplies. The rest of the road, until just north of Edmonton, had been gravel. Their wives, helped by sisters at the residential school, had packed a lunch of buns and sandwiches.

The men had begun to gather in the Mission hall, a garage converted into a meeting place, at 4 p.m. Sunday afternoon. It was already pitch dark and -50 degrees. "We left on Sunday so there would be no news leak out that we were coming. We wanted to be unexpected when we arrived in Edmonton Monday morning," said Father Plouffe. Two young Slaveys, James Metchooyeah and Victor Chonkolay, organized the men into groups of ten, each under a leader. The men were to follow without question the orders of their leader: keep silent, stay in line, obey. Anyone who disobeyed the regulations would be kicked out of the band for life.

In front of the Friendship Centre, an old run-down house near the railway tracks, the men stamped their feet, stretched and adjusted their ear muffs. With their thin windbreaker parkas stained with oil and dirt, jackets open down the front revealing heavy wool plaid shirts with a cotton shirt underneath, they all looked shabby.

A police escort arrived and the men formed quickly into a line, three and four abreast. The chief, Harry Chonkolay, led, with the four councillors in a line abreast behind him. Three of the councillors, Antoine Providence, Alexis Semianta and Paul (Big Paul) Metchooyeah, were aged, stopped men with sad eyes, stern unsmiling lips and grizzled hair. They were tiny, almost gnomes or trolls, some barely five feet tall, ageless and oracular. A fourth councillor, Harry Dodhoa, was a young man. The men carried large white placards which had been distributed among them:

HELP

WE WANT WORK

DON'T TREAT US LIKE KIDS BUT LIKE MEN

WHERE IS OUR FREEDOM?

WHERE DO YOU WANT US TO GO?

WE'RE PEOPLE FIRST, NOT JUST INDIANS

The men walked slowly off towards the downtown area, down the middle of the road in total silence, headed for the Alberta legislature and the office of Premier Ernest Manning. With them, farther back in the crowd, walked Father Plouffe and Hector Boissoneault. "We thought someone might throw a bottle at us. We didn't mind. We had nothing to lose," said Victor Chonkolay.

Father Plouffe described their mood: "The men were scared to death. They didn't want to hold the posters. Some were shaking and nearly crying. They didn't know what the result would be or what might happen to them. Except for the leaders, they only knew it was important for them to be there.

Not a word was spoken in the bus on the way to Edmonton."

Fewer than six of the 111 men spoke or understood English. Most had never seen a bus before. Only three or four had ever been in a city. "I don't want to go back to Edmonton. All those lights. All the cars going 'swish', 'swish'," remarked an old Slavey man.

Although the men were apprehensive, nothing happened as they walked, and no bottles were thrown. Edmonton paid little attention to this silent black troop, and only a few paused briefly on the sidewalk or at office windows to read the posters. It was a short walk, about twenty minutes, to the Legislature. Entering up the wide flight of steps, they assembled in a group in the marble rotunda of the legislature. They seemed even smaller (the tallest man in the band is only about five feet ten or eleven inches) and shabbier, against the shiny, polished marble, as civil servants in white starchy shirts and crisp blue suits interrupted their morning coffee to watch them. The men stood for more than an hour, not one word spoken, while the chief, councillors and the two young men, James Metchooyeah and Victor Chonkolay, met with Premier Manning.

"We are in an awful situation," the chief explained. He described how all his people, 1,800 divided among several reserves, were starving. There was no work. Everyone was on total maximum welfare and the welfare was half the provincial rate—$15 to $20 a month for a whole family. He told how the people lived in log homes with mud, leaking roofs, without any lumber to fix the roofs, how women and children were turned away from the nursing station because it was after hours. The people, said the chief, were living like animals, with no furniture, no lumber to make any and no money to buy any, so that they were sleeping on dirt floors at 50 degrees below zero.

Of the welfare which Indian Affairs gives the people in place of assistance towards making a living, the chief spoke slightingly: "My people do not want welfare," he said. "We want to work." And he objected to children being flown away hundreds of miles from home to go to school after grade nine. There were no training or vocational programs offered to his people. They had no way of getting out of Hay Lake and nowhere to go if they did.

Premier Manning pointed out to the chief and councillors, seated in a row across the table glaring at him with wide-spaced, intense eyes, that they were the responsibility of Indian Affairs, and that the province could not help them. The chief leaped up and banged his fist on the premier's desk, shouting at him: "You *are* our premier! " Mr. Manning and his cabinet ministers were impressed. Although he did not undertake to provide solutions to the problems which the Indians presented to him, the Premier sent a telegram to Prime Minister Lester Pearson demanding action from the federal government. The delegation could get no better response, and turned from provincial to federal offices.

Without stopping for lunch, the men regrouped and walked a few blocks to the Federal Building to see Indian Affairs' regional director, R.D. Ragan. Indian Affairs was not expecting them and Mr. Ragan was taken by surprise. He had nothing to offer, beyond suggesting that the men build a road on the reserve with a horse and scraper.

"Ha! " sneered Victor Chonkolay, an aggressive, highly articulate man who speaks fluent English. "We want Caterpillars." Mr. Ragan did not know what could be done.

"Ask me," snapped Victor.

Mr. Ragan rambled on, suggesting, pacifying, promising.

"Shut up, Mr. Ragan, it's time you listened to us," said Victor. "You are too small to deal with us. We will wait for your bosses to come. We will not come back to discuss this with you any more. If you don't do as we ask, you will hear from us again later on." With that, the leaders left.

Accommodation found for them in a shabby slum hotel, full of the usual drunks and rubbydubs, seemed a further insult. "Do we have to stay with all these drunk people? " the Indians asked. They went to bed without food, twenty- four hours after they had eaten last, but prepared to stay until their petition was answered. "We will stay until we have the answers we want and need," said Victor Chonkolay, the chief's son. "There is nothing to go back to. I am the only man with a job. The other men here have none." A bill to give the provincial vote to Indians was read in the Legislature that same day.

Later, the men moved from the cheap hotel to communal quarters at the Exhibition Grounds. The next day, Tuesday morning, the Salvation Army moved in to feed them. They had cots, army blankets and T.V. sets. The men sat, ate, smoked, talked quietly and watched T.V. Politicians came and made speeches; civil servants gave advice on how to deal with Ottawa. The implications of the requests and possible replies were discussed with all the men.

When an investigating team of government officials flew into Hay Lake the following Saturday, they found it infinitely worse than the Indians had said. Houses had no furniture but metal tubs on wood stoves for melting snow for drinking water, a few squalid, sagging beds covered with coats and dirty blankets, plywood and cardboard peeling off the floors, leaky roofs. Children, ragged and dirty, often half naked in below zero temperatures, pulled sleds loaded with firewood. A smell of rot, filth, smoke, wet clothes, permeated the fetid air of the log homes, large one-room buildings housing ten to fifteen people. The community, scattered between Assumption and Habay, was made up of over 100 homes, all equally wretched, their mud-chinked logs dung brown against the snow. From the rafters, inside, hung strips of smoked moose meat and dried fish — the staple diet of the people. This was the second phase of the march— an explanation, at least in part, of why the Indians went to Edmonton. Their main purpose was not jobs, not training, not angry demands but just to say: "Look at me."

On Saturday, the Indian agent was fired. He had been in Hay Lake only a year. He said he was not aware that he had fallen into disfavor with the Indians. Monday, the team of "bosses" left Hay Lake. The promised full-scale investigation had lasted three days.

Hay Lake was last heard of in March, 1965, when Ralph Ragan reported that a sawmill, diesel power units, a tractor and seven pre-fabricated cottages had been sent to Hay Lake. "More homes are planned for next year," he said. "We Want Work", the Indians had said, as clearly and loudly as they could. They got more welfare. They had not asked for a sawmill, nor chain saws, nor a tractor. All their important requests, the ones affecting their own freedom and future development, had been ignored.

Question: "What do you think will happen ten years from now when there are more people living here, wood is further away and moose and fish are a far distance from your settlement?"

    "Our people look back, never ahead, because they never know what is ahead."
    "We will die or disappear."
    "Maybe we will do as other people do."
    "The end of the world will come."
    "Our people learned to live off the land but now we are living in a new way. We would like to learn what is expected of us."

    The Hay Lake Indians gave that assessment of their future in 1968.

    The Hay Lake people have been settled only since 1953. They were named by the government in that year; before, they had been only numbers on Treaty Day. The Hay Lake band signed Treaty 8 in 1899 but had nothing more to do with white men until 1914, when an Oblate priest, Father Joseph Habay, for whom the settlement was named in 1952, entered the area. The Hudson's Bay Company established a trading post in 1920. Until 1953, the Slaveys had been nomads, following the moose and trapping fur-bearing animals through the bush and across the vast prairies near the Hay River. The people hunted in family groups, each led by the oldest and wisest man who knew best where to find the game and the best fur. Life was a daily gamble. The family lived off each day's hunt and fur was stored to be traded at the Hudson's Bay twice a year. If the game failed, the whole family would starve. The Indians were totally mobile, living in tents winter and summer. At first the tents were hide and poplar pole wigwams; later came Hudson's Bay Company canvas. The Indians' hide clothes also were exchanged for the wool and cotton factory-made apparel at the Hudson's Bay.

    The year followed a regular cycle based on spring trapping, summer fishing, winter trapping. Life was utilitarian and absolutely efficient. Each family unit was stripped bare of everything which did not contribute directly to survival, with no excess baggage allowed. It was a ruthlessly self-disciplined way of life, including the murder or suicide of those who became a burden through illness or age. When the population grew too large for the game in the area to support, the people began to die of starvation until the proper balance was restored. When the treaty was signed in 1899, the entire Slavey population was only 175.

The first link with civilization was established by the Hudson's Bay Company. The Slaveys began to move in diminishing circles around The Bay so they would be close enough to bring in their furs or get supplies when game ran low. Dependency took root. The circumference of the people's world became narrower, with The Bay in the centre. The family lost its self-sufficiency and the people became employees of The Bay. The fur trade bound the people ever more tightly to the company. The Indians were valued in terms of the amount of good fur they could bring in, and were paid not in money but in food. The more daring and successful a hunter was, the more dependent and enslaved he became to The Bay. The more fur he brought in, the more food he would receive. He and his family soon began to depend on this "store food" as the staple of their diet and in order to get it, the hunter would work even harder. By becoming an employee of The Bay, the Indian entered an economy which was not essentially different from that functioning in the rest of Canada. The Bay linked him, as a laborer and consumer, with the rest of Canada and with the world. The Slavey's produce—fur—found a world-wide market.

The Hudson's Bay Company was the only business in the area. The Indians bought their food from the same company to which they sold their produce. Money was unnecessary for fur and food were bartered. The Bay, completely in control, set the prices and the standards and the Indians were forced to abide by the decision of the Bay manager. It was simple for The Bay, dealing with an illiterate, non-English-speaking population over which it had complete control, to make sure that the value of groceries consumed by a family always equalled or exceeded the value of fur brought in, so that the people were perpetually in debt or breaking even. Although they were now laborers, they lived on the same subsistence level as before. All they had lost was their independence. Their relationship with The Bay contained no prospect of their becoming richer or more powerful and The Bay did not suggest to them that one day they too, the Indians, could be Bay managers or operate a store of their own.

In order to save time lost in hunting, The Bay would grubstake the Indian trappers before the season opened with enough food to see the family through. The normal economy was thus reversed, since the Indians got food first, and worked later. They had a big grocery debt at the store before they went trapping and they were expected to bring back at least enough fur to pay it off. A bad season put the Indians deeply in debt to the store. And it was not long before the whole community was under obligation to The Bay. The Bay would grant the most credit to the best trappers; a man's worth was measured by the size of his bill at the store. Debt made the Indians vulnerable to threats and pressure from the Bay manager. It was important to be friends with him or he would cut back credit, and this could mean death.

Pressure became severe in the period when The Bay was also the government. A resident Indian agent did not establish himself in Hay Lake until 1957. Until that time, the Indians received their government information and assistance, a family allowance, rations, pensions, through The Bay. The people couldn't speak English so the Indian agent consulted with the Bay manager.

A shattering change came in 1952 when the Oblate Fathers built a huge residential school on the reserve. The Slaveys were to be educated. Children had to attend school every day for ten months of the year. Suddenly, the balance swung from emphasis on the old leaders to emphasis on the children and the future. The hunting pattern was broken when the children began to attend school. It was then almost impossible for the parents to continue to follow the traplines. The necessary labor of the children—wood gathering, baby sitting, water-carrying—was missing, and no family wanted to leave its children for six months of the year. The Slaveys gambled on the future. They sent their children to school and settled down in their little log cabins around Habay and Assumption. The men continued to trap and hunt, but they were unwilling to leave their families alone for five or six months at a time. The circle shrank again.

They trapped closer to home. Soon the area was trapped out by too many hunters and game and fur became scarce. The people came soon to depend almost exclusively on The Bay for their food and game was a supplement, something to eat when the rations ran out. The population grew rapidly, since the food supply from the government and the store was inexhaustible. By 1963, the Slavey population numbered 767 and 33 children were being born every year. The little log cabins became crowded.

The simple act of establishing a school completely revolutionized the Slavey economy. Not only did trapping become almost impossibly difficult but the population soon destroyed the game. The Slaveys assumed, in all good faith, that the government which was insisting they attend school and thus abandon their way of life would provide new jobs for the children when they finished school and alternative employment for the men until their families were grown. But Indian Affairs found it easier to dole out increasing quantities of rations as the game dwindled. No attempt was made to retrain or re-employ the Indian men. By 1963, the entire community was on total welfare. The initial dependency on The Bay was multiplied into total dependency on government. The government now provided what nature had formerly supplied. The complete switch from subsistence based on the land to subsistence based on government handouts took only ten years.

The Hay Lake march on the Alberta Legislature began in 1963. Indian Affairs was spending $300,000 a year on Hay Lake against which the return in food, taxes and fur royalties was no more than $30,000. By 1973, the population would double, administration costs would triple to $900,000 and the financial return would be nil. Indian Affairs established a permanent agent in the community to hand out the relief. A health unit had been built and staffed with two nurses. The residential school had grown into an enormous establishment with a barn, garden, airstrip, chicken houses, residences for Fathers and teachers, power plant, a garage-turned-hall, 25 tanks of propane gas, as well as the two-storey white frame school. The school had 94 students and a staff of 16, plus nine

Indian employees. Over 40 families had settled down near the school, in a community called Assumption. At Habay, eight miles away on the lake, a day school was built in 1962. To what purpose all this education went no one knew. Education was an unknown quantity to the Slaveys. One adult had a grade eight education, highest in the community. Of the men, 68 had education between grade one and grade seven, and 71 were illiterate. The women had virtually no education at all. The educated men in the community were no better off than the illiterate, and only a few people spoke English well enough to be understood. Education hardly brought jobs, since only a few people were actually regularly employed. There were two clerks at the Bay store; there was a caretaker at the nursing station, and a few jobs at the school. The income from all employment was $92,550 in 1963. One-third of that came from trapping, $16,000 from fighting forest fires, and the rest from wages paid by Indian Affairs for wood cutting and other jobs around the reserve. Another $90,000 came from welfare, of which $65,000 was direct rations of clothing and food, and the rest family allowance, treaty money and old age pensions. The average yearly earnings from both employment and welfare for an able-bodied man was $661.00. Per capita income for the year was $14.72.

The rest of the $300,000 yearly investment in the community went towards expenses on the government establishments, especially maintenance and salaries for the schools. Rations totalling $5,000 were given out to everyone once a month. People flocked in from miles around The Bay to pick up their free food. The old age pensioners were the best off, with a steady income higher than the welfare given to an able-bodied man with a young, growing family. An elderly couple would get $150.00 a month between them; a man with five children might get $50 a month.

At Hay Lake in 1963, a community of Indians clustered around the Indian Affairs establishments at Habay and Assumption, white people lived in modern bungalows with running water, proper sewage disposal, and new furniture. The Indians had fewer possessions than they had had when they followed the trap lines. Dogs starved, strayed, or were killed; guns and traps rusted with disuse.

Half the population was under age 16, and 119 children were under six. Only 10 people were over 65 and only 63 people over 45 years of age. The reserve had 62 young people between 16 and 22 years of age. All were unskilled, unemployed and on welfare.

The Slaveys were not going to die or disappear. They were living, growing, multiplying and the birth rate was increasing every year as more and more young women grew to maturity. The population increased by 97 people in four years. Since the nursing station was established in 1953, the people were living longer, although they saw a doctor and dentist only about once a year. Health services for the Hay Lake band cost $50,000 a year, and the costs rose with the increase in population.

In spite of the poverty of the people, the Hudson's Bay generated pressure for them to acquire the material possessions of sophisticated urban life. The desire for these goods was reinforced by store catalogues, picture books at the school, and magazines. In 1950, The Bay stocked little except lard, flour, cloth, sugar and salt, but by 1963, the store was selling battery record players, $4.20 records, transistor radios, expensive plastic toys (a child's tractor selling for $13), bicycles, cameras, gas lamps, ready-made clothes in the latest styles and colors, leather jackets and boots, expensive children's wagons. The fruits of prosperity were dangled before Indians too poor to buy them.

This poverty and unemployment exists on a reserve of 30,000 acres, which is, with the exception of the lake and several hundred acres of marsh, magnificent timber and ranching country. There are 6,000 acres of potential arable or grazing land, and 1500 of natural prairie. Some of the best timber in Canada stands on or near the reserve. Between the reserve and the MacKenzie Highway, 500 million feet of marketable timber have been leased to outside companies. White settlers have bought up acres of grazing land to the north. To the south lies the Peace River country, a valley of good farm land. Before 1963, oil companies were beginning explorations in the area. In the middle of all this wealth and potential development, the Slaveys were living in idleness, misery, and growing anger, worse off than they had been before "civilization" had hit them. The system was, quite simply, that Indian Affairs did a lot of work and the Indians did nothing. All lines of communication ran to

Ottawa. Nobody outside of Indian Affairs knew that the Indians were there. An elaborate Indian Affairs bureaucracy routed Indian requests and communications through an assistant agency in Habay, an agent in Fort Vermillion, on to regional headquarters in Edmonton, and, if not quashed there, possibly on to Ottawa. Long delays or even total silence killed any enterprise which came from the Indians on the reserve. Even the occasional variations came without consulting the reserve, and without thought of their consequences. For example, one year, winter work was instituted. The project: shovel snow from the Indian agent's yard. The second winter, the agent gave orders for all trees around the houses to be cleared. The community was denuded. The parish priest requested that a spruce tree in front of his home be left standing. No discrimination: it was chopped down too. Because the winter works money, which replaced welfare, had to be spent during the winter, the men lost their chance to make a little extra money trapping or hunting. They could not afford to forfeit the winter works income.

Although $300,000 was being invested annually in the community, most of it went to support the government establishments. Very little, barely enough to maintain life, ended up in the people's pockets.

The band council met only twice a year with the Indian agent, once to draw up a budget and once on Treaty Day. The people had no form of functioning representative government whatsoever, and the chief and council did what the agent told them. They could vote in federal elections but not in provincial elections. They had no provincial MLA to look after their interests. The chief had been in office 25 years, and the band still appointed the chief under the old hereditary system.

The way of life had changed only in one respect—work was missing now. The people had been forced to live in an idleness which they never had experienced before. Their only apparent use was to produce children to fill the school. The value of the children changed. Out on the trap line, children had been valuable and useful, but now they were a liability, increasing the rations required without being able to contribute to the productivity of the family. This was the little box the Slaveys found themselves in in 1963. There was no prospect that this way of life would ever change.

Night, in the summer at Hay Lake, is twilight turning to dawn. In a large corral, the Indians are gathered in groups around small fires, smoking and talking. Seven drummers stand in line beside a large fire in the centre of the rings, beating their tamborine-drums in unison, eyes closed in concentration. A crowd of people, in two and threes, shuffles a two-step around the central fire in time to the beat. Most of the dancers are women, in kerchiefs and long skirts to their ankles, but teenage girls bright in lipstick and stretch pants shuffle too.

Men had brought cookies and cigarettes in large cardboard cartons to the onlookers. Everyone smokes. Two four-year-old girls puff and blow cigarette smoke in each other's faces until one coughs and chases the other out of the corral. Flags are hoisted on poplar poles around the outside of the ring. Most are sky blue and white, painted with the tree and animal symbols of the Slaveys. One Union Jack in shiny new silk hangs among them. Trucks and cars belonging to the local white people are lined up outside the corral. Their drivers, the Hudson's Bay manager, the nurses, remain outside leaning on the rails. Occasionally, a truckload of curious oil company employees drives slowly past without stopping. The Indians dance all night.

It is 1967, two and one-half years after the march. In the intervening years, the Hay Lake band has become rich, but the people still have little money, and they still live in mud-roofed log cabins. The band's new-found wealth, about one million dollars in the trust fund in Ottawa, did not come from the government. It was not in any way a result of the march. The money came from oil, after an oil company struck it rich on the Hay Lake reserve. A new corporation has replaced the Hudson's Bay Company. The oil company pays handsome royalties to the band for the right to drill wells on its property; it built the road betwen Habay and Assumption; it provides fresh water trucked in every second day for the whole community in return for permission to cross the reserve. It employs the men, and only 11 people are on welfare.

Oil rigs, dump trucks, bombardiers, pickup trucks thunder through the reserve at all hours of the day and night, but all this frantic industrial activity leaves the reserve and the Indians curiously untouched. They sit near the road inside an open teepee structure made of poplars with the leaves left on at the top, around a large smokey fire festooned with ragged chunks of moose meat. A whole family crowds inside this skeleton teepee, contemplating the world roaring by from between the wooden bars while the smoke makes their eyes smart. The moose meat hangs over them like raw, purple moss. Beyond the screen of smoke, swarms of giant mosquitoes drone like an airforce of tiny monoplanes. Furniture, benches, tables, and chairs have been moved outside. In their imagination, the people have moved to their summer fishing grounds, although in fact they haven't travelled more than ten feet from the front door.

Life is relaxed and somnolent as the smoke curls slowly up in the bright sunshine. The grass grows high and green in July and the marsh stretches for miles towards the lake. The Hay River is a small brown stream, and horses and cows with bells tinkling around their necks browse along the banks while a steady stream of bicycles pedal by along the road. The log cabins are quaint and scattered in the green bush. Where the brush has been cleared, the prairie stretches to the horizon. The silence is a faint hum — mosquitoes, wind, oil trucks, airplanes, helicopters chopping overhead carrying trucks and houses in giant nets slung underneath.

The rich royalties from oil have been deposited to the band's account in Ottawa, and have not been available to bring to the reserve what the people want, and the government has done little of what has been asked. About a dozen new houses have been provided. They are built in a rough, square townsite formation on a patch of bald prairie away from the rest of the settlement. Outbuildings have cropped up and horses graze nonchalantly between the homes. Each house, painted pastel colors, has a litter of tents, wooden wagons and smoke houses around it. Eight houses in the townsite have electricity. Other new homes have been located throughout the settlement and several men have used lumber cut by the sawmill to build their own. Most of the people still live in the old one-room log cabins with as little in the way of material possessions as they had before. A family with eight children occupies a small shack in Habay, although Indian Affairs had promised this would be the first family with a new home. Somehow, they were overlooked.

The homes in the townsite were those trucked in by Indian Affairs in the 1965 crash program. Since then, almost nothing has been added. The chief, 60 miles away in High Level, has had two new homes in four years. The sawmill is there but is not operating. It is run by a white man employed by Indian Affairs, and Indians work as woodcutters and sawyers for $1.50 an hour. They have to buy lumber from the mill for their homes and since they can make $3 an hour working on construction for the oil companies, the sawmill has trouble getting labor. "The sawmill is not ours," say the people. "It belongs to Indian Affairs. The white man runs it. Why can't we run it and use the lumber? " Most of the lumber from the mill is sold to the oil companies. The revenue disappears in Ottawa.

With the chief away from the reserve, local government has disappeared. All decisions are made by the chief and the Indian agent, and the council does not know what is going on. The money from oil royalties is paid by the oil company directly to Indian Affairs. The people have nothing to do with the transaction, never see either the cheque or the money, and do not know exactly how much they have in the trust fund in Ottawa. Estimates range between $1 million and $2 million. The agent will not tell them how much it is—he speaks only to the chief. The people are unable to get their hands on this money to develop the reserve. Without the chief, the council is disorganized and can come up with no definite proposals for spending the money, although the people have lots of ideas. The chief is determined to hang on to the death, since he is doing well. Until the people can organize themselves, Indian Affairs refuses to approve the expenditure of their revenue.

The community development officer was fired immediately after the march. The Indian agent is much like the previous one and speaks to no one. He is always busy. There is no one to help the Indians organize to get their money and they can't get money to hire anyone to help them organize. Many families are making money now—some have $2,000 in the bank—but the oil boom is, they know, temporary. The oil companies will pass on in a few years, taking their jobs and money with them, and Hay Lake will be abandoned. The people can stay and be poor or move with the company.

Victor Chonkolay describes the situation as it has developed: "Everything has swung back, just like it used to be. The oil company says 'go see the agent.' The agent says 'do it yourself.' It is time to push the chief and councillors away. People are fighting over the money in the band funds. The old people will never spend a penny. The agent says 'go cut cordwood, go fence.' That kind of talk has been going on for years, and the only change is that the agency office is four times bigger than before. He's now got four secretaries doing the work. People who come here to work with us get chased away by Indian Affairs. It breaks them, makes them quit."

There were 40 men who had signed a petition to depose the chief. Only two men, one crazy, had spoken in the chief's favor. But Indian Affairs supported him, nevertheless, and the chief refused to go. "It is just like it used to be."

Chapter 3
Home, Home on the Reserve

Treaty Indians in Canada number about 250,000—about one Canadian in 100 is an Indian. The identifiable Metis population is about the same, so that one Canadian in 50 is Indian or Metis. The Indians are expensive. On them, Indian Affairs spends about $175 million annually, in welfare, education, housing, economic development, and administration. Health costs reach about another $100 million. These figures do not include expenses borne by provincial governments for jails, police protection and services for indigent Indians who have left their reserves, nor do they reflect the expenses of the R.C.M.P., although much of their work in the West involves Indians. Family Allowance, pensions and unemployment insurance account for more millions.

For all this loss and investment, the government's only returns are in liquor and sales taxes. Most Indian reserves produce nothing—nothing, that is, except people.

Indians are the un-working class. Except for education expenses, the entire Indian Affairs budget is welfare or disguised welfare. Few Indians have permanent jobs. Many are employed on a seasonal basis, in sugar-beet work, potato picking, labor, construction, pulp cutting, fishing, and their jobs are often low-paying and hard manual labor. During off-seasons, they live on Family Allowance or unemployment insurance. Half of all Indian families earn less than $1,000 a year, and 75 per cent, less than $2,000. These "earnings" are not the actual income from employment or industry, but include Family Allowance and other government income which, on even the most self-supporting reserves, make up the bulk of the annual income.

Indians are becoming homeless, since new family formations are taking place at the rate of 1250 or more a year. Funds available for housing are insufficient to reduce the existing backlog of critically-needed Indian homes or to keep up with new family formations.

Indian communities are so deficient in utilities that minimum standards of health and decency are difficult to maintain. Income levels are so low that, in many instances, Indians find it impossible to pay the utility charges to keep them operating. Inadequate lighting affects the work of school children and the absence of basic plumbing facilities makes it difficult for Indian children to maintain a standard of cleanliness acceptable in public schools.

However much money the government is spending on Indians now, it is grossly inadequate to give them even a subsistence life. On reserves, where the economy remains static and the population increases, the Indians are in danger of starving and they would starve if Indian Affairs did not support them on welfare.

Half the Indian population is under 15 years of age. These children remain uneducated and often illiterate. Forty per cent of Indian children enter school unable to understand English or French; 61 per cent fail to reach grade eight; and 97 per cent fail to reach grade twelve. (The grade attained is often no indication of the level of the Indian child's achievement, since he is often promoted on the basis of size and age rather than competence.) About 35,000 adult Indians are now considered illiterate and virtually unemployable. The next generation is likely to be little improved.

For decades, reserve Indians have presented problems to the whites, who felt both responsible for producing the Indian problem and resentful of the costs which maintaining the Indians imposed. From the West, an agent reported in 1877:

> "They have a thorough and hearty aversion to working their land. They say to me: 'Give me a deed of my lot and I will have some courage to work.' This would do in some cases but in the majority of instances it would not do as they would very soon by their foolish trading be deprived of their land entirely."

The treaties provided farming equipment and the Indians proceeded to attempt farming with a pitiful supply of equipment allotted to them. The entire Indian population of Saskatchewan received, in 1877, two ploughs, two harrows, 13 spades, 18 axes, 41 hoes, four oxen, one bull and one cow.

"They have been furnished with inferior and old and worn out cattle, or cattle too wild for working and dairy purposes and with supplies of all kinds of the most inferior quality which would not be acceptable at any price by the ordinary consumer," stated a missionary.

The government's attitude was, frankly, that it was not prepared to support the Indians, buffalo or no, and the Indians could expect to get as little as the government could manage to give them. Often the seed arrived too late in the spring to sow and the Indians were so weak from sickness and starvation after the winter they could not find the energy to farm.

The Indians, whose surrender of land by the treaties had brought them to this situation, were bitterly resentful:

"Why does the white man want our land? You tell us he is rich and strong, and has plenty of food to eat; for what then does he come to our land? We have only the buffalo and he takes that from us. See the buffalo, how they dwell with us; they care not for the closeness of our lodges, the smoke of our campfires does not fright them, the shouts of our young men will not drive them away; but behold how they flee from the sight, the sound, the smell of the white man! Why does he take the land from us? Who sent him here? He puts up sticks and he calls the land his land, the river his river, the trees his trees. Who gave him the ground, the water, the trees? Was it the Great Spirit? No; for the Great Spirit gave to us the beasts and the fish and the white man comes to take the waters and the ground where these fishes and these beasts live—why does he not take the sky as well as the ground? We who have dwelt on these prairies ever since the stars fell do not put sticks over the land and say, between these sticks this land is mine; you shall not come here or go there."

Peigan chief

The plains Indians were starving in those years. Drought and fires destroyed the crops they managed to plant; measles and whooping cough killed them. The Blackfoot were described

as "skeletons", skin and bone covered with rags. Still, they were
expected to work for their rations:

> *"Strict instructions had been given to the agents to
> require labor from the able-bodied Indians for any supplies
> given them. This principle was laid down for the sake of the
> moral effect that it would have on the Indians, showing them
> that they must give something in return for what they
> receive, and also for the purpose of preventing them from
> hereafter expecting gratuitous assistance from the govern-
> ment."*

Indian Affairs report, 1880

All efforts were bent towards getting the Indians to settle
down and build houses. The house was supposed to bring with
it all the benefits of British culture. It had been obvious from
the start that there would never be enough money to make the
Indians self-supporting. The government adopted a strict "hold
the line" policy, and rigid controls were established over Indian
funds. Permission had to be sought from the agent before an
Indian could be given as much as a hoe or a bag of seed. There
never was any money, so the agent usually refused permission.

Everywhere in Canada, between 1900 and 1930, Indians
parted with enormous chunks of land. Much land for railway
tracks and roads was simply taken without compensation.
Towns like Kamsack, Saskatchewan and The Pas, Manitoba,
which now have "Indian problems", are built on former reserve
land. The land deals were made by the Indian agents, the chief's
signature was obtained (he couldn't read the deed), and the land
disappeared. Often, the band didn't know it had been sold.
What revenue there was has provided the money to support the
bands ever since.

The reserves stood still until 1946, then began to go
backwards. In 1944, 12,000 Indian children were without
educational facilities. The money spent on *all* roads on Indian
reserves amounted to the cost of one mile of trunk highway.
Indians were suffering from epidemics of gonorrhea and jaun-
dice; drugs were doled out by missionaries; R.C.M.P. constables
pulled teeth.

In 1943, Indian Affairs stated that reserves would be

abolished in 25 years. In the intervening period, the Indians continued to put forward objections to their treatment, and today, more than 25 years later, they are still on reserves and are still complaining about them.

The Hay Lake Indians wrote this brief to the Senate-Commons committee on Indian Affairs in 1948:

"We have nothing and our income is very small. We believe we should be exempt from taxes.

"What's the use of giving us the vote if we starve to death or don't know what it's all about? First give us the means of learning how to make a living and understanding what the vote is about."

Said the Nelson House, Manitoba people:

"Disgraceful treatments have been given to our ill people away which few never came back from hospital where for many years a most butchering doctor man hunting the annihilation of our races."

"We find it hard to vote for a man we never saw and we do not know what politics brings."

"We want protection against bad news makers, against angers from white men."

"In Morley, I got a piece of land close home. Plant garden. Too many stones, too hot by day. At night always frost. Can't make vegetables. Just the soil belong to Indians. Coal and oil underneath belong government. But I like garden. Can't eat stones. My boys in young life can't eat stones."

George Ebeneezer,
Stoney Indian.

"One day I try to make a living at Morley like white man. Make cabin and barn. Ask government for two cows. Government give me two cows, two calves. Got up to 32 head. Haven't enough hay. In March one winter lost almost all cattle. Start again, get up to 30. Lost again because can't put up enough hay. Can't raise more than 25. Why don't the government treat us to good land to grow lots of hay? Then

we go forward and raise up children good with milk and vegetables.

Johnny Lefthand,
Stoney Indian.

If a band did get ahead and make money through selling land or raising cattle, the money went to pay the wages of the Indian agent and to cover the administrative costs of writing letters to Ottawa as well as taking over all the functions previously provided by Indian Affairs. It didn't pay a band to progress.

"Would you say you were wealthy if you lived in a city which had millions of dollar of buildings and not one building which you could use? A band fund is of that nature."

Indian

"If we are attributed free houses, the Indian Agent or some other white persons may walk in at any time to tell us: do this, do that. If we are unable to accomplish what they ask, we are liable to be thrown out and our houses given to someone else.

"Practically, to us the Indian Act amounts to this: avoid offending the Indian agent or the Hudson's Bay Company to make sure we get the necessities of life."

Indian, 1960

Low living standards and Indian hopelessness are to be found on both "rich" and "poor" reserves. The Indians are fully aware of the stupidity of many of Indian Affairs programs, but are unable to do anything about them. Indian Affairs likes to take credit for any successes on the reserves: "We started that," or "*Our* program has been a success." The "we" and "our" always refer to the Branch, never to the Indians, who are given credit only for the failures. The Indians have always taken the blame for mistakes and inadequacies on the part of Indian Affairs. No wonder they have such a bad reputation.

Indian reserves today are like jails, with inmates confined together in overcrowded conditions for reasons they do not understand or accept. Values of reserve society are those of prisons: do no work, do not co-operate with the guards, lie, let each man take care of himself, everyone's belongings are fair game, keep out of sight. Indians who show too much friendliness to white people are "stoolies." Indians, like prisoners, give alcohol as an excuse for all their misbehavior.

The Indian, like the prisoner, suffers "civil death." Deprived of his freedom and his responsibilities, the Indian is confined to his reserve by psychological bars. He has lost his citizenship; he is rejected and ignored. On reserves, the strong "gorillas" rule, while the weak are ridiculed and persecuted.

Chapter 4
Norway House

The River

Lake Winnipeg spills over, at its northeastern tip, to form the Nelson River which flows, with increasing momentum, through a series of lakes, until it empties into Hudson Bay at York Factory.

The lake is messy about dying. Much of it just oozes away for miles on either side of the Nelson's banks, forming great stretches of muskeg covered with scraggly spruce, scrub and coarse grass. A few rocky promontories jut out from the squishy morass. A man can sink up to his waist or, in fact, out of sight in this bog when it is wet in the spring. It can grow grass, but is almost always too wet to allow cattle to eat it or men to mow it. In the summer, the muskeg produces clouds of mosquitoes which rise like a pestilence from stagnant pools.

Here, the Nelson is filled with islands, large and small. On these islands, for hundreds, perhaps thousands, of years, Indians camped. On one of the rocky promontories, just downstream from where the lake empties into the Nelson, the Hudson's Bay Company built a fort and, shortly after, James Evans, Methodist, built a church. Around these two foreign objects, these two intruders, the tissue of a community formed—a school, log cabins, frame houses.

Until the coming of the railroad to western Canada, Norway House was the heart and head of the western fur trade. All water routes to Hudson Bay from Alberta and Saskatchewan led to Norway House.

Norway House (called that because The Bay post was built by a couple of Norwegian carpenters) was a booming frontier town, a crossroads. Settlers and supplies were channelled south down the lake to Red River. Explorers and traders went west. Furs were shipped north. The community, if it could be called that, was based on the principle of transience. Since everyone, except for a small handful of executives, clergymen and Indians, was going somewhere. Norway House made sense only as a junction, a refueling stop, a jumping-off place. It produced nothing itself.

Some of these people dropped off to form a kind of scum, sediment, which clung to the river's banks and islands. Bay men married Indian women, built houses and raised families. The Indians came to depend more and more on the post and settled more closely around it. Boat men and traders would retire and settle down or form casual liaisons and raise children. Illegitimate children, products of brief encounters, grew up and stayed in Norway House, the only home they knew. In 1873, the treaty with the Indians gave them a stretch of land along the south shore of the river, including the fort's point of Rossville, and solidified their community.

Fur began to get scarce, prices dropped and, by the time the railway went through in the south, the Hudson's Bay Company was beginning to close out its operation at Norway House. After the railway came, supplies and people no longer passed through from Lake Winnipeg, York boats rotted on the shore, and the economy receded rapidly. The transients left for good, leaving Norway House to fend for itself as best it could, a few hundred people scattered in log shacks through the rocks and muskeg, a couple of churches, a school.

Norway House is a dank and dark place. The air is heavy and damp even in winter. The lowness, flatness of Norway House are sensible, tangible, immediately—a shallow bowl with slippery sides. Seen from the airplane window, Norway House is a blot. 400 miles north of the blank whiteness and scrubby wilderness of the Interlake, it may be anticipated as a relief; instead, it gathers up and intensifies the desolation, and provides the human counterpart of wilderness.

The first glimpse of Norway House is of a large black and white jail-like structure with a huge blackened chimney belching smoke which befouls the snow around the barracks for several hundred yards in every direction. The barracks, dirty white with black trim, is the center of a black puddle it has spewed over itself while, for miles around, the snow is white.

The community grows like mould along the shores of the river. A few solid core growths are connected by filaments of houses. It creeps for almost ten miles south from Rossville, down both sides of the river and covering, with a loose network, two large islands, Fort Island and Mission Island.

The community floats on the surface of the water in suspended animation, as if it had, like green scum, grown out of the river. The grass and dark scraggly trees creep out of the river. The slime on the bottom has solidified—it is difficult to know where water ends and land begins. The river shore is vague, fuzzy, shifting as if it were floating, heaving with the undulations of the water. The river itself is huge and sprawling, dwarfing the dull, monotonous trees. Near Rossville, two miles across, it is almost a lake. It flows everywhere, forming channels, streams, bays and inlets. The land is an excrescence of no value. The river is everything. It is made on a different scale.

The river reduces the human to insignificance. In the winter, the glare of its expanses of white ice makes the white-painted buildings of the settlement look grey, dirty, false. Square, neat, painted buildings are an absurdity in this fluidity. They look like toys, silly child's blocks, yellow, red and white. Every building, house, school, hospital, church, is built to face the river. Men do not look at one another but rather gaze at the water or at the ice, separately, all in a row, entranced by the space, the brightness.

The river has all the light. Even in winter when the water is buried under ten feet of solid ice, the river flows with blinding, reverberating, roaring light, and in the summer too, the light on the water, not the water itself, gives a sense of continual motion. In summer, because of the break and sweep of the waves, the light moves faster, flickers, while in winter it is solid, steady, heavy.

When the river is frozen, the pinks, yellows, blues and purples which bounce off the ice are so clear and brilliant that even fresh paint looks drab and faded. Only the river reflects light; everything else absorbs it. The new yellow, turquoise and brown government buildings look old and ugly; white paint is grey, and the drab brown and grey wood Indian homes are not seen at all.

The land has no light, no color at all. The trees are dark: murky greeen-brown-black, an indeterminate color. The shore is simply a dark shape, a place where the light ends, filled with hidden quagmires. It is shadow. The land has no color. Everything is black and white. The people too.

White people live in white or colored buildings on the

rocky promontories at Norway House—the bright, light places jutting into the river. The promontories are also the highest points of land.

Brown people live in brown or grey buildings in the bush—in the dark, brown, shadowy places, hidden by trees. These places are lower than the rocky points, and marshy.

Clearings

Rossville is the largest and most organized of the white clearings in the bush at Norway House. The Hudson's Bay Company built its fort on the outermost tip of granite on a large peninsula extending into the river from the south shore.

The Methodist church is beside it, on the highest windy crag in the area with a splendid view downriver. Behind the church and fort on their desolate promontory cluster the Indian Affairs complex of buildings, the United Church residential school and, farther back behind the school barn where the trees begin, several dozen Indian homes.

A Roman Catholic church and school occupy another large rock south on the peninsula. The Indians' homes are scattered along the river banks. At the very tip of the point stands a stone cairn in memory of James Evans. The residential school surrounded by a wire fence is the building which, from the air, looks like a jail. From the ground, the ashes from the chimney are more noticeable. The hospital used to be here until it was moved to Fort Island, on its own promontory.

The Indian Affairs buildings are white with green trim, as is the Roman Catholic school. The United Church school is white and black. The old fort was white, but only its main gate remains. The new Bay store is yellow and jaundiced green, the church on the point is cream and brown and all the buildings are frame.

Behind the school barn, out of use since the policy of making Indian school children raise hogs has gone out of fashion, two rows of Indian homes straggle off towards the trees. Most are whitewashed log cabins with unpainted shingle roofs, the whitewash turned a pleasant weathered grey. Most have woodpiles as high as the roof, so the visual impression is of a great heap of logs, out of which a tumbledown, sagging cottage takes form. Chips and sawdust cover the ground in front. Some of the houses are covered with artificial-brick tarpaper, a few new ones are pre-fab plywood and one is painted bright pink. A similar group of homes clusters around the Roman Catholic complex to the south. The white men's churches and government buildings look stiff and incongruous perched on the rocks, as though dropped helter-skelter by some giant gull. Their drab cream and bilious yellow colour is visible for miles, each unique in shape, color, style.

The Indians' homes seem to have grown out of the ground, even the pink one. They are not a healthy, natural or beautiful growth, but like fungus, and have the same vague monotony as the trees. Each log shack looks like every other log shack. They have been built to an Indian Affairs plan—same size, same whitewash, same shingles, same windows, same people. This monotony makes them nearly invisible.

The second white community, and the most important, lies a mile directly upriver from Rossville, on Fort Island, a swampy island which takes up most of the river, leaving a narrow channel on each side. This community is built around the hospital, a low brown and yellow building flanked by white clapboard nurses' residences and the yellow building of the administrator which, like the yellow church in Rossville, is high on a rocky point, commanding a broad view of the river. The airplanes land and take off in front of the hospital, and around it are the hydro plant, the telephone building, and the community development officer's house-office. Along the northern shore of the island are a second Hudson's Bay store, a post office, school, airline office and the only hotel. Just as at Rossville, the institutions stand out in the landscape, while Metis homes are scattered and hidden for miles along the river shore. Indian and Metis homes are located on the opposite side of the island at its other end. Across the channel from the hospital, Metis homes straggle for miles along the shore. The only institutions on the northern shore are a Pentecostal church and a school. Farther upriver, past Fort Island, the darkness increases. Three small clearings have been made in the bush, for a Roman Catholic Mission and school, an Anglican mission and school across from it on Mission Island and, upriver, a second Anglican school and a United Church building. Indian and Metis homes are located on Mission Island and on both shores.

The community of Norway House stretches, all told, about ten miles upriver from Rossville. Within that ten miles live 2,700 people. Treaty Indians number 1,700; Metis 700 and whites 250, and all these people form a community of great interdependence. These people are served by nine schools. Many people are illiterate and speak almost no English. They are cared for by six churches representing four denominations. Few people attend church. The white people provide services for the Indian people. The Indians permit themselves to be serviced by the white people. Allowing themselves to be cared for is the daily occupation of 2400 people at Norway House.

There are no other occupations. The fish to be caught will feed only a handful of families, and too few animals are left to make trapping a source of livelihood. There is no industry or agriculture. A few years ago, Indian Affairs shipped up some cattle by barge but they have since disappeared. Some drowned, some starved, some froze, many were eaten. Some were shot: "This guy from the government came in one day to my place and shot all my cattle with a gun. He said they weren't any good. I never got any more." Some were probably diseased.

(One bull, which had apparently gored someone to death, was put ashore on a small island off Rossville point. The bull was covered with tar and ignited, according to local legend. Its agonized bellows could be heard throughout the community. For a long time the island was called Bull Island. It is now called Drunken Island, for different reasons.)

An Indian agent who had either seen or heard about the luxuriant grass at Norway House was not apprised of the fact that the grass grows in water, and is, in most years, impossible to harvest. The cattle starved in the winter for want of hay. An attempt to grow potatoes and other vegetables suffered similar inundation.

Occasionally, odd construction jobs will come up or men will leave their families in the community to work outside. The rest work for the white people who are there to work for them. Or they don't work at all and allow themselves to be serviced to the maximum by unemployment insurance, welfare, and Family Allowance.

Tracks

The way a community functions internally can be seen best in the winter when everything is thrown into relief by the snow, and the tracks that people make are visible. The widest and most worn trails lead to the important places, the school, the store, and the hospital.

In the summer, the river is the road at Norway House. It is a chaos of speeding motor boats, big, ponderous scows, powerful RCMP boats, little canoes almost vertical in the air with the thrust of a heavy outboard. The air is filled with an incessant roar, even at night when the Indians steer by landmarks in total darkness, gauging the speed and distance of other boats by the sounds of their engines.

In the winter, the river is still the road (Norway House has no real roads) but the only vehicles are some bombardiers and a few skidoos. These are owned by important government people (Indian Affairs has a bombardier; so does the hospital) except for a few Indians who run a bombardier taxi service around the community at 50 cents a trip, $5 to charter. Everyone else travels on foot.

The most important tracks are made by the airplane from Winnipeg which comes in and goes out three days a week. It is the only contact with the outside besides radio-telephone. The outside, where all decisions are made, controls Norway House and that is why the plane is so important. It brings inspectors, agitators, writers, visitors, politicians who might have an important effect on the settlement's life. It takes away sick people, important people, lucky people. The plane brings all the mail, newspapers and gossip. Everybody's pay cheque comes in on that plane, and it brings food and clothing from the mail orders.

The hospital gives the airline a lot of business by sending sick people to Winnipeg. The plane lands in front of the hospital to be close to the patients, and a hospital staff person is usually on the plane or meeting it. The hospital is, therefore, the first to get any news. It knows everything sooner than anyone else in Norway House. This liaison with the airline, TransAir, is an important source of power in Norway House, for the hospital personnel can easily give the impression of having information they do not in fact possess. They know, at least, who gets off every flight, what that person is doing in Norway House, and whether he is likely to be a threat to the hospital.

The Un-working Class

A window in the boys' recreation room on the second floor of the United Church residential school in Rossville overlooks the school's backyard with its unused barn, trampled playground, and sheds. To the left are the two scraggly rows of Indian shacks. Straight ahead hidden in the bush, blocked off by a wing of the school, are more Indian homes. Near the barn, a thin metal pipe about three feet high sticks straight out of the ground. On the end is a tap. A man comes from behind the barn, walking slowly and deliberately across the open space. He carries an aluminum pail in each hand, goes to the tap, sets one pail underneath, fills it, sets the other in its place and fills it too. He turns the tap off, picks up both his pails, turns, and walks even more slowly and deliberately back in the direction from which he came, slopping a little of the water on the snow as he goes. He appears again on the other side of the barn, heading between the two rows of log shacks, and finally disappears behind a house. By this time another man is at the tap, with one pail. He had come from the opposite direction. He fills it and carries it out of sight. In a few moments, a woman comes along, pulling two pails on a toboggan, accompanied by two small children. All these people move at a leisurely, methodical, deliberate pace. Looking more closely at the tap, a well-worn trail can be seen leading up to it and away. The snow around it is trampled into mud.

That tap is the water supply for the 109 Indian homes of Rossville. The path that leads to it is the most important in the community. If someone were to stand at the window in the school for a whole day, he would probably see a person from every household come to that tap with a pail. It is a new path, three years old. The people used to take their water from the river, hauling it out more or less in front of their houses. The river was found to be polluted in 1964. Now they use the school water supply, which is chlorinated.

Water-getting is an extremely important ritual in Rossville. A large number of men come to that tap, young, able-bodied men carrying pails a child could handle. These men have no other jobs, so they make water-getting into a job, a symbol of their ability to provide at least that much for their families. Water carrying consumes a lot of hours in a day, particularly if small pails are used. It can take up as much as three hours of a day.

You look at these men, coming one after the other, each with his silly little pail and you think: How stupid! If that man carried two large pails and walked at twice the speed, he could carry four times as much water in half the time. Or better still, why don't they get together, all these individual men, and pay one man with a large water wagon or barrels to deliver water to the entire community? With the time they'd save, they'd be able to work more, make more money.

Work at what? There is no work. That's why these men carry water. They are not stupid. Save time for what? To sit around?

If these men were too busy to carry water, they'd *have* to hire someone.

This path tells many things about Norway House—the slow, deliberate round of daily chores performed for the sake of having something to do, every day almost exactly the same as the one before it. By the time a man has been carrying water 200 yards three times a day every day for three years, it is an important routine in his life. He depends on it. His family depends on him. What if he is offered a job? How can he take it? Who will provide water for his family? He will turn the job down or will take it and quit after two weeks in order to go back to hauling water. He has turned into a housekeeper. In order to survive the idleness of having no job at all, he magnified the importance of basic family chores until he equates them with work. What was, in a tougher age, women's work, is now man's work. He feels insulted if anyone suggests he should stir himself to find a job. He is already working. Instinctively, he makes it as slow, inefficient and time-consuming as possible so he will be able to convince himself that it is really laborious.

Ritualized inactivity is hard to destroy. It is difficult for a man accustomed to the ritual of fishing or trapping to adjust to a world where there are no fish and no fur-bearing animals. He simply applies his skills to something else—meaningless work, and, by doing so, makes it meaningful to himself. The biggest mistake that any vocational counsellor or job-placement advisor could make is to assume that these men are unemployed. They aren't. They are working very hard at not working. A counsellor, to tempt them into something more productive than carrying water, has to redirect all the energy which is being poured into the un-work.

By ordering the Indians to use the water out of the tap, the white community at Norway House provided an excellent alternative for the genuine work which is not available. The water has to come from the tap because the river is polluted. The white men polluted the river. Therefore, the white men have provided work for the Indians, just as they promised. No one is unemployed at Norway House.

The Bay is the only building in Rossville which faces inland, its back to the river, its door towards the people. It is the only building you don't have to walk half way around to get in the front door. From this door a well-worn path leads across the mile or more of open ice to the second white community, the hospital community, and past it down Fort Island to the Anglican mission at the bottom of Mission Island. This path, invisible in the summer, in the winter is the most obvious route in the community.

From the Rossville point, a procession of little black figures can be seen wending its way across that blank stretch of open ice, exposed to the north wind in the full, intense cold.

Most of these pilgrims make the trip on foot, although a skidoo will occasionally scoot across, or a blue bombardier lumber along, shooing people out of its way. These people are Indian or Metis, old and young, men and women, going to, or coming from, The Bay. For many, it is a two or three mile walk each way. Some older women in cotton stockings, print cotton skirts and black nylon windbreakers, pull toboggans with bags of groceries but many of them carry nothing. All walk at the same unhurried pace, feeling neither the wind nor the cold.

These people too are working. They are going to The Bay. On this particular day, that is the most important thing they have to do. The people of Norway House, scattered up and down 10 miles, have no news medium which tells them what is happening in Norway House. So news is carried by people. In summer, it is easy to do by boat, but in winter news must be carried by foot.

For the Indians and Metis, The Bay is the newspaper and the radio station of the community. Half an hour of standing around at The Bay brings a resident up to date on all the latest developments—who has arrived or left, a birth or death, a bit of scandal, prospects of jobs. The women cluster inside the store, near the door where they can see who comes in and who goes out. Everyone's purchases are also closely evaluated, since income can be estimated very accurately from a bag of groceries. The men stand outside in a row along the wall. From this point looking in towards the community, they can see everyone, where he is going, who he is talking to.

Going to The Bay is, like water-getting, an inactivity which, by nature of repetition, turns into work. It symbolizes the acquisition of food and clothing even though, in nine trips out of ten, nothing may be purchased. Or the money will be spun out so some little item can be bought each day. The long walk is also time consuming. If the weather is cold, the person has an excuse to stay longer in the store to get warm.

The Gossip Industry

Gossip, an important part of any community, becomes a pre-eminent occupation, a key industry, in an idle community. Closely related is the practice of people-watching or, less politely, spying. In Norway House, a knot of people is gathered in all seasons around the front door of The Bay. The store has provided benches for the gossips to make them more comfortable. Since nothing important ever happens in Norway House, only trivial information is exchanged. This information is frequently related to the private personal conduct of Norway House residents and is discussed with the solemnity and exhaustiveness of political debate.

To live in Norway House is to live a totally public life. Everyone has known each other from childhood; every habit, gesture and attitude is familiar. Any change of dress, mood or expression is immediately noticeable. Every word betrays, and even to fail to do something is significant. Gossip, cumulative, exchanged and re-circulated at the Bay, generates new speculation which radiates out through the community. The Bay is a news market and everyone who trades there is expected to contribute something to the exchange. A person's status in the community depends on the importance of his information. This obligation can be a burden, especially for people who are unpopular or on the fringe of the community, and to enhance their position, people will exaggerate trivial events, embroider, elaborate, distort. Although the gossip is distorted by the many personalities and prejudices of its purveyors, everyone believes it because everyone has contributed to it. Even the people who suffer from the gossip believe it.

Gossip, covering the community as a self-protective myth, creates the community's image of itself. Information which does not help to do this disappears, while the information which is considered important is that which satisfies the people's needs. If a community feels a sense of injustice, frustration and bitterness, the information circulated will justify and enhance those feelings. Information tending to disprove the collective prejudice will not be listened to or repeated. Everyone bearing his little load of information to The Bay makes an initial selection, asking himself what his listeners *want* to hear. If he tells them something that bores them, he will be shunned. He chooses the tidbit he thinks will please most, perhaps adding some embellishments for effect. What is left out of the gossip circuit can tell as much about a community as its legends. In Indian communities like Norway House, the legends revolve around the white man's injustice and Indian attempts to "go white" in white communities.

In Norway House, the importance of talking, listening, watching has become exaggerated. Going to The Bay to talk has replaced the vanished former occupations of Norway House, and material wealth has been replaced by a wealth of story. The principles are the same as the water-carrying industry. It takes time and skill to learn to gossip well; once these skills have been learned, gossip becomes a job. The men standing in front of The Bay are working.

Old people are the key people in the Norway House gossip circuit. No new information is coming into the community so the people are forced to pass around the stock on hand, the shop-worn stuff. Old people are best at this, simply because they've been around the longest and know everybody's history and family connections intimately.

It is easy for gossip to remake reality in a place like Norway House because it is physically and socially isolated. Miles of muskeg separate it from other communities; Indian Affairs and the provincial bureaucracy separate it from political involvement. Barrenness cuts its economic ties. There is no reason to go to Norway House; there is no reason to leave. Norway House has become introverted. Private lives become public business, for the community sits in perpetual judgement on itself. Because people are not working or have jobs which have no value in the eyes of the community they cannot be judged in terms of their contribution to the community or the formal role they play in it. They are judged, therefore, on the basis of their personal conduct, habits, idiosyncracies, ambitions. Only popular men, who have been approved by the information mongers, are given positions of power in Norway House. These are the men who tell the people what they want to hear; they enforce the collective prejudice. The prejudice becomes, through these men, respectable and institutionalized.

Privacy is impossible and, in fact, frowned upon. Every family squabble, every slap and spanking is public knowledge within hours. Friends talk; children talk because there is a ready market for this inside information. Members of a family which attempts to achieve privacy will find themselves spied upon. Friends will cease speaking to them and the community will ignore them. They will find themselves cut off from sources of information because they have refused to participate by allowing themselves to be spied upon. Gossip will be turned against this family, and lies circulated about them. They will be talked about twice as much as before. Silence will fall in a group when they approach. The spread of ugly rumors about fighting, liquor and fornication will bring persecution from other sources; the priest or minister will come around and ask questions; the RCMP might arrive; a social worker or health nurse might investigate. The family will get the reputation of being a 'bad' family.

This kind of social pressure can mean starvation. If the Indian agent or a social worker hears the bad rumors, the father may find his welfare cut off, or find himself last in line for any jobs that come from the agent. The community will provide nothing in an emergency. The children may be blamed, wrongly, for offences at school and may even be sent away to reform school. Some rebels leave the community and never return, while many use liquor as their protection, dropping out of the community and becoming an embarrasssment to it. They become slovenly, so poor, so irresponsible that no slander can make their reputation any worse. Gossip cannot touch them, for they have forfeited their good names.

Gossip in Norway House is not only conservative, based on the habits and views of the gossipers, it is also turned towards gaining the favor of the bureaucracy. In gossip, the Indians compete for favors and, by attacking each other's reputations they enhance those of the officials while destroying their own. Gossip fictionalizes life, and actually creates for each member of the community a role which he is expected to play, and does play. Each person knows his role, accepts the stereotype which the gossip has made of him, and acts it out from day to day. If a man is known for his slow speech, he will speak even more slowly so that his characteristics are even more noticable. If a man has a peculiar laugh, he uses it again and again. The Indians behave like actors carefully trained for parts in a play.

The script is written daily, and the scenes acted impromptu, with everyone in full costume. Most outsiders mistake the set for reality. They think these people are standing around doing nothing. "We must bring in jobs," they say. "The people must work. Industry Relocate. Upgrading." The cast of thousands doesn't move or relocate. They *are* working. To live is to act and acting is work. They are carrying water. They are going to The Bay.

Cops and Robbers

The hospital at Norway House, called "the compound," is surrounded by a modest wire fence beyond which its staff is not encouraged to venture. Outside the compound is native territory.

The hospital administrator (who has left Norway House since this was written) spent several years in Malaya and the Belgian Congo before taking up his post at Norway House in

1964. He is an elderly man with silvery white hair and a ruddy complexion bronzed by the tropical sun reflected off the river's ice. He wears, under his overcoat, summer pale khaki gabardine trousers, and a zipper jacket. Underneath, a sky-blue starchy shirt matches his eyes, which are candid and slightly squinty from staring down gun barrels in the bright sun. The furniture in the Administrator's house is Early American Colonial red maple. It is fittingly provided by the hospital. The doctor himself has added many trophies and souvenirs of Africa, tooled leather cushions, a white wool rug, assorted tusks and horns, brass and silver ornaments. The effect of all the red and polished wood is an exotic and appropriate decor which could be described as "Imperialism" or "Britannia Rules". On the desk is a framed photograph of the doctor in a red military jacket with gold braid, sword and medals.

Since the white people at Norway House wear uniforms, the place makes a strong military impression. The nurses all wear white dresses and the doctors white jackets. They have regulation navy blue nylon parkas with red and yellow braid trim for winter wear. The navy blue parkas are also worn by Indian Affairs people, and by most of the school teachers and other civil servants. Those civil servants who do not have blue parkas have khaki ones, as do the RCMP, who wear, of course, police uniforms. Priests and ministers are garbed in black and the nuns in grey.

The Indians wear black or motley. They have, of course, black hair and brown skins, but the blackness is intensified by general use of black windbreakers, black stretch slacks, black trousers, black kerchiefs and skirts, black shirts. A navy blue parka with red and yellow braid is never found on an Indian. Parkas cost too much. Even the young people give the impression of total blackness, from head to foot, although they may—girls particularly—wear bright pink slacks or a red cap. This one color seems to heighten the blackness. On others, colors and patterns are jumbled, faded, patched so that every garment cancels out the others and the total effect is zero. Plaids, stripes, floral patterns, solid colors, wool, cotton, nylon, gabardine are all worn at once. An Indian's clothes match only if he's in black.

The Indians' clothing has a peculiar quality. Their dress is like that of war refugees, camp followers tagging across the face of the earth after some massive imperial army. The people clothe themselves with the refuse of this army. They live in the smoke and grime from the battles being fought on the distant front. Men and women wear army surplus clothes, khaki parkas, old and out of style, heavy hobnailed boots, serviceable galoshes, drab green pants. This military clothing comes from Indian Affairs which handed it out as rations for years and probably still does, although most of it looks old. Some of it was inherited by men who joined the army and went overseas in World War Two; now it is ragged and patched, but still wearable.

In these clothes, the Indians slouch, lounge or straggle. They do not stand up straight, but are hunched over, leaning to one side, bent, walking with a shuffle. Their gestures are vague, half-formed, indecisive, their bodies limp and shapeless. This peculiar shambling quality, with each part of the body moving at a different rhythm in a different direction, makes them seem out of focus, and they become blurry, vague, cloudy. After a while, one doesn't notice them any more.

The Hospital

The hospital is the principal institution at Norway House. It is the main employer. Sickness is the primary industry.

The hospital, as in African communities, gives Norway House what structure and meaning it has. It is a northern Lambarene. The hospital, or the hospital mentality, controls the entire community, Indian, Metis and white, and the hospital administrator, as the highest ranking civil servant, is, in effect, the Administrator of the community. Everyone depends on the hospital. It is today what the Hudson's Bay was a century ago.

1963–In Rossville, the children are vomiting. Children with poisoned bowels are admitted to the hospital daily. They are its most frequent users. Not infrequently, a small child or baby, untreated, will starve to death from rejecting all his food or, weakened with malnutrition, will fall sick with pneumonia. Filth causes this diarrhea and vomiting. Doctors despair of the slovenly housekeeping of the Indian women in Rossville: "They just will not learn to keep things clean. They can't see the connection between a dirty privy, a fly and a sick child. Then they blame the hospital. They leave food out uncovered until it goes bad or all kinds of flies and dogs and things get into it. You should see some of their water pails, all scum. Haven't been washed for years. With those kind of homes, what can you do? Mice and lice and God knows what running through everything. At least the kids get clean at the hospital."

A public health nurse is employed to make home visits, checking up on sick children and attempting to teach the women the importance of cleanliness. She doesn't make much headway, and the children continue to get sick.

"My kids were sick all the time, throwing up. I couldn't get a job. I had to stay home all the time, getting water, chopping wood to keep them warm. I couldn't leave them. As soon as one would get better, another would be sick."

Sam Anderson got a job as assistant to the health nurse. He was hard-working, anxious to learn and it would keep him close enough to home to help his family. He had been raised in Norway House, knew everyone, and spoke Cree better than English. It was his job to interpret to the Indian women the importance of cleanliness. Sam and the health nurse spent a lot of time looking into outdoor privies in Rossville, most of them filthy. "Dirt," Sam lectured the Indian women in Cree, "makes little animals like lice, only much, much smaller, so small you can't see them. These are called germs. When the germs in this dirt get on food or into water, they make it bad. Your children get sick from eating these germs." The women giggled. Imagine not being able to see an animal. Sam, they thought, must have got converted to some new white man's religion (the Pentecostals had been active in the area). Disinfectant was, however, issued free to the women and some of them sloshed it around with a will. The children continued to get sick.

Every day, someone from each of the 109 families in Rossville would walk to the river bank a few yards in front of his house, pail in either hand, and scoop out buckets of clear, cold water. Norway House people had always taken their water from the river. There is nowhere else; inland water is brackish from the muskeg.

"I learned how to test the water to see if it is pure. One

*day, I tested our drinking water from the pail. It was
poisoned. Then I went to the river and took a sample from
there. It was poisoned. I took a lot of samples from the
river—everywhere the water was not good."*
—Sam Anderson

In the hospital, two miles upriver from Rossville, a patient
flushed a shiny white disinfected toilet. In a rush of water, the
excrement disappeared like magic, proceeded along a network
of hidden pipes and, minutes later, was excreted into the Nelson
River, raw, untreated, unprocessed. It proceeded on its way
downriver to Rossville. Patients, nurses, doctors, cooks, janitors—130 people—used that sparkling running water system at
the hospital every day. What happened to all the blood, the
dirty dishwater, the contents of bedpans, the vomit? It was
pumped into the river. Two miles later, the people of Rossville
dipped out what was left and drank it. Their children got sick.
They went to the hospital. There, they produced sewage which
went into the river.

"How could I tell them? They are powerful white people.
I'm just an Indian."

Sam sent away his water samples to experts in Winnipeg.
They verified his findings. Armed with his letters, Sam broke
the news to the administrator. "The hospital is making the
children of Rossville sick."

Sewage still goes into the river but it is treated first. Even
so, the people of Rossville have to carry their water in pails
from the residential school.

Sickness has been good business at Norway House since
the hospital was first built at Rossville in 1923. Almost as soon
as it opened, it was overcrowded. It was a pathetic venture. A
puny white clapboard two-storey structure with one doctor was
expected to treat all the sick Indians of northeastern Manitoba.
Moreover, the doctor had to recruit his own patients, flying
little monoplanes into isolated lakes and bringing his sick people
out to Norway House.

The Indians were very sick, sicker even than the outside
doctors suspected. Tuberculosis and malnutrition were almost
universal, starvation was frequent, and epidemics of measles,
diphtheria, and whooping cough carried off hundreds of children

every year. Pneumonia and venereal disease were commonplace, and smallpox was a recent memory.

To the idealists, the hospital, perched on its barren rock, was a beacon of hope. To the cynics, it was a fortress. The hospital has never lost its military connotations as a bastion in the war against disease, and against sick people.

> Indian: *"The hospital is death. The doctors there killed the Indian people. Some say they tortured them to death, cut them open alive. Nobody who went to the hospital came back. We knew that as soon as the doctor said a man had to go to the hospital, he was a dead man. Many sick people would hide in the woods when the doctor came. They wanted to die at home, in their own place."*

Because the hospital was so small, only the sickest people could be taken there, and many of them were on the verge of death. The hospital became a kind of terminal care institution. The Indian could see no point in going to a strange building to die. Facilities were inadequate at the hospital and, as in any hospital, some people died who shouldn't have died or who would have lived with better care. The white man promised life and produced death. Those patients who were not so seriously ill would be treated on the spot in the community, and their recovery was usually attributed to natural causes rather than to the doctor.

Hospitals do not normally recruit patients. Teams of interns do not patrol the streets, pouncing on unsuspecting passers-by, punching needles in them, stripping them and subjecting them to an instant physical examination. Those diagnosed as sick are not apprehended and locked up until cured or dead in a strange institution in a state of quarantine, away from friends and relatives. Doctors do not canvass from house to house, banging on doors, demanding to examine all the people inside. They do not make threats about the terrible fate awaiting those who refuse to be examined. Hospitals and doctors expect people who feel ill to seek them out.

In times of crisis and extreme emergency, however, hospitals become authoritarian and aggressive—if for instance a community is stricken with the plague, typhoid or polio. Then the hospital takes over the whole community. Norway House has been in a state of crisis and epidemic since the hospital opened. The alert is always sounding. Nurses patrol the community, searching for the slightest sign of incipient disease. Northern Manitoba is an epidemic area. Disease must be sought out and eradicated. Pain involved in the cure is secondary. The hospital is doing battle with death itself.

The panic which is felt by the staff of a small, understaffed and inadequate hospital in the middle of a plague has never decreased. Every Indian is seen as a potential patient, a source of infection, and Indians are bodies to examine, treat, cure.

Patients are actively recruited, sometimes impressed. Almost every pregnant Indian woman in its region is flown into the hospital at least a month before delivery time (at public expense) and boarded in the community until the baby is born. She is then flown home with the baby. This kind of red-carpet treatment certainly provides an incentive for the women, married or not, to have children—one month's paid holiday by air. All this fuss and expense could be virtually eliminated except in problem births if there were enough nurses and trained mid-wives in the communities. Children, accessible to the hospital when at school, are watched even more closely. They are examined for everything and popped into the hospital at the drop of a hat.

There is a strong element of religious crusade to the hospital's zealous battle against disease. The public health nurse is the knight in the field. Cleanliness is her doctrine. Illustrated tracts under her arm, she travels from house to house, keeping a sharp eye open for lice, impetigo, coughs and rickets in the children while she talks about disinfectant and toothbrushes. She hopes to be able to apprehend any people who are already sick, and to prevent future sickness from occurring by giving sound advice. The attack has recently become more discreet. Because health units have been set up in many isolated areas, doctors no longer drop out of the sky in airplanes. The bombardier service, which was operated in winter to pick up sick people and bring them in, has been discontinued because the Indians used it as a free taxi. Because the emphasis has lately shifted from cure to prevention, the doctors no longer are in direct touch with so many people, and the war against disease has taken on some of the appearance of an intelligence operation, in which the Indians serve as the spies.

Hide and Seek

Because the health nurse cannot visit every home in the community in a week, or even in a month or two, she must rely on the gossip industry to tell her who is sick. This is how, in its search for sickness, the hospital first became tied up with information-getting. The onus is on the nurse to find the sick people, not on them to find her. The nurse becomes a detective. The people, for their part, hide their illnesses when possible and develop fake diseases to confuse her and waste her time. There is usually a high turnover in health nurses in the North (they marry Bay managers) which makes the people's job easier. It takes at least a year for a new nurse to learn the community and by then she's ready to leave.

The War on Sickness involves the whole community, white and Indian. School teachers, of course, are the best allies in the white community and the priests cover the adult front efficiently. Bay managers, Indian Affairs employees and other civil servants also pick up a good deal of stray information by overhearing conversations, assisted by the telephone, which a few Indian homes possess. (The Indians are beginning to realize their handicap and are requesting phones with private, not party, lines). The hospital, probably quite by accident, has hit upon the ideal method of obtaining information first-hand. It hired Indians and Metis. All its menial staff, nurses' aides, cooks, laundresses, cleaning women, janitors, are now natives, though no Indians or Metis hold positions of authority. The hospital is the chief, and almost exclusive, employer of native labor in Norway House, and about 80 to 100 people work there. They are not allowed to live in the compound but commute back and forth every day from their homes, so that they are in constant contact with the other Indians. This large staff provides the hospital with its essential window into the Indian settlement at Rossville and the Metis area across the river. It is a route along which flows the information the nurses need. Here, within the confines of the hospital, in a sterile, formalized atmosphere, the two communities meet. The native labor is cheap, abundant and highly proficient. The people are hard, conscientious workers. The hospital gets a fringe benefit—the ability to say that most of its staff are Indian or Metis.

The Indian staff members are made to feel an important part of the hospital's battle against germs. They are told that by working at the hospital, they are helping their community to be a better, healthier place to live. The most menial job seems important; the nurses and doctors are friendly and praise the staff's work; and the job also gives them status in their own communities. The fact that they are employed and making good wages makes them automatically superior to most of the rest of the people, who are unemployed and on relief.

These employees soon become dependent on their jobs. The money means the difference between poverty and relative affluence. There are dozens of people waiting and able to take the job away from them if they make a slip. They enjoy the praise and the feeling of being useful and important, of being community benefactors. So they are only too willing to co-operate with the nurses and administrators, to give the information desired. They consider it their public duty, a matter of importance, to tell who has been looking poorly or coughing badly lately, who is keeping a dirty home, who is neglecting the children. This information is given in an informal way, in the course of casual conversation. This system into which the hospital has slipped is well known to bureaucrats in other places, where, under the name of "milieu control," it provides the government with essential information about the people which it governs.

It can be argued that, under the circumstances of mass chronic disease of every kind, the hospital had no alternative but this militant ferreting out, this drastic crash program. It was an emergency in northern Manitoba in 1923. However, the people of Norway House, all 2700 of them, have now become physically and mentally dependent on the hospital. Sickness is habit-forming. By being cared for so completely, totally and efficiently, with no financial obligation on their part, no obligation even to seek out a doctor or a nurse, the people have accepted emergency care as normal. Norway House is a community of out-patients, who are often perfectly well, physically, but who have the mentality of patients. Why should they take precautions against illness if the nurse is going to do it for them?

So the emergency persists in Norway House. People who are overlooked by the nurse do not arrive at the hospital until it is almost too late to save them. When they die, the people become angry. Why has the hospital gypped them of life? It promised life.

When the nurse fails to anticipate the people's illnesses they become extremely resentful. "She is not doing her job," they complain. Health is something which is provided for them in the hospital, an inalienable right, like in the treaties.

The hospital works frantically at curing and preventing illness, but the harder it tries, the more passive and sick the people become. The hospital thus creates its own patients, along the lines of a capitalist enterprise. Indian and white attitudes work towards one end — to perpetuate the present arrangement.

Lots more information besides that connected with sickness passes through that umbilical cord from the natives to the compound. Almost through a process of osmosis, the hospital authorities find they know almost everything that is going on in the Indian and Metis communities. They are well-informed of the private lives of most of its major figures and know a good deal about what activities are being planned.

As The Bay is the connection on the telegraph line within the native community, the hospital is the key connection between Indian and white communities. The administrator, because he is in control of the hospital, is therefore in control of the information, and is the most powerful man in the whole community.

If the hospital were suddenly to break down or go away, the community would be thrown into a panic, and the people would feel they were going to die. This kind of panic has recently afflicted several communities in northern Manitoba where nursing stations have closed down. The people are terrified without the nurse there, although the main reason the health service can't get nurses to staff the stations is because the Indians make their lives miserable with complaints and demands.

The Cowboys

The white community in Norway House is as rigid and stereotyped as the Indian. Everyone is completely identified with his job, his position in the community. There is the Bay Man, the Hydro Man, the Telephone Man, the Indian Agent, the Health Nurse. Names are used seldom, but when they are, a tag is usually added: "This is John Smith, the Hydro Man." Doctors, of course, have their titles built in, and both the Roman Catholic and Anglican ministers use the term "Father" before their names. The nuns use Sister.

Initials are used as a kind of a code to refer to institutions or people. The Bay is a good example of an abbreviation. The churches are called UC and RC. The Indian Affairs is IAB; Community Development Officer is the CDO; Manitoba Telephone System is MTS.

The white community is a community of institutions. The visual effect is startling. All these institutions are grouped together, around The Bay at Rossville and around the hospital on Fort Island, each set in its own little compound, surrounded by a fence. It is a community made up only of government buildings—utilitarian,antiseptic, severe, each a world unto itself. There is no hodge-podge of stores, theatres, garages to soften the austerity.

There are no private homes within these compounds. The Indians' homes are carefully segregated towards the back. The white people who operate the institutions live in houses, but these are provided by the government according to a standard model and look more like official buildings than homes. None has any touch of individuality, and all are designed and painted to match the institution with which they are affiliated.This total bureaucracy has a military look, as if it were a POW camp in the depths of a tropical rain forest. The schools are barracks and inside each one, the jail-like UC school and the ugly, battleship grey RC school on Fort Island, is an army of little prisoners, 90 to 100 Indian children between six and 15 years old.

The clearings around these buildings are kept obsessively

clean. There is no garbage, no litter around the institutional buildings. Even one discarded cigarette package would, in winter, be a relief from the whiteness. The only spot of bright colour in the institutional community is the Canadian flag which flies over The Bay, the post office and the R.C.M.P. building.

Across the line in the Indian community the first thing noticed, sharply, is the litter. It is the litter associated with any summer cottage where there is no garbage pickup—discarded furniture, bottles, broken children's toys. Also, there are the wood piles with saws and axes lying around, washing sagging on the lines, tarpaper left over from covering the house. "The Indians are dirty, sloppy," say the white people. "They live in a garbage dump." This litter looks like a garbage dump only in contrast to the sterility of the institutional community.

All these institutions deal in people because people are the only raw material Norway House has. The hospital processes sick people into well people, the schools process ignorant children into educated children, and the churches make Christians out of heathens or Protestants out of Catholics (and vice-versa). Indian Affairs makes Indians out of people. Hydro and the telephone system are secondary; they assist the people-processors by making life easier for them.

The other institutions—churches and schools particularly—share the hospital's aggressive militancy. The residential school grabs the Indian children out of their homes at the age of six and locks them up in an ugly, dark, cabbage-stinking barracks ten months a year for ten years. The children sleep in tiny white iron cots in large dormitories, side by side. There is no privacy. The school is being phased out, so in 1966 its enrolment was down to 60 children. When it had a full enrolment of 160 in previous years, beds were crammed into the dorms so tightly that the children had to walk across them to reach their cots, and the floor was barely visible. It was built in 1952, but looks 60 years old. The halls and classrooms are dark and small, the whole three-storey structure is wood, all the furniture is old and broken, and classrooms are bare of even the minimum equipment and pictures. The building is a firetrap. The school is segregated with girls on one side, boys on the other. Although they eat in a common basement dining room and share the school rooms, indoor recreation areas are also segregated and duplicated, and are too small to do anything in.

The children are tight-lipped and uncommunicative, and have to be pumped for information. Boys of 11 and 12 wet their beds regularly. All speak poor English with a thick, slurred accent. It is slang English, the language of the lower class, television and crime. Their chief indoor recreation is playing pool, which they do with a will, using the thick end of the cue. Most of the students would be graded as retarded or dull-normal IQ, between 50 and 85.

One boy, who seemed a bit slow but by no means an idiot, has an IQ of three, I was told by a teacher in the school. Tommy, who speaks excellent, rapid, colorful English (the best English in the school) at 11 can neither read nor write. He is a bright, alert boy and a leader among the others, with an extensive spoken vocabulary. He has been raised in white foster homes. Everyone has tried to teach him, but he can not concentrate long enough to learn. He blanks out and is called unteachable. Many other students are also considered unteachable. They pass from grade to grade but learn little and care less.

At Easter in 1967, plans were being made to take 20 of these children to Expo in Montreal. The money—$4500—was being donated by the institutions of Norway House. The Anglican minister and a couple of the United Church school teachers were taking the children and paying their own fares. Some of the children would be from Norway House, the rest from the North. Plans were being made by an all-white committee. The Indian and Metis people were deliberately excluded from making arrangements. "If we got the community involved, they'd just haggle and bicker and mess things up and we'd never get anywhere," a young teacher told me. The children are sponsored by someone who puts up the money for their expenses; they are selected by the teachers and school administration.

"They aren't taking my boy anywhere," shouted one Indian woman at a band council meeting. "God knows what they're going to try to pump into his head now." Why wouldn't the school let her know what's happening? It must be something bad. Her son would not go to Expo under such humiliating conditions.

The Church

The Anglican church is a quaint old log building hidden in the woods on Mission Island, four or five miles upriver from the white settlements and very isolated. On Easter Sunday, 1967, its old dark oak pews are jammed with about 100 people, the majority of whom are Metis. Huge sheets of tinfoil are looped across the ceiling to reflect the heat. The walls are insulated with an inner wall of white heavy paper, tacked down with wooden slats. Dusty artificial flowers and wreaths adorn the altar. The flags are stained and brown with age. The stained glass window has been painted with poster colors. The people, with eroded brown faces and gnarled bodies, are bundled up in brown and black winter jackets and heavy boots. They sing the hymns in a thin, tuneless wail, half-tempo and everybody at a different place in the lyrics. Father Benard, who has the thin lips and wide-set hooded eyes of a Van Dyck portrait, wears a white surtout with lace along the bottom. He preaches a simple colloquial sermon about the Resurrection, about how John and Peter ran to the tomb and John got there first, but it was Peter who ran inside panting, to touch the place where Jesus had lain. Jesus and the disciples seemed like real people, fishermen like the men crowded into that church.

Most Sundays, the Anglican church draws only a dozen or so, but still it has a larger total congregation than either the United Church or Roman Catholic church. The annual collection at the Anglican church totals $1,200, also more than either of the other churches can muster. For years Father Benard talked about a new church but could draw no spark of interest from his congregation. What would happen if the old church just fell down? "That is an interesting question," said Father Benard. What about a church-without-a-church, just lay people? "You still need a building." The Anglican Church would be humiliated if it folded up in Norway House. It would be a terrible defeat. The United, Anglican and Roman Catholic churches have been involved in a knock-down, drag-out battle for Indian souls for 120 years. In most northern Manitoba communities, (but not Norway House) a partial truce has been declared.

There is an unwritten agreement between the Anglican and

United Churches that they will not take converts from each other. Catholics are, however, fair game.

Most isolated Indian communities are homogenous, according to which denomination got there first. The shepherds guard their flocks with jealous eyes. "In many plces the Catholics have come in, spent a lot of money and built a big church, but they have made only a few converts ," commented Father Benard with satisfaction. Norway House is one of the last battlegrounds.

Originally, the churches were able to exercise their power through the auxiliary services they provided, schools and medical care. The chaotic school system of Norway House is a result of this rivalry, in which every child locked up in school was counted a convert. Every mission had its school—in addition, before doctors and nursing stations came to the North, the priests and clergymen dispensed drugs and performed minor operations as well as last rites. The Indians, sensibly enough, developed the habit of going to the church with the best school or the best medical facilities. Keen competition developed among the churches as to who could provide the best facilities and therefore get the biggest congregation. A clever Indian would be baptized in two or three denominations, get educated, and stay healthy in the process.

> *"The church is becoming less and less important. Norway House is different from other northern communities. It is half-way to Winnipeg. Other agencies have taken over — Indian Affairs, the hospital, schools."*
>
> Father Benard

The church, standing alone on the merits of Christianity, is falling. All the small denominational schools are being replaced by a large, central public school run by the government. The hospital long ago took over the medicine. The churches are now building their own tombs. The United Church built a large, expensive hall in Norway House in 1966. No one is allowed to use it except church groups. Therefore, few people use it. Because the United Church has its new hall, the Anglicans feel obligated to counter with a new church,whether the people want it or not. The Bishop was alerted to the seriousness of the situation (how the wretched Catholics would crow) and the church is being provided, occupied or unoccupied. If the Anglican church is built, the onus will then be on the Catholics to produce a new structure.

An entente has been established between the United Church and the Anglican priest. They co-operated on the Expo venture to the exclusion of the Catholics. (One reason the community was not involved might have been that it would have enabled the Catholics to manoeuver some of "their" children on the trip.) All the clergymen spend a great deal of time in the white communities, and they have lost direct influence over the Indian and Metis people. They maintain that power indirectly by subtly influencing the other agencies. Father Benard spends a lot of time at the UC school and takes boys home with him for weekends. He also visits in the community, making friends, carrying news, listening. He is friendly, good-natured, intelligent, sympathetic, and everywhere he gives advice discreetly, helpfully. The Indian agent and his wife attend the Anglican Church. The Roman Catholic priest, Father Fleury, is highly respected by the Administrator. Father Fleury is also ubiquitous, here, there, everywhere.

The two Fathers (the United Church minister seems to lack the talent and inclination for intrigue) know all. Because they officially represent Morality, they comment and give opinions on community affairs which others are hesitant to give. Any dogmatic opinion expressed by any authoritative person in Norway House almost certainly originates as a reflective observation by Father Fleury or Father Benard.

Parties

This institutional community has its own highly efficient lines of communication. It has, of course, the telephone, which links all the important people during the day. The hospital is the entertainment centre of Norway House, partly because it is the biggest institution and partly because it has a large supply of single girls. Many Bay managers are single, as are the R.C.M.P. constables and assorted school teachers.

The compound has a curling rink, and a recreation hall is being built for dances. Movies are shown twice a week. Parties, however, provide the principal method of communication.

"Why, when you see the girls at the parties all dressed up in their pretty little formal dresses, it shows that life up here need not be any different, or any worse than in any city. I encourage them to dress up in their good clothes. They mustn't let themselves go just because they are in the north. I try to set certain standards of behavior. It's so easy to slip. You have to be careful not to let yourself slide."

The Administrator

Sometimes the decorum goes awry. One evening the nurses planned a Bavarian beer garden party, with checked table-clothes, candles, songs and, of course, beer. A bunch of very exuberant beer-drinking construction men from the telephone company showed up and got into the spirit of things by drinking vast quantities of beer. The Administrator called them a bunch of drunks and ordered them out of the compound. So lonely is life in Norway House for the institutional people that they depend on these civilized entertainments, these formal social evenings of cocktails and gossip as their main amusement. It is, therefore, important that they do nothing to alienate the Administrator or the hospital staff for fear of being socially ostracized and perishing from loneliness.

Because they suffer from the same boredom, white people in Norway House have evolved a gossip circuit identical to the Indians'. Everyone's private life is enquired into, assessed, and passed around, and strangers are relished and painstakingly cross-examined. Those who do not conform to middle class standards do not last long at Norway House. This gossip exchange operates to reinforce fear and dislike of Indians exactly as the Indians' stories reinforce dislike of white men.

Their creed is: We do not adapt to become like the natives. We must make the natives become like us. We must be careful, vigilant. We must preserve the cocktails, the chitchat, the Christmas turkey and the formal gowns in the depths of the jungle. We must not go native. We do not talk to natives and do not mix with them socially.

The fact that the government people, and the Indians, believe in the myth, in the ideology which this society is trying to project instead of daily reality, creates this peculiar half-reality in the shifting world of Norway House. The people believe mythology to be real; human experience is subordinated to the claims of doctrine. The people no longer believe the evidence of their senses.

The people in the compound are able to keep up appearances because the hard labor is done by the Indian servants who usually come in the morning, clean the house, cook and go home in the evening. Like the hospital employees they are an excellent source of information and they depend upon the money from their jobs.

Charlie is an Indian employed as handyman and part-time carpenter around the hospital. "Charlie comes in and has his tea with us every day," the Administrator told me benevolently. "He should come in any time now. You can see where Charlie's been here," the Administrator said, pointing at a large black footprint on the white rug. Charlie came in but he had his tea in the kitchen.

Ogima

From inside Norway House, the Administrator and the Bay Man and the Indian Agent look like powerful people. From outside, they, and Norway House, are insignificant. Living at Norway House is a game which is played according to rules laid down by somebody else. All the information and gossip which circulates within the community is important only in relation to the outside. All really important information is transmitted along the radio-telephone lines or the airline connecting Norway House with Winnipeg and Ottawa. No important decisions are made in Norway House. All decisions are made in Winnipeg and Ottawa. In Norway House, the white men are ogima or boss-man. These bosses have bosses outside who make the rules of the game, since Norway House is only an institution, governed by an outside bureaucracy. The white people are servants of the government.

Rules and orders which are set down formally by authorities in Winnipeg determine the structure of the community. All the people in Norway House are dependent, helpless, frightened. Rules are changed at any time, capriciously, by men on the outside. The wilderness which the institutions are fighting is not the noncommittal forest, not the native population, but rather the fear which comes from ignorance and helplessness. God is up there on Parliament Hill, or in the Manitoba Legislature. He issues edicts which must be obeyed and gives no reason for them. There is no way the people can map out and plan their futures—a telegram can change everything.

While the Indian and Metis hospital staff and servants are useful sources of information to their employers, the system works the other way as well. The employees keep their ears open, and carry large quantities of valuable news from the outside back with them when they go home at night. The Indian people, who are dependent on the institutions which are dependent on the bureaucracy, need to know as quickly as possible what is happening on the outside. The servants tell. In this way, in their fear of the outside, the white and Indian communities are bound closely together. Their interest is mutual, and inmates and the guards are on the same side when it comes to dealing with inspectors or politicians.

Although the community seems so split and the two camps are antagonistic, there is a deep, powerful bond uniting them. The hospital needs patients and the patients need the hospital. The Bay needs customers and the customers need The Bay. The hiders need seekers and the seekers need hiders to seek. Everyone is content. Change must be prevented at all cost. In this task, Norway House is united to the death.

The gossip industry, held together by the servant class, is Norway House's protection against the outside. Every bit and scrap of news or speculation about the outside is passed around the entire community. Instinctively, everyone works out a unified way of coping with a threat. Gossip, by creating a total, inverted, looking-glass universe, keeps outsiders outside. Many government people come into Norway House to poke around, so many in fact that the hotel is always full of directors or inspectors or supervisors or MPs, and the airline does a booming passenger business. They are confronted with an irrational world where everyone works at not working, where private lives are public, where trivial things are crucial. Everyone talks about things which are of no interest. Visitors can't find out anything. The government inspector takes it for a couple of days, then scrambles back, glad to forget about the place. Everything seemed fine; he'll just let it go. Norway House is reprieved. The dangerous people are men who make decisions without coming to visit, so Government must be kept satisfied. Things must be done according to the rules. Norway House must go on the way it has always gone on. Nothing positive must be done. No action, no agitation, no crisis must arise. The attention of the Government must not be directed towards it. Be quiet.

But mistakes are made. Clever young men like Sam Anderson learn too much and take their jobs too seriously. It was bad enough Sam found out about the water pollution, but by calling in outside experts he did a dangerous thing. News about the polluted water at Norway House spread outside. All kinds of people found out about it (thank God not the newspapers). Had Sam simply told the Administrator, the hospital could have quietly corrected it and the Administrator could have taken credit. It was too bad Sam found out at all; it should have been a nurse or doctor. Then the Indians need never have known.

The hospital was shaken. The Indians were angry. The hospital had lost face with them. Its omnipotence was shattered. Now the Indians knew what they had suspected all along—the hospital made them sick. Its power and authority were questioned. Worse, the bosses in Ottawa were furious, and the reputation of the whole department was at stake. The hospital was purged. People were threatened, fired; control was tightened.

But the old equilibrium might have been re-established had another mistake not happened. A man in Island Lake, Manitoba, an Indian community about 100 miles north of Norway House, was in the airline's shed one day when he noticed what seemed to be a baby's arm sticking out of a cardboard box which had been kicked into a corner. The arm was sticking out because the box had been so badly damaged. The man discovered that the box was addressed to him, and it was, in fact, the reason he had come to the shed. The body of his stillborn baby daughter was being shipped back from the Norway House hospital to Island Lake for burial. It had been some time since the baby had been born and he had been wondering what had happened to the body. The body was in the cardboard box. Sealed closed with masking tape and put on the airplane, either no one knew what it was, or it had been lost in the shuffle, so it had lain, frozen, in the shed for some time.

Within hours, the story had been circulated through Island Lake. In days, it had reached many Indians in the North and certainly the Indians of Norway House. The hospital again was embarrassed, frightened, shaken. Another unfortunate accident, and again an Indian had found them out. The hospital which, until then, had been tense but secure in its authority within the community, became frightened. Instead of sitting happily on the central circuit for all information, the hospital felt vulnerable.

Since 1960, there had been trouble in surrounding Indian communities: a demonstration in Thompson, sensational press reports about starvation in Nelson House, a strike of Indian employees at the Hydro dam in Grand Rapids. The hospital felt that some vast subversive plot was afoot to start an Indian uprising and it was the next target.

Because the hospital was sensitive to pressure from above, it started to pressure the people underneath it whom it felt responsible for the trouble, the Indians. The system for gleaning information, the cord of servants and employees, turned into a system for exerting pressure, pressure to keep quiet, not to make any more mistakes. This pressure has made the Indians afraid too.

Because everyone now fears trouble, trouble is always anticipated. Anyone who visits the community is a potential trouble-maker, not a potential benefactor.

The hospital finds itself operating a kind of "protection racket". Those individuals who co-operate with it will receive medical care. Those who do not co-operate might find themselves ignored. The hospital has made the Indians dependent on it by giving them total care for free. Even a slight cold has been treated as a kind of emergency. Now, it begins to withdraw that service, slowly. For the Indians, who see the hospital as meaning the difference between life and death, this withdrawal is terrifying.

The hospital's retreat from the community, the cutting of contacts, is done in several ways. A rumor is started that the hospital might close down. The Administrator himself is the chief bearer of this indirect threat:

"There is absolutely no legal reason why we should provide anything in the way of medical care for these people at all."

He is right and the people know it.

The Administrator throws doubt on the competence of the hospital and its staff:

"The hospital is too small. We can't attract good doctors up here. All we get are inexperienced young interns right out of medical school or some incompetent old fellow who can't tell one disease from another and never could. It should be turned into a teaching institution. Good hospitals are needed in places like this. These people deserve as good care as city people." That's a bit alarming, for a hospital administrator to say his own staff is second-rate, and does not inspire confidence in the Indians. Unless the hospital is reformed it would be better to take everyone into Winnipeg hospitals, says the U.C. administrator. If the Indians make life too difficult for them, the doctors and nurses might simply resign. It would be weeks and months before they could be replaced and how would Norway House like that?

The bombardier service which transported patients to hospital in winter was cut off. "I had to put my foot down," said the Adminstrator. "Too many healthy Indians were using it as a taxi service to get to the beer vendry. It was being abused." The Indians, many of whom live five to ten miles away, have to arrange their own transportation, and it costs $5 to hire a bombardier.

The Indian and Metis employees at the hospital found themselves under more direct pressure: obey or be fired. Because the hospital controls most of the jobs in Norway House it can also control the community. Many of its employees are intelligent, strong-willed young people who would like to take an active part in community affairs. They cannot do so.

Sam Anderson was on the band council at Rossville when he was hired as assistant to the health nurse. He wanted to run for chief, but he was told that because he was now a federal civil servant, he could not hold elected office. He had to choose between making a living and being on the council. He resigned from the council and did not run for chief. All the other hospital employees are in the same position, so the affairs of the community are left in the hands of old age pensioners. The hospital decrees the political structure of Norway House by whom it hires and fires. Potentially dangerous people are kept on staff and treated with special favor. All staff members get little special considerations, and they know these will disappear if they displease the administration.

People have been fired and not replaced from the community. Advertisements have appeared in outside newspapers for persons to fill their jobs. The hospital doesn't trust the Indians any more. It is cutting back. White people will be brought in to take over the whole operation. The Indian people have responded by becoming violently antagonistic to the hospital. The Indian staff members keep their eyes and ears open for scandalous stories which they can ferry back to the community, stories of drinking and parties and feasts, of affairs, intrigues and mistakes. Grievances against the hospital have become institutionalized. Tales of injustice grow into legends.

"The hospital is evil, poison! " exclaimed one man, tense and shaking with emotion. "They will not send their bombardier to get our sick people because it is too busy taking the hospital staff to their parties."

The chief accused the Administrator in public: "You have no right to take the bombardier away from us. It is your duty to serve us. It is our right. If we weren't here you wouldn't have a job." "If the Indians want an ambulance service so badly, why don't they provide it themselves? " asked the Administrator.

The hospital staff is cursed and plagued with complaints about its service. "Whatever you do for them it is never enough," sighs the Administrator. "Always, they are demanding more. They do not ask, they demand. I have been here three years and I just don't understand these people. I don't understand what goes on in their minds."

By removing the bombardier, the hospital broke the rules of the sickness game. It told the people, in effect, they had to start getting well on their own. The vital link between hospital and patient was shattered. Until then, the patients had felt a part of the hospital routine. They accepted its power, and they accepted being servants. They accepted the parties and wine and social gatherings from which they were excluded. Patients, they knew, had no right to these things. They didn't resent the wealth and fun because they knew certainly that those strong, wealthy people were there to serve them, the patients. As long as they had a comfortable bed to lie in, daily meals and blood transfusions to keep them alive, they were content. They were secure.

As soon as the hospital pulled the bombardier out, attitudes towards the hospital began to change. Contentment turned to outrage and hate. That bombardier was the connection with the hospital world. Now the people hate the hospital which has turned against them. Now that they are no longer served slavishly by it, they hate its superiority. They hate the ostentatious display of wealth, the food, the wine, the dances. They hate being menial servants when the hospital refuses to serve them. They hate all the white people of Norway House, the people that might, any day, like the hospital, pull out and let the community die. They don't hate them because they are white or because they are unpleasant, they hate them because they are guards, wardens, doctors with absolute power. They hate them because they are afraid of them.

This hate erupts like a plague in Norway House. The first people to suffer are those in limbo, the native employees on the hospital staff. Not only does the hospital intimidate them, but their own community turns against them. The people suspect the employees have been "bought" by the hospital. They think that, in exchange for their jobs, the staff people have agreed to supply information about the Indian and Metis people. An informal, valuable relationship is now seen as deliberate and evil. The staff personnel are, in the eyes of their own people, stoolies and informers. They are suspected, shunned, threatened. All the importance they once possessed has disappeared.

Russell Balfour is a band constable at Norway House. He is paid by Indian Affairs and recommended by the band council to preserve law and order on the reserve. The R.C.M.P. is also responsible for preserving the peace in Norway House, both on and off the reserve. Since there is usually only one R.C.M.P. constable to supervise the whole community, Balfour was asked to team up with the R.C.M.P. man on occasion. Balfour agreed and began to go around on investigations with the R.C.M.P. man. He was immediately branded by the community as a stoolie. He was spying and informing on them for the police, the people said. Balfour explained he was the police. Yes, but he was *their* police. The R.C.M.P. was different. Balfour's life has been threatened, and he has been beaten up by men he has grown up with and knows well. He has been told that unless he quits being seen with the R.C.M.P., he will "get it." The men mean it. One day, Russell Balfour will be found floating in the river, or accidentally shot.

The people have nothing against Balfour in particular, or against the R.C.M.P., with one constable for 2700 people spread over ten miles. Everyone is suspected of being a hostile spy. Casual conversations are analyzed: What was he trying to find out? What did she mean by that? Everyone must have a good excuse for being wherever he is. People talk in whispers. The gossip industry has turned into a spy industry. The information is no longer harmless, but is used to inspire fear and suspicion. The community is divided into Good Guys and Bad Guys; each person makes his own assessment, but there are no neutrals. From a philanthropic enterprise—the establishment of a hospital—a situation of racial hatred has arisen. It took 40 years. A mission of compassion, help and equality, has bred hate, destructiveness and segregation.

Outsiders

Norway House is a compound. The fences and walls are invisible but very real. The people have depended for so long on the institutions — the hospital, the churches, the schools, Indian Affairs, even the telephone — that they now see themselves as incapable of living without them, incapable of living outside Norway House. The people have become "institutionalized." They are perpetual offenders, recidivists. Freedom is a terrifying thing.

Their complaints are not directed at having to live in this compound but along the lines that it is not run efficiently enough. Norway House people do not complain that the hospital intimidates them by threatening to close down, or by firing members of its staff. They complain that the bombardier service is cut off. They do not appear to be able to see that the bombardier service was another lever the hospital could use to intimidate them and they are better off without it. When it is suggested they supply their own ambulance service, financed by the government grants, the people make no effort in this direction. They would rather complain about the hospital's meanness than provide themselves with a bombardier.

Support for genuinely dangerous protests mysteriously evaporates. White people in Norway House use the labor of jail inmates — Indians doing time for liquor offences — to build halls, auditoriums and do chores. When the Indians recently asked the R.C.M.P. to be able to use inmate labor on their band hall, they were refused.

Many Indians and Metis in Norway House see the jail as a real grievance; they feel persecuted by the fact that so many Indians are arrested for drinking. It seems incredible that one policeman can intimidate 2,700 people, but they see him as a symbol of the totalitarian authority of all government institutions. The police tend to be lenient; the stories circulated about them describe how a cop pushed an Indian downstairs. One incident is magnified to typify police behavior in general.

One man drew up a letter of protest to the Attorney-General. He asked for an investigation of the whole police and legal process in Norway House in order to clear up the people's complaints and explain what is happening. No one else in Norway House would sign the letter. It will go to the Attorney-General as one man's complaint and likely be brushed aside. The Norway House people will, of course, complain when they are brushed aside. They will verbally attack the Attorney-General.

Norway House's grievances will never be settled. By making half-hearted complaints and backing out at the last minute, the people anger the government. They are worse off than before. The people seem to be willing to sacrifice themselves and their children to be able to take revenge on the government by causing it annoyance.

"The people here have lost their ability to think. They just don't think anymore. The young men lie around in the shade playing cards and smoking, drinking. You can't tell the people how to bring up their children properly. They won't listen.

"I go to talk to some of the women about improving things like health and the schools. They will hear what I have to say and then just laugh and turn to some other topic.

"The council is controlled by old people. We will talk to one of the councillors about a proposal to make at the meeting. He will agree to mention it. He will lose the piece of paper with the proposal written on it. He will forget to speak about it. 'Eh, what was that you told me again?' he says later. My own father is on the council and he won't speak out about the way Indian people are treated here.

"I don't know what we can do, the people can't read or write most of them. I have to fill out their welfare forms and do all the writing for them, it takes up all my time. They can't do anything for themselves; they take all their letters to the agent to have him read them. 'Oh, well,' they say, 'I'll just take this over to the agent. He will do it for me'."

Maggie

If a person is dependent on the Indian agent to read and write and fill out welfare forms for him, he is not likely to do or say anything which will anger the agent.

Frustration and emotional tension are high in Norway House. What does a man do with a sick child and no way to get to the hospital because neither the hospital nor the band will provide transportation? He weeps when he tells about the anxiety of having to walk the five miles or wait for a friend to find some transportation. The people show tremendous anger at describing injustices of the police; they shake and their eyes blaze. The emotional reaction is disproportionate to the event or complaint related; the people seem to be trying to express a whole lifetime of helplessness and servitude by relating one incident. The emotion is generated by their impossible position.

Community Development Officers have been assigned to Norway House to help the Indians. Some of these officers have been able to assist with little caretaking jobs. One helped the fishermen organize a co-op to harvest what fish were left in the lake. A residents' association was organized, and is dominated by white people. Indians are excluded because they are on the reserve, and in the eyes of the whites the Metis aren't really residents, but squatters. The whites are only temporary renters.

A school committee was formed to control and unify the multitudinous schools. The committee, however, perceives its function in terms of supplying blackboard erasers and making sure the schools are warm. The first two CDOs played house with all their little toy committees which had no power. The CDO was busy from morning to night, calling meetings, picking people up to take them there, sitting through hours of irrelevant debate, taking people home, listening to grievances, reporting illnesses and indigent cases to the proper authorities, writing reports to headquarters. His house was built just behind the hospital, next to the Hydro Man's. He was automatically absorbed into the white compound.

The people, white and Indian, understood what his real job was. The CDO was there to help the institution run more smoothly, to iron out any kinks and bumps, to be a go-between, a shuttle between patients and doctors, inmates and guards. He was, in effect, a resident social worker, another institution. He would supply another service. The Indians would allow themselves to be community-developed. The CDOs failed, as everyone before them, to break the Indians' habit of seeing themselves as consumers. Their appetite for community-development was as voracious as for medicine. The CDO could never do enough, and the Indians themselves, of course, did nothing.

The CDO's technique was to become absorbed into the community—to become inconspicuous, friendly, good-natured, intelligent, sympathetic; just, as a matter of fact, like the two Fathers. Like them, his influence was to be unobtrusive. His advice would be casual. He could encourage people to think for themselves. He would anger and alienate no one. His ideas would be adopted unconsciously. Such a technique can improve a system's operation. It can never change one system into another.

Two members of the Company of Young Canadians arrived in Norway House in March 1967. One was Benny Baich, the Jesse James of the North—hero of a strike in Grand Rapids, organizer of a march in Thompson, instigator of the press scandals about starvation. Fear came to the surface in Norway House. The people were going to be roused, organized. There would be an uprising, murder and mayhem, riot.

Baich called a public meeting. The United Church

refused to rent him their new hall (the CGIT, all nine girls, was using it). He was accommodated in the small auditorium in the residential school in Rossville. No one would rent him a bombardier to get to the meeting. The Administrator refused to attend, but sent his secretary, who took shorthand notes. Indians filled the front of the room, while the white people sat at the back. Father Fleury was literally shaking, and Father Benard gave a passionate plea for peace in his opening prayer. Everyone expected an oration, a call to arms.

They might have got it, but the Indians had been working. The chief and council sat up at the front with Baich, and instead of letting him get close to the audience, they kept motioning Baich away from the front row of the spectators so that several feet separated him from the audience. As he spoke, one of the councillors made insulting remarks in Cree: "Don't listen to this dumb white man. Who is he? " The interpreter who was translating Baich's English into Cree became deaf and speechless with fright. He had been hired because he was fluent and accurate—under ordinary circumstances. But he could not hear what Baich was saying, and asked him to repeat every phrase. He garbled the Cree, had to stop and go back to repeat and would interrupt Baich in the middle of a sentence.

The passionate oration which everyone feared was scuttled. Baich, however, never intended one. On a large sheet of white paper, he had drawn a big circle in black ink. On the inside of the circle, he wrote "Indian people," while on the outside, he wrote "White people." Around the outside edge, he listed the institutions: hospital, schools, churches, R.C.M.P., airline, Indian Affairs. He held the circle up for the people to see. That, he said, is you, Norway House. The Indian people are all in here, on the inside. The white people are surrounding you. They keep you in there. They have the power.

He told the people what they looked like; he told them what they were worth— nothing. He talked about the money— the millions of dollars—that was being invested in Norway House and the return—nothing. Do you, he said, think the government and the people of Canada are going to let this situation, this drain of their resources, continue?

He held up his finger. Norway House is a finger of Canada. That finger is sick. It makes the whole body sick. He let the people work out the implication of what happens to sick fingers when they cannot be cured.

"It was the first time anyone had come in to Norway House and talked about the past, present and future. The CDO had just busied the people. 'They're children; you're a Communist,' the Roman Catholic father told me. The community was tense, so tense the interpreter couldn't hear. Everyone is afraid that other people are stool pigeons. If a man talks out of turn, he will be threatened that he'll lose his job. The Indians have got to act inferior if they want to survive. 'These people have failed me time and time again,' the Father told me.

"Norway House is a luxury. When is the day coming when they decide whether they shoot dogs or kids? When do they bring the soldiers? The government isn't trying to abandon Norway House—it's pouring in more money, bigger institutions. A new $3 million school is going to be built; they're making roads from nowhere to nowhere. This place is like a zoo when the animals start killing each other. The people have nothing else to do."

Benny Baich

When Benny Baich finished his speech and nothing happened, the white community was joyous. The uprising had been averted. Baich was branded a troublemaker, a Communist, and an aphorism went about the community about the Company of Young Canadians being "neither young nor Canadian." For two days after the meeting, though, the Indian people flocked to Baich with their problems, their hates, their grievances. For the first time, they expressed their feelings. They knew that what they had been shown was true. Fight, Baich told them. Free this place. Organize yourselves into a secret group, sworn to stand by each other. Write letters telling about the people being fired, the threats and pressures. Write to the premier, to all the white people in Norway House. Break open this secrecy. Tell everybody what is happening. "Like a bird, I fly over and look at a place," says Baich. "I don't stay. I have other work to do. But I can tell you what you look like to me. If you don't like what I show you, it's up to you to change it. I can't change it for you."

Baich went away, and the revolution didn't happen. The secret organization was not formed. The people lost their nerve.

In a few days, things which had seemed so clear at the meeting looked fuzzy. The rumor of Communism filtered down to the Indians. Was Baich really suspect? Who were they to believe? Perhaps things would improve. Perhaps nothing drastic need be done.

Sam Anderson sits there, eyes glowing, soaking up every scrap of information, every idea he can, thinking, planning, hoping.

"This place Norway House is a trap. It is poison. I could not speak English until four years ago. I used to go and hide under a canoe when I saw a white man, or even an Indian who was dressed strange. Rossville was like a big city to me. My father told me to quit trapping. 'I do not want you to get TB,' he said. A few years ago, the ambition of all the trappers was to catch a silver fox. Fathers told their sons about the silver fox. It was the most valuable of all furs. To trap a silver fox was the highest achievement. It was worth $500. Where has it gone now? It is being produced in fur ranches in the south. The silver fox up here is worthless now, I know. The Indians would trap baby foxes and sell them to the white ranchers from the south." Sam is looking for his silver fox—a nickel mine that will save Norway House.

His people hate. They nourish it with anecdotes and outrage. They clutch their grievances around them, licking their wounds. Their wails make a pleasant noise in their ears; it is better than silence. They have begun to enjoy their hate. What would they do without it?

Chapter 5
The Tramp of the Multitudes

More than one enthusiastic Indian chief or councillor, convinced the government is cheating his people out of their treaty rights, has written away to Ottawa to get a copy of his treaty, in order to outmaneuver the Indian agent who is trying to pull the wool over his eyes. The chief is astounded when he receives, by return mail, a little nine or ten page pamphlet bound in plain white paper and issued by the Queen's Printer. This little booklet, which looks more like a liquor commission price list than an official document, is his treaty. The Indian is dumbfounded. His treaty is supposed to be a huge, sacred document, written on parchment and bound with seals of everlasting fidelity. It is supposed to contain all sorts of guarantees. How can all these promises be written in nine printed pages? But nine pages is all there is, and it isn't much:

> ". . . the following articles shall be supplied to any band of the said Indians who are now actually cultivating the soil or who shall hereafter commence to cultivate the land, that is to say: two hoes for every family actually cultivating, also one spade as per family aforesaid, one plough for every ten families, five harrows for every twenty families, one scythe for every family, and also one axe and one cross-cut saw, one hand saw, one pit saw, the necessary files, one grind-stone, one auger for each band, and also for each Chief for the use of his band one chest of ordinary carpenter's tools; also for each band enough of wheat, barley, oats and potatoes to plant the land actually broken up by cultivation by such band; also for each band one yoke of oxen, one bull and four cows; all the aforesaid articles to be given once and for all for the encouragement of the practice of agriculture among Indians."

In this treaty Her Majesty also agreed that $1,500 a year would be spent by herself "in the purchase of ammunition and twine for nets for the use of said Indians." These promises, or "rights," were contained in Treaty No. 3 which served as a model for all the treaties which followed. It was signed at the site of the present town of Kenora on October 3, 1873. Indian leaders of the Lake of the Woods area had been notified in advance and had gathered at the meeting place. Her Most Gracious Majesty Victoria the Queen of Great Britain and Ireland spoke through the mouth of Alexander Morris, Lieutenant-Governor of Manitoba and the North-west Territories, who, in turn, spoke through the mouth of his Metis interpreter, James McKay. Her Majesty made herself clear at the start:

". . . it is the desire of Her Majesty to open up for settlement, immigration and such other purposes as to Her Majesty may seem meet, a tract of country bounded and described as hereinafter mentioned, and to obtain the consent thereto of Her Indian subjects inhabiting the said tract, and to make a treaty and arrange with them so that there may be peace and good will between them and Her Majesty and that they may know and be assured of what allowance they are to count upon and receive from Her Majesty's bounty and benevolence."

The "tract of country" mentioned was northwestern Ontario, with the exception of the tiny pockets of land reserved for the Indian people. There was certainly no doubt in Victoria's mind that the Indians were Hers and Her subjects. They were a conquered people, dependent on Her bounty and benevolence as, indeed, they have been ever since, and they were expected to live on an "allowance" in exchange for the country. The Indians were of course, being bought. In exchange for the Queen's bounty, the Indians ". . . do hereby cede, release, surrender, and yield up to the Government of the Dominion of Canada for Her Majesty the Queen and Her successors forever, all their rights, titles and privileges whatsoever to the lands . . . " Then follows a description of the area given up, five thousand square miles "to have and to hold the same to Her Majesty the Queen and Her successors forever."

In return for all this, the Queen set aside some of their own land for the Indians:

". . . the Queen hereby agrees and undertakes to lay aside reserves for farming lands, due respect being had to lands at present cultivated by the said Indians and also to lay aside and reserve for the benefit of the said Indians, to be administered and dealt with for them by Her Majesty's Government of the Dominion of Canada in such a manner as

shall seem best, other reserves of land in the said territory hereby ceded . . ."

The reserves were to be set aside where it was deemed most convenient and advantageous by the commissioners, after conference with the Indians.

Reserves were measured on the scale of one square mile for each family of five, more or less depending on the number of children. The government also reserved the right to sell, lease or otherwise dispose of reserve land "with the consent of the Indians first had and obtained." As far as this reserve land was concerned, the Indians had no rights whatsoever. They were living on government land which would be administered for them by the government. Even their reserve was not their own. The treaty could not have made it clearer that the Indians are wards and dependents of the government with no rights of self-government. Reserves were intended as government owned and operated farms which would support the Indian population, "to be administered and dealt with *for them* by Her Majesty's government."

> *". . . to show the satisfaction of Her Majesty with the behavior and good conduct of Her Indians She hereby through Her commissioners, makes them a present of twelve dollars for each man, woman and child belonging to the bands here represented in extinguishment of all claims heretofore preferred."*
>
> *". . . each Chief duly recognized as such shall receive an annual salary of twenty-five dollars per annum and each subordinate officer, not exceeding three for each band, shall receive fifteen dollars per annum."*

Each Chief and band councillor was also promised a new suit of clothes every three years and the chief, in recognition of the signing of the treaty, was given a "suitable flag and medal." Once a year, each Indian would get five dollars.

Four important agreements were made on the part of the government. These promises have been the source of most of the ensuing bitterness and conflict. The government promised to provide schools on the reserves, "whenever the Indians of the reserve shall desire it." Indians were forbidden to drink alcoholic beverages on the reserve. This regulation was not suggested by the government but by the chiefs themselves. Today, many of the older people on reservations are still strongly opposed to liquor within the reserve and many reserves are, legally, "dry."

The most controversial treaty clause and the one which has caused the most ill-feeling between the Indians and the government deals with the Indians' use of the land:

> *". . . The Indians shall have the right to pursue their avocations of hunting and fishing throughout the tract surrendered . . . subject to such regulations as may from time to time be made by Her Government . . . and saving and except such tracts as may, from time to time, be required or taken up for settlement, mining, lumbering or other purposes by Her Government or by any of the subjects thereof duly authorized by the said Government."*

This is, of course, a completely meaningless promise. It has resulted in the Indians having virtually no hunting or fishing rights whatsoever as settlement has gradually encroached on the land surrounding their reserves. Regulations such as the Migratory Birds Act made it illegal for Indians, as well as anyone else, to shoot game birds out of season. When the federal government turned the control of natural resources over to the provinces, new regulations were brought into force which further limited the Indians' hunting and fishing freedoms. Licences for trapping and fishing were required by the province from everyone, Indian and non-Indian. Most Indians, under the impression that the right to free hunting and fishing was a treaty right, did not bother to apply for a licence or did not even know a licence was required. Hundreds of them found their traplines and fishing grounds taken over by white men who had acquired licences from the government. The Indians, naturally, felt cheated. But the Indians were actually given no rights to hunt or fish at will in the treaties. Between mining, lumbering, farming, game preserves (which also bar Indians) and legal agreements, Indians have little freedom left. The only distinction which remains is their ability to hunt game animals, deer and moose out of season, much to the envy of their non-treaty compatriots. These animals provide an important food supply but not a living for an Indian. To make a living, he must have a licence like anybody else.

> *". . . Such sections of the reserves above indicated as may at any time be required for Public Works or buildings of*

what nature soever may be appropriated for that purpose by Her Majesty's Government, due compensation being made for the value of any improvements thereon."

Visit any reserve in Canada and you will be told a tale of woe of land taken away by the government without what the Indians consider to be "due compensation". No regulations were set up about who would decide what compensation was to be given and there was no right of appeal. Often, the Indian agent arranged with the chief to give the band a certain quantity of cash or food or equipment in exchange for land required for a railway track, highway or other purpose. Little was put in writing and what was written down has, in most cases, been lost. In many cases, the band would be satisfied at the time that they had received enough, but later would feel that they should have asked for more. When they saw land that was worthless to them being made productive by some enterprising farmer, its value increased in their eyes and they remembered that once it had been theirs. In many cases, no compensation was given when land was simply taken over by settlers who were not pushed off. Land has been sold by Indians to individuals and to cities, but the records of the sales, kept in Ottawa or lost altogether, are gone, and the Indians do not realize that the land was sold, although often for a pittance, and feel now they gave it away. It has become virtually impossible for even the most diligent lawyer to make a distinction between land legally sold and land stolen, when the transaction took place verbally 60 or 70 years ago. No written documents remain and the Indians themselves don't remember too clearly what happened. The treaties, apparently, gave the Indians very little, but the Indians, on their part, gave up a great deal. They yielded what rights they had as inhabitants of Canada:

". . . Solemnly promise and engage to strictly observe this treaty and also to conduct and behave themselves as good and loyal subjects of Her Majesty the Queen. They promise and engage that they will in all respects obey and abide by the law and that they will maintain peace and good order between each other and also between themselves and other tribes of Indians and between themselves and others of Her Majesty's subjects, whether Indians or whites . . . and they will not molest the person or the property of in-

habitants . . . or the property of Her Majesty the Queen or interfere with or trouble any person passing or travelling through the said tract . . . and they will aid and assist the officers of Her Majesty in bringing to justice and punishment any Indian offending against the stipulations of this treaty or infringing the laws in force in the country so ceded."

This paragraph makes the self-contradiction of the treaties clear. The Indians were not given "separate status" but "double status". They were to be both Canadians and Indians. Although they were to live on reserves separated from the rest of the population and governed by different rules, they were, at the same time, to be subject to all the rules of British justice to which normal Canadians are subject. The Indians, therefore, become subjects twice over.

The treaties, of course, are not really treaties at all. They were actually deeds of sale by which the Indians ceded their land to the government. By calling them treaties, the government led the Indians to believe that they were being treated as independent. Actually, behind all the high-flown language of the documents, the government was taking the position that the Indians were not really an independent political group, and by signing the treaties, the Indians unintentionally acknowledged that they were subjects.

The use of the word "subjects" is the clearest illustration of this. A government does not make "treaties" with its subjects. The government regarded the Indians as subjects; the "treaty" was a multi-purpose document by which these "subjects" ceded their land, and gave up their independence. The Indians fell into the trap and signed, and the government had in one step gained the land and destroyed the Indians as a separate political power which might have to be dealt with.

The repetitive use of "Her Majesty," "The Queen," and "Great Mother" in the treaties is also a subtle and deliberate misrepresentation. The Indians were not, as they were led to believe, negotiating with Great Britain but with Canada; to this day, many Indians are still under the impression that if they have any citizenship at all it is British, not Canadian. The Indians were not made aware of the fact that a new, untried government existed in Ottawa; they were led to believe they were dealing with a remote and omnipotent deity.

But this treaty arrangement, not even a technical surrender, was even less advantageous than a real surrender would

have been. The so-called "treaty rights" were not rights but
restrictions. Every "right," every "freedom" was dependent on
the bounty and benevolence of the Queen. They were fake
rights, as the treaty was a fake treaty. Reserves were set aside
for the Indians to assure them that they still possessed freedom
and independence, that not all their land was being expro-
priated, but the reserves were still to be Crown land, owned by
the government and "to be administered and dealt with *for
them* by Her Majesty's government, in such a manner as shall
seem best." The Indians, therefore, would get their own land,
separate from Canada, yet it would be administered by Canada
and would not be theirs. Similarly, the Indians' freedom to hunt
and fish would be preserved as long as it did not interfere with
the other desires of the government. The treaties gave the
Indians neither rights as Indians nor rights as Canadian citizens.
The Indians became wards of the government. Although the
government used the word "subjects" in the treaties, after the
signing, the Indians became a very special kind of
subjects—Indians—and henceforth they were treated as a separate class of citizens. The treaties put the Indians in Canada, but
prevented them from being a part of Canada.

So the British government—and later the Canadian
government—created an identity, a status for the Indian, and
embodied it in the treaties. By signing the treaty, the Indian
accepted the position in society and the personality which the
British imagined for him. He became a figment of the
Anglo-Saxon imagination. He is at least in his official, legal and
public self, an artificial creation. The Anglo-Saxon Canadian
invented the Indian.

The Great Mother

Treaty No. 1 with the Indians of southern Manitoba was a
direct result of the Riel rebellion of 1869. Although the Indians
did not farm, like the Metis, and had taken no active part in the
revolution, land had become an important issue to them. The
Metis' fear of being shoved back and dispossessed spilled over
onto the Indians, who became extremely worried. News of their
agitation was soon carried to Ottawa. It was obvious, after Riel,
that some agreement would have to be made with the Indians.
Although settlers had been in the region since 1812, it had not
been thought necessary until 1869 to negotiate with the
Indians. The fear and vindictiveness with which the federal

government reacted to Riel, who was more French than Indian, undoubtedly influenced its dealings with the Indians. The Indians were told to sign; if they did not, the implication was clear that they would be persecuted like Riel. Had the Riel rebellion not occurred, it is difficult to say whether the treaties would have been signed at all.

A.G. Archibald, Lieutenant-Governor of Manitoba and the North-West Territories, negotiated Treaties 1 and 2. His successor in office, Alexander Morris, negotiated Treaties 3 to 6. Morris has left an invaluable account of the proceedings, including verbatim transcripts of the conversations between government spokesmen and the Indians, newspaper accounts, and his own memos to his superiors, published as a book in 1880: *The Treaties of Canada with the Indians of Manitoba, the North-West Territories and Kee-wa-tin:* (Toronto, Belfords, Clarke and Co., 1880). The book also includes brief accounts of Treaty 1 and Treaty 7.

The treaties were modelled roughly on the Robinson Treaty of 1850 with the Indians of Lake Superior and Lake Huron. The Robinson Treaty initiated the concept of total surrender in exchange for money, and the Indians' right to occupy certain portions of Crown land and to hunt over unsettled land. The Robinson Treaty, however, paid money in a lump sum, 500 pounds sterling a year, to the band, not to each individual. It also provided for an increase in the annuity if the land surrendered became productive to the government.

> *" . . . In case the territory hereby ceded . . . shall at any further period produce an amount which will enable the government of this Province without incurring loss to increase the annuity . . . then, in that case, the same shall be augmented from time to time . . . "*

Robinson suggested the increased payment, if made, should not exceed one pound sterling per Indian, but the amount was left to the discretion of the government. The Indians of Lake Superior and Lake Huron are, therefore, entitled to a large portion of the annual income of the province of Ontario. The treaty provided that, if the size of the band dwindled, the annuity would dwindle proportionately. It provided no schools, no agricultural equipment and no buggies. Liquor was not forbidden. The principle of the reserve, with ownership vested in the federal government, was established.

Treaty 1 signed at Red River in 1871, was more specific:
Each family of five was allotted 160 acres, more or less,
depending on the size of the family. Treaty money was set at $3
per capita, payable in goods or cash, at the Government's
discretion. A school was promised for each reserve. Liquor was
forbidden, either on reserves or off. No mention was made of
hunting or trapping rights. Memoranda to the treaty mention
gifts which were not actually specified in the agreement. Special
dress was to be given to each signatory chief, along with
ploughs, harrows, and buggies, and cattle which were to remain
the property of the government.
The idea of surrender is very clear:

*"The Chippewa and Swanpy Cree Tribes of Indians and
all other Indians inhabiting the district hereinafter described
and defined do herby cede, release, surrender and yield up to
Her Majesty the Queen and successors forever, all the lands
included within the following limits . . . "*

The Indian chiefs who trooped into the Stone Fort at Red
River on July 27, 1871, to begin negotiation, included Bird
Forever, Lying Down Bird, Centre of Bird's Tail, Flying-round,
Whippoorwill, Yellow Quill, and Red Eagle (otherwise known as
Henry Prince.) Lt.-Gov. Archibald addressed them as they sat
on the ground under a canopy:

*"Your Great Mother, the Queen, wishes to do justice to
all her children alike . . . while her arm is strong to punish the
wicked man, her hand is also open to reward the good man
everywhere in her Dominions. Your Great Mother wishes the
good of all races under her sway. She wishes her red children
to be happy and contented. She wishes them to live in
comfort. She would like them to adopt the habits of the
whites, to till land and raise food and store it up against the
time of want. She thinks that this would be the best thing for
her red children to do, that it would make them free from
famine and distress and make their homes more comfortable.
But the Queen, though she may think it good for you to
adopt civilized habits, has no idea of compelling you to do
so. This she leaves to your choice, and you need not live like
the white man unless you can be persuaded to do so of your
own free will.*

"Your Great Mother will lay aside 'lots' of land to be used by you and your children forever. She will not allow the white man to intrude upon these lots. She will make rules to keep them for you, so that as long as the sun shall shine, there shall be no Indian who has not a place that he can call his home, where he can go and pitch his camp or if he chooses, build his house and till his land.

" . . . you will still be free to hunt over much of the land included in the treaty. Much of it is rocky and unfit for cultivation . . . beyond the places where the white man will be required to go at all events for some time to come. Till these lands are needed for use, you will be free to hunt over them . . . but when the lands are needed to be tilled or occupied, you must not go on them anymore. There will still be plenty of land where you can go and roam and hunt as you have always done and, if you wish to farm, you will go to your own reserve where you will find a place ready for you to live on and cultivate."

Morris,Treaties, p. 28.

Indians have suggested that the treaties were frauds because the Indians didn't know what was happening. This is not so. All statements were meticulously interpreted to the Indians. They knew precisely what was happening and even took Archibald by surprise. He wrote:

" . . . The Indians seem to have false ideas of the meaning of reserve. They have been led to suppose that large tracts of ground were to be set aside for them as hunting grounds including timber lands, of which they might sell the wood as if they were proprietors of the soil.

"I wished to correct this idea at the outset. In defining the limits of their reserves, so far as we could see, they wished to have about two-thirds of the province. We heard them out, and then told them it was quite clear they had entirely misunderstood the meaning and intention of reserves . . . and then told them it was of no use for them to entertain any such ideas, which were entirely out of the question. We told them that whether they wished it or not, immigrants would come in and fill up the country, that every year from this one twice as many in number as their whole people there assembled would pour into the Province and in a little while would spread all over it, and that now was the

time for them to come to an arrangement that would secure homes and annuities for themselves and their children.

"If they thought it better to have no treaty at all, they might do without one, but as they must make up their minds if there was to be a treaty, it must be on the basis like that offered."

Morris, Treaties, p. 30.

On one side of the tent, the chiefs sat with their few warriors armed with arrows; on the other side sat the Lieutenant-Governor, surrounded by soldiers with guns. The Indians signed. They were, in fact, anxious to come to terms. They were not hostile; they welcomed civilization and wanted to be part of it:

"The Indians ... have a firm belief in the honor and integrity of Her Majesty's representatives and are fully impressed with the idea that the amelioration of their present condition is one of the objects of Her Majesty in making these treaties ... Indians give great assistance in gathering in the crops ... I found many farmers whose employees were nearly all Indians.

" ... There is no reason to fear any trouble with those who regard themselves as subjects of Her Majesty. Their desire is to live at peace with the white man, to trade with him and, when disposed, to work for him; and I believe that nothing but gross injustice will induce them to forget the allegiance which they now claim with pride or molest the white subjects of the sovereign whom they regard as their Supreme Chief.

"The system of annual payment in money I regard as a good one, because the recipient is enabled to purchase just what he requires when he can get it most cheaply and it also enables him to buy articles at second hand, from settlers and others, that are quite as useful to him as are the same things when new. The sum of three dollars does not appear to be large enough to enable an Indian to provide himself with many of his winter necessaries, but as he receives the same amount for his wife or wives, and for each of his children, the aggregate sum is usually sufficient to procure many comforts for his family which he would otherwise be compelled to deny himself."

Wemyss Simpson,
Indian Commissioner,
Nov. 3, 1871.

The Indians were obviously so dissatisfied with the pittance they received in the treaty, a bare piece of land and a school, that Archibald added the plow, cattle and buggies later to induce them to sign. But this treaty was an elaborate pretense. Manitoba had become a province of Canada in 1870. The land they were haggling over had been lost to the Indians for over a year.

"Our Hearts Are Like Paper . . ."

In 1873, in different circumstances, the Indians almost won. Then, as now, there was only one way to get from eastern to western Canada without entering the United States—through the dense bush north of the Lake of the Woods. In 1873, traffic still used the rivers. All transport followed the Winnipeg River to Rat Portage and crossed the Lake of the Woods to the Rainy River. The rivers and lakes were controlled by the Indians. For generations, canoes and steamers had used this route to the West. Thousands of settlers, troops and traders had passed back and forth through Rat Portage, at the Northwest Angle of the Lake of the Woods. No treaty had yet been signed with the Indians, and Wolseley's troops going through to quash Riel in 1869 alarmed the Indians. Fur traders they didn't mind; they were willing to overlook steamers with captains who chopped down trees along the way for fuel. But flotillas of war canoes filled with hundreds of men armed with guns moving against a man who represented, in part at least, the Indian cause, made them balk. The Indians of the Northwest Angle began to agitate for a treaty.

Alexander Morris, the Queen's representative, arrived at the Northwest Angle, now Kenora and then only a Hudson's Bay post, on September 25, 1873, and was accompanied by troops to make a good military impression. The Indians pitched their tents along the river. A number of traders had also been attracted to the spot, trying to persuade Indians to buy trinkets with the loot they'd get from the treaty. About 800 Indians milled about. The men, their faces garishly painted, squabbled and fought. Several different factions were present; each had a strong chief and none was willing to give precedence to another. They could not decide among themselves what to ask for or what to threaten. Each was jealous of his power and fearful that others might achieve greater advantage.

The governor was nervous; this treaty was crucial. If the Indians became angry and did not sign, they could, if they wished, stop all traffic between east and west, and commerce and government transactions would have to be rerouted. Because of the strategic importance of the Northwest Angle, concessions were made in this treaty. The Indians were to be offered one square mile of land instead of 160 acres. Hunting and fishing "rights" were also spelled out, although they were revealed, on close reading, not to be rights at all. Annual treaty payment was to be raised to $5 a head from $3. Another $1500 a year was guaranteed for the purchase of ammunition and twine.

The Indians were again promised schools, farming equipment and cattle as in Treaties 1 and 2. Liquor was to be forbidden.

Morris opened with a platitude which clearly reveals that he regarded the Indians as already conquered, treaty or no: "We are all children of the same Great Spirit and are subject to the same Queen." The Indians didn't share his point of view and showed a strong sense of real estate. "All this is our property where you have come," said one called Mewedopenais. "The Great Spirit has planted us on this ground where we are, as you were where you came from. We think where we are is our property. We ask $15 for all that you see [the people] and for the children that are to be born in future. This year only we ask for $15; years after, $10; our chiefs $50 a year and other demands of large amounts in writing, say $125,000 yearly."

"We are all of one mind," said another chief. "We do not wish that anyone should smile at our affairs as we think our country is a large matter to us."

Morris refused to negotiate with them. The Indians could take the treaty as is, or leave it. Morris would not tamper with the Queen's Word. The Governor's only weapon was to make the Indians feel they were missing an opportunity.

It was a masterful bluff, and both sides knew it. Morris knew that if the Indians refused his terms, it meant war or the total severance of communication between eastern and western Canada. The Indians knew that the government placed great value on their bush and waterways: "Our hands are poor but our heads are rich, and it is riches that we ask so we may be able to support our families as long as the sun rises and the water runs," said one chief. "The sound of the rustling of the gold is under my feet where I stand; we have a rich country and it is the Great Spirit who gave us this, where we stand upon is Indians' property, and belongs to them. The white man has robbed us of our riches and we don't wish to give them up again without getting something in their place." The chiefs stood firm: "You see all the chiefs here before you as one mind; we have one mind and one mouth. If you grant us our demands, you will not go back sorrowful."

Not only did the chiefs know what was happening; they proved to be tough negotiators. Had the bargaining ended there, the Indians, as they knew, could eventually have claimed their own price for right-of-way through the Northwest Angle. Western Canada and the federal government would have been at their mercy. The Canada from sea to sea of which Sir John A. Macdonald was dreaming would have been impossible. He would have bought that dream at any price. But one, Lac Seul Chief, was willing to accept the government's charity:

> *"We are the first that were planted here, we would ask you to assist us with every kind of implement to use for our benefit, to enable us to perform our work. We would borrow your cattle, we ask you this for our support; I will find whereon to feed them. The waters out of which you sometimes take food for yourselves, we will lend you in return. If I should try to stop you—it is not in my power to do so; even the Hudson's Bay Company—that is a small power—I cannot gain my point with it. If you give what I ask, the time may come when I will ask you to lend me one of your daughters and one of your sons to live with us; and in return will I lend you one of my daughters and one of my sons to live for you to teach what is good, and after they have learned, teach us."*

The Indians had welfare-minded leaders even in 1873. Morris was jubilant:

> *"I have heard and I have learned something. I have learned you are not all of one mind . . . What the chief said is reasonable. I wish you were all of the same mind as the chief who has just spoken. Should you want goods, I mean to ask you what amount you would have in goods so you would not have to pay the trader's prices for them. He wants his*

children to be taught. He is right. He wants to get cattle to help him to raise grain for his children."

Ultimately, the chiefs capitulated, and began bargaining, not on *their* basis, owning all the land the government wanted passage through, but rather, they bargained on the government's terms. The details of a treaty were negotiated:

Morris: This year, instead of ten dollars we will give you twelve dollars to be paid to you at once as soon as we sign the treaty. This is the best I can do for you. I wish you to understand we do not come here as traders but as representing the Crown and to do what is just and right.

Chief: One thing more we demand—a suit of clothes to all of us.

Morris: . . . suits will be given to the Chief and headmen and as to the other Indians, there is a quantity of goods and provisions here that will be given them at the close of the treaty. The coats of the Chiefs will be given every three years.

Chief: Once more; powder and shot will not go off without guns. We ask for guns.

Morris: What I have promised is as far as I can go.

Chief: You must remember that our hearts and our brains are like paper; we never forget.

Another Chief: I see your roads here passing through the country, and some of your boats—useful articles that you use for yourself. Bye and bye we shall see things that run swiftly, that go by fire—carriages—and we ask you that us Indians may not have to pay their passage on these things but can go free.

Morris: I think the best thing I can do is become an Indian. I cannot promise you to pass on the railroad free, for it may be a long time before we get one; and I cannot promise you any more than other people.

Chief: All the promises that you have made me, the little promises and the money you have promised, when it comes to me year after year—should I see that there is anything wanting, through the negligence of the people who have to see after these things, I trust it will be in my power to put them in prison.

Morris: The ear of the Queen's government will always be open to hear the complaints of her Indian people, and she will deal with her servants that do not do their duty in a proper manner.

Chief: I want a copy of the treaty that will not be rubbed off, on parchment.

Chief: One thing I find that deranges a little my kettle. In this river, food used to be plentiful for our subsistence. I perceive it is getting scarce. We wish that the river should be left as it was formed from the beginning—that nothing be broken.

Morris: That is a subject that I cannot promise.

Excerpts from The Manitoban
Oct. 18, 1873, quoted in
Morris, Treaties, *p. 45*

The chiefs showed an extraordinary grasp of the future, and foresaw the railway, the disappearance of wild game and fish, and the broken promises of the government. They felt strongly that they were being robbed. If they did not accept the government's terms, the alternative was a war which Indians knew they could not win without great cost. They gambled on peace.

The chiefs were silent and apprehensive as they signed the treaty. "First I must have the money in my hand," said one sly, ancient chief. Morris immediately held out his hand and told the interpreter to say to the chief: "Take my hand and feel the money in it. If you cannot trust me for half an hour, do not trust me forever." The chief smiled and signed.

The final gesture of Chief Mewedopenais was that of a defeated king:

"I take off my glove and in giving you my hand I deliver over the birthright and my lands; and in taking your hand I hold fast all the promises you have made, and I hope they will last."

Not to be Rubbed Out ...

In September of the following year, 1874, Morris and the commissioners moved out over the sun-burnt prairie dotted with bleaching buffalo bones to Fort Qu'Appelle and Fort Ellice where Treaty 5 was signed with the Crees and Saulteaux.

The terms of the treaty were the same as Treaty 3, except the ammunition and twine was reduced to $750 a year and each chief got a flag. Again, Morris travelled with troops and stayed at the Hudson's Bay post.

There was a series of disagreements, some arising from hostilities between the Crees and the Saulteux, others from Indian objections to the encampment of the militia. Finally, the actual negotiations began. Morris' opening speech contained subtle threats:

> *"The Queen knows that it is hard to find food for yourselves and your children; she knows that the winters are cold, and your children are often hungry; she has always cared for her red children as for her white. Out of her generous heart and liberal hand she wants to do something for you, so that when the buffalo get scarcer, and they are scarce enough now, you may be able to do something for yourselves . . . she would like to take you by the hand and do as I did for her at the Lake of the Woods last year.*
>
> *"I cannot believe that you will be the first Indians, the Queen's subjects, who will not take her by the hand. I have opened my hands and heart to you . . . I have put before you our message, I want you to go back to your tents and think over what I have said and come and meet me tomorrow. Recollect that we cannot stay very long here. I have said all."*

Quibbles and internal disputes stalled the negotiations for three days. The Indians would not speak clearly. Something was troubling them. They would neither agree nor disagree to the treaty; they offered no counter-proposals. Morris tried to wheedle a response out of them:

> *"I want you to look me in the face, eye to eye and open your hearts to me as children would to a father, as children ought to do to a father, and as you ought to the servants of the great mother of us all. The promises we have to make to you are not for today only but for tomorrow . . . the promises we make will be carried out as long as the sun shines above and the water flows in the ocean . . . We are your true and best friends who will never advise you badly, who will never whisper bad words in your ears, who only care for your good and that of your children."*

These words of Morris'—these promises—were never written down in the treaties, but the Indians remembered them. They were accustomed to listening acutely and memorizing what was being said. The phrases which Morris used here have become almost the stock language of Indian-white relations. Indians, priests, Indian agents use this childish jargon, and the concepts— "children," "father," and "great mother"—which Morris spun out of his own head, now accurately describe the relationship which has built up between the Indians and the government.

Many Indians are under the impression that the phrase "as long as the sun shines and the rivers flow" is actually written in the treaties. It is not. It was a phrase which first appeared during the signing of Treaty 3 and which Morris picked up. The negotiations, as they proceeded from treaty to treaty, seem to take on the quality of a chant. When Morris heard a phrase he liked, he used it at the next encounter and thus it was passed on from band to band. Similarly, the Indians picked up his phrases and used them. A strange diplomatic language grew up which was limited to about 10 very important words. In this way, "as long as the sun shines" grew into a classic promise associated with the treaties although it was never more than rhetoric.

The Indians finally confessed the reason for their anger. The Government had bought the Hudson's Bay Company's rights to the Northwest Territories. The Bay had been given 300,000 pounds sterling and enormous parcels of land, in a treaty made with The Bay before any had been made with the Indians. The Bay had staked off its property which was, technically, still Indian property. The Indians were outraged; they wanted The Bay dispossessed or an equal agreement. One chief took Morris to task:

> *"The Company have stolen our land. I heard that at first. I hear it is true. The Queen's messengers never came here and now I see the soldiers and the settlers and the policemen. I know it is not the Queen's work, only the Company has come and they are the head, they are the foremost; I do not hold it back. He [the HBC] does whatever he thinks all around here. Let this be put to rights."*

This chief, The Gambler, like the chiefs at the Northwest Angle, showed an acute perception of the realities of colonialism. The Gambler made an association between The Bay and the government which was accurate; the government was working in the company's interests.

The Gambler: When one Indian takes anything from another we call it stealing, and when we see the present we say pay us. It is the Company I mean.

Morris: What did the Company steal from you?

The Gambler: The earth, trees, grass, stones, all that I see with my eyes.

Morris: Who made the earth, the grass, the stone and the wood? The Great Spirit. He made them for all His children to use, and it is not stealing to use the gift of the Great Spirit. The lands are the Queen's under the Great Spirit. The Chippewas were not always here. They came from the east. There were other Indians here and they used the wood and the land, the gift of the Great Spirit to all, and we want to try to induce you to believe that we are asking for the good of all. We do not know of any lands that were stolen from you, and if you do not open your mouths we cannot get the wall taken away. You can open your mouths if you will; we are patient but we cannot remain here always.

Pis-qua: [pointing to Mr. McDonald of the Hudson's Bay Company] You told me you had sold your land for so much money, three hundred thousand pounds. We want that money.

The Gambler: The Indians want the Company to keep at its post and nothing beyond . . . I do not want to drive the Company anywhere. What I said is, they are to remain at their house. Supposing you wanted to take them away, I would not let them go. I want them to remain here to have nothing but the trade. I do not hate them; we always exchange with them and would die if they went away.

Morris: The Queen and her Councillors may think you do not want to be friends, that you do not want your little ones to be taught, that you do not want when food is getting scarce to have a hand in yours stronger than yours to help you . . . you will not let so little a question as this about the Company, without whom you tell me you could not live, stop the good we mean to do.

Already, in 1871, the Indians were totally dependent on The Bay. Yet still they had the courage to oppose it. The Gambler's arguments are irrefutable. Morris was forced to take refuge in petulance:

> *"I am sorry for you. I am afraid you have been listening to bad voices who have not the interests of the Indians at heart. If because of these things you will not speak to us we will go away with hearts sorry for you and your children who thus throw in our faces the hand of the Queen that she has held out to you."*

It is clear what the government's trump card was: the Indians were starving. They had to have food from the government; to get it, they had to sign the treaty. When it appeared that these Indians too were anxious about the future, Morris told them what he had done about the treaty at the North-West Angle:

> *"I would have it all written out, a true copy made on skin, that could not be rubbed out, that I would send a copy to his people so that when we are dead and gone the letter would be there to speak for itself, to show everything that was promised ... I did so and sent a copy of the treaty written in letters of blue, gold and black to the Chief Maw-do-pe-mais whom the people had told to keep it for them. I told them (the Indians of Treaty No. 3) I could not give them what they asked, and when they understood that, and understood the full breadth and width of the Queen's goodness, they took what I offered and I think if you are wise you will do the same."*
>
> Morris. p. 114

The Tramp of the Multitudes...

When Morris arrived in northern Saskatchewan in 1876, the Indians there were desperate. They had heard stories of the land being taken away, the buffalo were disappearing, and the Indians, ravaged by small-pox, were starving. As early as 1871, the Cree chiefs had pleaded with the Hudson's Bay manager at Edmonton House to help them in obtaining government assistance. Nevertheless, the Indians were apprehensive, and had their own ideas about what was to happen to them in a few years. There were statements that white men would come until they outnumbered the Indians, and there were reports that the Indians warned the intruders:

> *"A few weeks since a land speculator wished to take a claim at the crossing on Battle River and asked the consent of the Indians, one of my Saulteaux friends sprang to his feet and pointing to the East said: 'Do you see that great white man (the Government) coming? ' 'No,' said the speculator. 'I do,' said the Indian, 'and I hear the tramp of the multitudes behind him and when he comes you can drop in behind him and take up all the land claims you want, but until then I caution you to put up no stakes in our country."*
>
> Rev. George McDougall,
Morris, p. 174.

But by 1876 any Indian resistance had entirely eva-porated. They had indicated that they wanted negotiations, wanted supplies, and when Morris arrived, the Indians were prepared to accept what he would offer.

> *"The whole day was occupied with discussion on the food question . . . The Indians were, as they had been for some time past, full of uneasiness. They saw the buffalo, their only means of support, passing away. They were anxious to learn to support themselves by agriculture but felt too ignorant to do so and they dreaded that during the transition period they would be swept off by famine or disease. Already they have suffered terribly from the ravages of measles, scarlet fever and smallpox . . . they were not exacting but they were very apprehensive of their future and thankful, as one of them put it, 'a new life was dawning upon them.' They asked for an ox and cow for each family; an increase in the agricultural implements; provisions for the poor, unfortunate, blind and lame, to be provided with missionaries and school teachers; the exclusion of firewater in the whole Saskatchewan; a further increase in agricultural*

implements as the band advanced in civilization; freedom to cut timber on Crown lands; free passage over government bridges or scows; other animals, a horse harness and wagon and cooking stove for each chief, a free supply of medicines; a hand mill to each band; and lastly in case of war they should not be liable to serve.

"Then Poundmaker rose and said . . . he did not see how they could feed and clothe their children on what was promised. He expected to have received that; he did not know how to build a house or to cultivate the ground . . . I replied to them, with regard to assistance, that we could not support or feed the Indians, and that all we would be able to do would be to help them to cultivate the soil. If a general famine came upon the Indians, the charity of the Government would come into exercise.

"James Senum, chief of the Crees at White Fish Lake said that he commenced to cultivate the soil some years ago. Mr. Christie, then chief factor of the Hudson's Bay Company, gave him a plow but it was now broken. He had no cattle when he commenced but he and his people drew the plough themselves and made hoes of roots of trees, Mr. Christie also gave him a pit-saw and a grind-stone and he was still using them. His heart was sore in spring when his children wanted to plough and had no implements. I had then presented Sweet Grass his medal, uniform and flag, the band playing, 'God Save the Queen' and all the Indians rising to their feet.

"I thought the desire of the Indians to be instructed in farming and building most reasonable and I would recommend measures be adopted to provide such instruction for them. The Indians are tractable, docile, and willing to learn . . . advantage should be taken of this disposition to teach them to become self-supporting which can best be accomplished with the aid of a few practical farmers and carpenters to instruct them in farming and house building. The universal demand for teachers, and by some of the Indians for missionaries, is also encouraging. The former the government can supply; for the latter they must rely on the churches . . . the field is wide enough for all and the cry of the Indian for help is a clamant one."

Morris, Treaties, p. 185-194.

The Vision of Alexander Morris

"I cast my eyes to the East down to the great lakes and I see a broad road leading from there to Red River. I see it stretching on to Ellice, I see it branching there, the one to Qu'Appelle and Cypress Hills, and the other by Pelly to Carlton; it is a wide and plain trail. Anyone can see it, and on that road taking for the Queen, the hand of the Governor and commissioners, I see all the Indians, I see the Queen's councillors taking the Indian by the hand saying we are brothers, we will lift you up, we will teach you, if you will learn, the cunning of the white man. All along that road I see Indians gathering, I see gardens growing and houses building; I see them receiving money from the Queen's commissioners to purchase clothing for their children; at the same time I see them enjoying their hunting and fishing as before, I see them retaining their old mode of living with the Queen's gift in addition.

"Since I was a young man my heart was warm to the Indians, and I have taken a great interest in them; for more than twenty-five years I have studied their condition in the present and in the future . . . the first words I spoke in public were for the Indians, and in that vision of the day I saw the Queen's white men understanding their duty; I saw them understanding that they had no right to wrap themselves in a cold mantle of selfishness, they had no right to turn away and say 'Am I my brother's keeper?' . . . I saw them saying the Indians are our brothers, we must try to help them to make a living . . . as I came here I saw tracks leading to the lakes and water courses once well-beaten now grown over with grass; I saw bones bleaching by the wayside; I saw the places where the buffalo had been and I thought what will become of the Indian? I said to myself, we must teach the children to prepare for the future; if we do not, but a few suns will pass and they will melt away like snow before the sun in springtime."

Morris, Treaties, p.231

"The allotment of lands to the Indians, to be set aside as reserves for them for home and agricultural purposes, and

which cannot be sold or alienated without their consent, and then only for their benefit . . . I regard of great value. It at once secures to the Indian tribes tracts of land, which cannot be interfered with by the rush of immigration, and affords the means of inducing them to establish homes and learn the arts of agriculture. I regard the Canadian system of alloting reserves to one or more bands together, in the localities in which they have had the habit of living, as far preferable to the American system of placing whole tribes in large reserves which eventually become the object of cupidity to the whites and the breaking up of which has so often led to Indian wars and great discontent . . . the Indians have a strong attachment to the localities in which they and their fathers have been accustomed to dwell and it is desirable to cultivate this home feeling of attachment to the soil. Moreover, the Canadian system of band reserve has a tendency to diminish the offensive strength of the Indian tribes should they ever become restless, a remote contingency if the treaties are carefully observed.

"The fact of the reserves being scattered throughout the territories will enable the Indians to obtain markets among the white settlers for any surplus products they may eventually have to dispose of. It will be found desirable to assign to each family part of the reserve for their own use, so as to give them a sense of property in it, but all power of sale or alienation of such lands should be rigidly prohibited. Any premature enfranchisement of the Indians, or power given to them to part with their lands, would inevitably lead to the speedy breaking up of the reserves and the return of the Indians to their wandering mode of life and thereby to the recreation of a difficulty the assignment of reserves was calculated to obviate. The Indians are fully aware that their old mode of life is passing away. They are not 'unconscious of their destiny'; on the contrary, they are harassed with fears as to the future of their children and the hard present of their own lives. They are tractable, docile, willing to learn. They recognize the fact that they must seek part of their living from 'the mother earth' to use their own phraseology.

" . . . The cattle given to them will expand into herds. It is true the number assigned to each band is comparatively

limited, and the Government are not bound to extend the number. This was done advisedly . . . for it was felt that it was experiment to entrust them with cattle, owing to their inexperience with regard to housing them and providing fodder for them in winter and owing, moreover, to the danger of them using them for food if short of buffalo meat or game. Besides, it was felt that as the Indian is, and naturally so, always asking, it was better that if the Government saw their way safely to increase the number of cattle given to any band it should be not as a matter of right but of grace and favor and as a .reward for exertion in the care of them and as an incentive for industry.

"What is to be the future of the Indian population of the North-West? I believe it to be a hopeful one. I have every confidence in the desire and ability of this present administration, as of any succeeding one . . . to extend a helping hand to this helpless population . . . with the machinery at their disposal, with a judicious selection of agents and farm instructors, and the additional aid of well-selected carpenters and efficient school teachers, I look forward to seeing the Indians faithful allies of the Crown, while they can gradually be made an increasing and self-supporting population. They are wards of Canada, let us do our duty by them.

"But the Churches have their duty to fulfill. There is a common ground between the Christian churches and the Indians as they all believe, as we do, in a Great Spirit. The transition, thence, to the Christian's God is an easy one.

"Let us have Christianity and civilization leaven the mass of heathenism and paganism among the Indian tribes, let us have a wise and paternal Government faithfully carrying out the provisions of our treaties, and doing its utmost to help and elevate the Indian population, who have been cast upon our care, and we will have peace progress and concord among them in the North-West; and instead of the Indian melting away, as one of them in older Canada tersely put it 'as snow before the sun' we will see our Indian population, loyal subjects of the Crown, happy, prosperous and self-sustaining and Canada will be enabled to feel that, in a truly patriotic spirit, our country has done its duty by the red man of the North-West and thereby to herself. So may it be."

Protecting the Aborigines

The tone of Governor Morris' addresses to the Indians reflects accurately the attitudes of the Canadian conquerors. The traders who sold the Indians bad liquor and the merchants who relieved them of their furs for a few pots and pans did not concern themselves with rhetoric and polite phrases. But the politicians were concerned with the morality of the white man's influence. The effects of civilization upon the Indians were apparent in the destitution, drunkenness and epidemics which threatened to exterminate them altogether. Reluctant to admit responsibility for these plagues, politicians expressed fear that, in the words of one British group, "not one of all their race will remain in whom the purer and nobler features of our character may be reflected." Commercial imperialism was accompanied by an ideological imperialism. Both were aggressive. Not only was the Indian to be separated from his wealth and his land, but he was also to be separated from his religion and his traditions. Missionaries helped provide a cloak of benevolence. Alert for the work of the Devil on every side, they soon discovered it. They found it, oddly enough, in the white people, particularly the fur traders. The Indians, as far as the missionaries could discover, needed saving only from the pernicious influences of rum and whiskey dispensed by the unscrupulous traders. Chief among the offenders, they found to their horror, was the illustrious Hudson's Bay Company. The missionaries wrote outraged letters back to England.

> *"They were all drunkards, with one exception; not drunkards in a limited sense but the most abandoned and unblushing sots imaginable; they were never sober when they could procure anything to intoxicate them; they were idle in the extreme never attending to any business except hunting."*

The missionaries' work in converting the heathen was futile as long as they were in a state of perpetual intoxication. Missionaries' letters were circulated and published and the stories of starvation and exploitation caught the sympathies of a sentimental nation. The missionaries considered the commercial enterprises antagonistic to their own religious interests and to the best interests of the native people. Strong hostility developed between the traders and the missionaries or other "do-gooders" who wanted to protect the Indians from the very civilization which they represented.

The desire to protect the Indians from exploitation was a humanitarian and laudable motive. Its weakness was that it sought the protection not by reform and control over the vicious trading methods, but by artificially sheltering the Indians from them. It was a defensive act; the missionaries and the humanitarians were not prepared to curtail the activities of capitalist enterprise on principle, but only in relation to the Indians. The missionaries' solution was not to help the Indians work out a better arrangement with the traders, based on justice and equality, but to separate them from the traders altogether. Any idea of unionism or bargaining was as foreign to the missionaries in Canada as it was to the bourgeoisie of Great Britain. Their failure to take a stand against the concepts of free trade and the exploitation which it entailed meant that they were giving tacit support to the exploitation which they, at the same time, condemned.

Two conflicting interests, commercial traders and missionaries, were thus firmly established in Canada before Confederation. They represented two major drives of the British soul: the lust for wealth and the lust for respectability. Both had to be satisfied by the politicians. The treaties were, therefore, forced to pay lip service to the Indians' right to their land, even when this right had already been cancelled out in the interests of political expediency. The Indians were promised money, education and protection when, in fact, the government knew it was unable to provide those things. The Indians who had, apparently, been corrupted by Western civilization, were to be reformed, enlightened, rescued by that same civilization.

Interest at this time in the "natives", as they were called in Britain, was intense, fanned by the hellfire and brimstone letters of the missionaires. An Aborigines Protection Society was formed to look after the interests of natives of all British colonies, including the Indians. Indians were perceived in Rousseauist terms as noble savages and were, like Rousseau's Indians, treated like characters in a book. Indians were, according to the missionaries, to shun the corruptions of civilization, business, trade, money, fun, sex, and retreat into idyllic pastoral life. They would farm and become religious, calm, sober and industrious.

The Canadian government actually tried to implement Rousseau's dream with real savages. The treaties were to be the social contract. Missionaries and Indian agents would stand around like benevolent creators, making sure nothing went amiss on the farm.

The reserves are an expression of these attitudes towards the Indians. Indians could be propertied, like proper English-men, and yet could be supervised, and separated from evil influences. The reserves gave to the Indians land, farms, educa-tion and protection. The Indians would be treated as foreigners in the country. Such separation of the races effectively solved the problem of how to treat an ignorant, debauched savage as a British citizen—he would be a "probationary citizen." This trend to apartheid was strong in Canada as early as 1836, when the Governor of Upper Canada, Sir Francis Bondhead, wrote to a British politician:

> *"I feel that before the subject of the Indians in Upper Canada can be fairly considered, it is necessary to refute the ideas which so generally exist in England, about the success which has attended the Christianizing and civilizing of the Indians, whereas, I firmly believe, every person of sound mind in this country who is disinterested in their conversion and who is acquainted with the Indian character, will agree:*
> *1. That the attempt to make farmers of the red men has been, generally speaking, a complete failure.*
> *2. That the congregating them for the purpose of civilization has implanted more vices than it has eradicated and consequently,*
> *3. That the greatest kindness we can perform toward this intelligent, simple-minded people is to remove and fortify them as much as possible from any communication from the whites."*

Extracts from Papers and
Proceedings of the Aborigines
Protection Society, Report, p. 36

The desire of the missionaries to civilize and establish colonies of Indians was matched by the desire of the government to get rid of them. Many considerations made the need to deal with the Indians pressing. By 1870, Canada was faced with an influx of settlers. The Indians had made some threatening gestures when survey lines went through for the telegraph and the railway; isolated incidents of Indians tearing up settlers' fence posts and kicking them off their homesteads had been reported. The British government and, later, the Canadian government felt an obligation to protect these colonists from the Indians. The Riel rebellion and news of Indian uprisings and serious warfare in the United States increased the concern. There was genuine fear of massacre.

The treaties were as much a strategy to gain peace and the friendship of potentially hostile Indians as they were an attempt to give them a start in a new life. The political expediency of a government anxious to avoid violence united with humanitarian concerns. The Indians were protected; they were also rendered harmless. The Indians thought: "The government will help us get back on our feet." The government thought: "Ah, we've finally got rid of them."

Chapter 6
Behind Polished Desks in Swivels:
The Indian Act

"I never thought of thinking for myself at all."

Sir Joseph Porter, K.C.B.

"The Indians are off left. The Indians are always off left."

The Fantasticks

"I am the chief and many times I am distressed and cast down in spirit over my people. I feel powerless at times when I want to make some advance for their well being. You know that when a captain steps aboard his ship, he has all his papers and power to control his ship. So then why should not I, as chief, not have my papers and power to have full control over my people, power that will make my word law and order on my reserve?

I want my copies and paper and report blanks for each month and when I have received my copies I will send them back for your and his Majesty's signature. It is no good to give me orders as a chief and give me no power to show as a sign for the people to fear. When I want to defend the law, they snap at me, that's when I need the power from the throne."

Chief, Poplar River, Manitoba, 1947

"Any plans or policies formulated by the department are not revealed to the Indians. We recognize the need for secrecy in warfare but the department has not declared war on the Indians so we question the need to be kept in the dark."

Indian

"The Indian agent's duties are becoming more and more like the commander of an internment camp of a defeated enemy."

Mohawk Indian

"As I looked at the sick boy, I looked up and I saw the Holy Ghost looking over the back of the boy's bed. He was dressed in very high class white man's clothes."

Indian

"I do not vote. I am an Indian. I do not wanted to be turned a white man. I want to remain an Indian until the end of the world."

Indian

"There is an underlying fear among our people that at some future date there is always the danger that an unscrupulous or thoughtless government might again betray us."

Blackfoot

"We do not even know what we've done wrong until we've been caught."

Indian

"To them, Ottawa is the Indian Affairs Branch and it's all in one building—Parliament."

Indian Affairs official

"Indian Affairs uses gestapo methods. We all have that feeling. There is not one chief here who has not the same feeling. We are marked."

Indian chief at meeting

"There are two Indian children going to school in Winnipeg. The white children are running after them calling 'woo-woo-woo-woo.' The sister tells the other not to listen to them. That is why we are against integration, especially in the cities because the white children do that."

Indian

"The term person means an individual other than an Indian."
Indian Act of 1880, Sect. 12.

That particular phrase was not used in subsequent Indian Acts, but the attitude which produced it persists. It is interesting that even the Eskimo, who was every bit as 'uncivilized' as the Indian, was not included in the non-person category.

The stereotype of the Indian which exists today can be traced directly back to the definition of "Indian" which was set down in that early Indian Act. The Indian Act was written to be read by white Canadians with legal knowledge. It was not read by Indians in 1880, and it is not read by many Indians now. A very few Indians have ever read it, and even fewer have managed to make their way through this thicket of legal jargon. The only people with a thorough knowledge of the Indian Act are the Indian agents and superintendents.

"A band is any tribe, band or body of Indians who own, or are interested in, a reserve, or in Indian lands in common of which the legal title is vested in the Crown."
Act of 1880

From the start, the Indian Acts reflected a peculiar and erroneous notion that reserves are communes and that, therefore, Indians lead a communal life. If today Indians on reserves lead a communal life, sometimes sharing liquor and wives as well as food and clothes, it is because they have been forced to live that way. The government has imposed a communal system on them from the beginning. The reserve not only was a commune, but was a commune to which the Indians did not have legal title. The treaty was a lease which defined the government-landlord's rights and duties. The rent the Indians paid was the forfeiture of their right to Canadian citizenship.

The reserve system was originally conceived—certainly by Alexander Morris, the principal negotiator of the treaties—as a homestead system whereby each Indian family would cultivate its own section of land, much as did the immigrants to Canada. The only difference would be that the Indians' land was leased from the government, not purchased outright. Each Indian family would be relatively independent. Those who worked hard would thrive; the lazy would fall behind. The government, however, interpreted the reserve as belonging equally to every Indian band member, with the equipment, finances and produce to be shared by all. The Indians could, therefore, progress only as rapidly as the band's slowest member.

Today's stereotype of the Indian is the unambitious Indian. It reflects the economic circumstances which the government created with the reserve system. The reserve is also responsible for the myth of idyllic Indian communal life.

The popular stereotype of the Indian is reflected in the language of the Act, dealing with requirements for the enfranchisement of an Indian:

> *"The Superintendent-General shall authorize some competent person to report whether the applicant is an Indian who, from the degree of civilization to which he or she has attained and the character for integrity, morality and sobriety which he or she bears, appears to be qualified to become a proprietor of land in fee simple . . . "*
>
> Act of 1880

Before the request for enfranchisement even went to Ottawa, it required the consent of the band council and forwarding by the local agent. The approval of the Superintendent-General was to be followed by at least three years' probation for the Indian before final assent to enfranchisement was granted. Two other clauses in the Act reinforce the impression of the view of Indian character on which the Act is based: Chiefs were to be elected by vote of the band "for a period of three years unless deposed by the Governor for dishonesty, intemperance, immorality or incompetency." Elsewhere, it is made a specific offense under the Indian Act for any person keeping a bawdy house to allow an Indian woman in for the purpose of prostitution.

"What's your number? "

The easiest way to tell a real Indian from an enfranchised Indian or a white man is to ask him his number. "What's your number? " is often used as a taunt by treaty Indians to humiliate non-treaty Indians who attempt to speak on behalf of Indian people. An Indian's name and number are written on a list in Ottawa and also "posted in a conspicuous place in the superintendent's office that serves the band."

A treaty number is the same as a surname. One was given to each male Indian who took treaty status at the time the treaty was signed. Many Indians did not have surnames, or if they did, they were incomprehensible to the white men taking the census, so a number was used instead. The number is, like a family name, passed down through the male line. A wife takes her husband's number when she takes his last name at marriage, and their children also have the same number. If one of the children has an illegitimate child, the child takes its mother's number. A widow keeps her husband's unless she remarries.

An Indian who becomes enfranchized loses his treaty status and his number as well. An Indian woman who marries a white man or an enfranchised Indian loses her Indian status, and her number is thus removed from the list. The list, which contains the names and numbers of all the Indians in Canada, is referred to officially as the Register. Any Indian whose name does not appear on the Register is not a "pure-blooded Indian."

The Lord of the Manor

The legal system of land tenure under which Indians function is not unlike the feudal system, and the levels of administration can be compared to feudal ranks. The Indian Affairs Branch is the lord of the manor. The Indian agent is the local manager. The lord has total control over the lives of his serfs, who neither own their land nor rent it. They are "crofters" permitted to live on the land and farm it, but not for their individual benefit. The lord or manager tells them what to plant and when to sow and harvest; he provides the equipment; he tells them when to sell the crop and at what price. He can, if he wishes, tell them to plant nothing at all. Thus, the Indians, on their own reservations, actually work for Indian Affairs. The revenue from their work goes to the Minister, as the lord is called. Often amounting to millions of dollars, these funds are kept by Indian Affairs to be spent at the Minister's pleasure. The Minister draws up "projects" on which to spend this money, plans for model villages, schemes for economic efficiency and even proposals to move people from one part of the country to another.

But he treats his Indians with charity. They are given the opportunity to be Christianized and educated, and are provided with houses, food, clothing, money for liquor, and medical care. The system is predicated on the Minister's treating the Indians as a responsible patron would treat inferiors.

Within the last ten years, this feudal system has been influenced by the surrounding capitalist economy sufficiently to make the relation of Indian to Indian Affairs move closer to that of employee to employer. He is a "professional Indian", and the Queen's bounty and benevolence laid down in the treaty has become a salary. The Indian is paid to be an Indian and, since in most cases he is living in poverty, he is paid to be a peasant.

The minister has virtually total authority over reserve land. He may expropriate it by paying the individual holder a token fee, and the Minister is the final arbiter of the amount to be paid in cases of dispute.

Reserve land can be divided into parcels, and in such circumstances, each family is given a certificate of possession for its parcel of land. This certificate is more commonly called a "location ticket." It says simply that that particular Indian family has the permission of the Minister to live on that piece of land. Technically, the band council allots the parcels of land to band members. However:

> "... the Minster may, in his discretion, withhold his approval and may authorize the Indian to occupy the land temporarily and may prescribe the conditions as to use and settlement that are to be fulfilled by the Indian."

Office Consolidation, Indian Act, Revised to 1961

In such cases, the Indian receives only a certificate of "occupation" and may be expelled from the property by the Minister at the end of two years.

If an Indian improves his land and then for some reason (such as enfranchisement) leaves it, compensation for his improvements will be determined by the Minister alone. Again, the Indian is without right of appeal or arbitration. An Indian cannot transfer his parcel of land to a fellow band member without the approval of the Minister. His certificate of possession is therefore nothing like ownership, since it gives him no right to *give up* possession. It is an empty document. If an Indian cannot give up possession, he does not have real possession. And even this empty possession may be taken at will, since the act empowers the Minister to cancel a location ticket which was, in his opinion, obtained through fraud or error. The government thus has the power to take away any Indian's right of possession without demonstrating to the Indian or to any other authority that an error or a fraud actually did occur.

An Indian band or an individual Indian has no power to permit an outsider to lease land on the reserve or even to live on the reserve without approval from the Minister. The Minister can grant permission for an outsider to lease or reside on a reserve for one year or perhaps longer if he sees fit. The clause which sets this out is provided to keep white men from leasing reserve land for farming purposes without Ottawa's knowledge. The one-year lease attempts without success to discourage farmers from renting reserve property because their capital investment would be insecure. It does keep white men from establishing stores, garages or other business•on reserve property. The Indians still spend their money in white men's businesses, but they have to go several miles to do it.

Most important, this aspect of the Act and its administration keeps the reserve intact and the band homogeneous and isolated. Not only can no white person establish residency on a reserve, even with the permission of the band, and thus desegregate it, but no Indian belonging to another band can live there either. The members of the various bands, even though they may belong to the same tribe (Cree, Saulteaux etc.) are thus not allowed to move from reserve to reserve except through marriage. To counteract this, much "visiting" takes place between related families on nearby reserves. Visits will last weeks and months, with two or three families sharing the same house. Indian Affairs officials will cluck about "overcrowding" and romantics will coo about the joys of communal life but there are simply no regular accommodations for the visitors' use.

> *"30. A person who trespasses on a reserve is guilty of an offence and is liable on summary conviction to a fine not exceeding fifty dollars or to imprisonment for a term not exceeding one month or to both fine and imprisonment."*

This section has helped to keep white people from going on Indian reserves, and has contributed more to segregation and misunderstanding than the reserve system itself. The Indian has always felt perfectly free to leave his reserve and wander about the countryside, visiting towns in his area. Townspeople, on the other hand, have often been afraid to set foot over the invisible line which marks off a reserve for fear that an Indian constable will leap out to arrest them for trespassing.

This clause has given Indian Affairs a free hand on the reserves, screened from the gaze of the casual passerby. Poverty, ineptitude, injustice have gone unnoticed. No white person will notice that the roads on Indian reserves are potholed, rutted, mud or gravel trails one car wide until he tries to drive down one and he will not try to drive down one if he feels he will be arrested for trespassing.

An Indian cannot sell the grain or cattle he raises on reserve land. Indian Affairs sells it for him, and takes the profits.

Indian bands are expected to keep their own roads, bridges, ditches and fences in good shape. If they do not, the Indian agent can have the work done himself and charge the cost up to the band.

A band may not sell all or part of its reserve. It first must surrender the property to the government, and the government then sells it. The money goes to the government, to be spent on government projects.

An Indian's will has no validity unless it is approved by the government. The will can be declared void by the Indian agent for any one of a number of reasons. The government is lawyer, executor and judge, not only of what the Indian wants to say in his will but of his right to leave his belongings to whom he pleases. An Indian may not leave his possessions to anyone outside the band.

The restrictions of the Act, and the bad effects of its good intentions turn up again and again. Because the reserve land is not subject to legal seizure (Clause 29) Indians without property to use as security find it difficult to obtain credit. The Act covers such a great part of everyday life that the Indians have no freedom of action for themselves. They depend completely upon the competence and good will of the Minister.

Paid Leisure

Because the Act provides authority for the Indian agent to farm vacant reserve land himself, using Indians as laborers , or lease it to others, a pattern of leasing of reserve land has evolved. Since the proceeds from such rentals go in part to individual Indians in possession, and in part to the account of the band, some money actually comes in to Indians from the rents. When he farms the land himself, he does the work, has no authority over planting or sales, and sees any profit go to the government in Ottawa. When he rents the land, he need do no work, and actually sees some cash from the land.

By working his land himself, the Indian gets nothing. Not working, the Indian gets a couple of hundred dollars by allowing someone else to work it. In this way, the Indian has been able to transform himself into a kind of capitalist. All he need do is let his land go to waste, "uncultivated and unused" and then lease it to the white farmer next door. Free of his responsibility to farm, he can travel around the country, picking up odd jobs here and there, living with friends, going on welfare when his lease money runs out. Everyone, except the government, is happy. The Indian has more money than he had before and no work. The white farmer is making a fortune off the good land he is renting. It is becoming difficult to find an Indian reserve on farm land in Western Canada. Virtually the entire acreage of every reserve, except for a tiny patch around the Indian settlement, has been leased out to neighboring farmers.

There is one step more in the process. The Indian, to make a little more money, hires himself out to work as a laborer on his own land which he has leased to the white farmer. He drops from "capitalist" to a low rung of the economic ladder, migrant farm labor. The Indian is conscious of the irony of having to work for a white man in order to make his own land, granted him as long as the sun shines, yield some cash revenue. He knows that he could own and farm that land himself had the government permitted him to do so. The white man has, in fact, taken his reserve land. The government has allowed and encouraged this by making it impossible for the Indian to farm it himself. The white farmers drive new Cadillacs and Chryslers these days. The Indians drive 1948 Fords.

Share the Wealth

In Ottawa, the government has two bank accounts for each Indian band. One is a capital account, the other a revenue account. The money from both accounts is spent *for the Indian band by* the Indian agent. It is spent only for projects which are to benefit the whole band in common, not for any particular individual. Indian Affairs decides what is beneficial. Capital comes from the sale or surrender of reserve land or capital assets of a band. All other band income is revenue money. Half the profit from a sale of land or oil rights can be distributed equally among band members on a per capita basis, and the other half goes into trust. It disappears.

Band capital is used by the government to build and maintain roads and bridges on reserves, build fences, to purchase land for the band, to "buy out" an enfranchised Indian, to buy cattle and farm machinery for the band, to build any public works the Minister feels desirable. It can go as small loans to band members. It can be used to build houses on the reserve and to meet administration costs for land management. Band capital can be used "for any other purpose that in the opinion of the Minister is for the benefit of the band."

In order to maintain its reserve, a band has to sell its reserve. The capital money is used for public works, roads, lighting, ditches, etc. to make the reserve habitable, but the money to do this comes from the sale of reserve land. The capital funds are acquired by sale of the property for which it should be spent.

When the reserves were established, the government realized that great expenditure would be required to set the Indians up as farmers, living in the neat little frame houses everyone envisaged for them. So the government pointed out to the Indian chiefs that the bands had a great deal of land which their few members could never use completely. Land could be sold to white settlers, and would yield money to set up farming for the Indians. The Indians sold. From that initial sale of land, which for most bands took place between 1900 and 1930, they are still drawing their capital income unless they have, like a few, been lucky enough to strike oil. This capital income has been grossly inadequate to maintain the Indian bands in anything resembling adequate living conditions, but it is the only source of income they have, unless they sell even more of their reserves. By initially advising the Indians to sell their reserves, and by setting up the Indian Act so that their public works money *must* come from that source, the government, in effect, broke its treaty promise. It made it impossible for Indians to maintain a decent standard of living on a reserve. An Indian band in Western Canada is trying to maintain itself at a standard which was considered adequate for rural Canada in 1885 or 1915, because their capital has been frozen at that level, at the time of the land sale.

Their poverty has been built in, inescapable.

The actual operating expenses of the band are paid from interest on the capital. This makes up the land's revenue, and must meet the annual budget. The revenue may be spent by Indian Affairs for any purpose that will "promote the general progress and welfare of the band or any member of the band." The money may be spent "to assist sick, disabled, aged or destitute Indians of the band and to provide for the burial of deceased indigent members of the band and to provide for the payment of contributions under the Unemployment Insurance Act on behalf of employed persons . . . out of moneys of the band." Revenue is also spent by the government for "the destruction of noxious weeds" and control of insects, pests and vegetable diseases. It is spent to control the spread of disease, whether or not the disease is communicable. This can be interpreted to mean the construction and maintenance of a hospital, entirely from band funds. Revenue money is used to destroy, alter and renovate homes and other buildings on the reserve; "to prevent overcrowding of premises on reserves used as dwellings" and to keep both private and public buildings in a sanitary condition. Boundary fences are built and maintained from revenue money.

Sometimes the Indians themselves have control over the use of and allocation of their own revenue income, if they can convince the government to grant them "the right to exercise such control and management over lands in the reserve occupied by the band as the Governor-in-Council considers desirable." To obtain self-determination, the Indians must obtain the consent of the federal Cabinet, and there are no standards, no tests, and no uniform code which a band may follow to achieve the object. The decision appears to be an arbitrary one, and is influenced largely by political considerations, with Indians in the constituencies of powerful politicians more easily able to win self-determination than those in other areas. And it is only since the Indians were given the vote in 1960 that many bands have been able to win more control over their own affairs. But even if, after a long struggle, the band council gains control over its own revenue, there is little it can do beyond housekeeping and minor public works, because the revenues are so slender. And the limited capital makes for difficult choices. The more capital that is spent on public works, the less revenue the band has. It has to make a choice between good roads and poor weed control, or good sanitary conditions and no drainage ditches. Of course, both capital and revenue funds are spent on public works, and separation of the two makes no sense. It is impossible to have sanitary living conditions without a decent water supply, yet one is a revenue expense and the other comes under capital expense, and the band can generally have one only if it foregoes the other.

If the band does not have enough revenue to maintain even the bare minimum in decent living conditions for its people it exists on government charity. The money comes from public funds, instead of the band's account, and the government will provide the revenue in the form of a "grant." Rich, or potentially rich, reserves are discriminated against. The more revenue they have, they more they must draw on their own welfare funds for unemployment insurance, health care, weed and pest control, house renovation, sanitary inspection. By the time all these expenses are met, there is little, if any, money left to invest in the reserve or in fringe benefits. The rich reserves do not get government grants, and its expenses may be so high that the individual members of the band are as poor as those Indians who live off government charity.

There has been no means for Indian bands which have been fortunate enough to have rich revenues from oil, timber or real estate to invest their money in a way which will produce ever-increasing revenue for the band. The money has been frozen in trust in Ottawa and frittered away on maintenance expenses, rather than being ploughed back into the reserve economy in a sensible business-like way. The money has been used unproductively and the bands have lost incentive to make money, perceiving that the poor Indians are as well off as they. The universal tendency in Canada has been for rich reserves to become poorer as they slowly devour their resources.

Who Governs?

Indian reserves do not, like municipalities, make their own bylaws. The bylaws are made in Ottawa and apply uniformly to all reserves. The government even sets the penalty for breach of these regulations, which range from poolroom licensing to speeding regulations—$100 maximum fine or three months in jail or both. Indian Affairs provides all municipal services to the Indian. It is Conservation Officer, Health Nurse, Sanitary Inspector, Building Inspector, Police, Highway Traffic Act, Department of Agriculture, Humane Society and Pound, Hospitalization and Medicare, Engineer and Finance Company. All these services are expected from the Indian agent, who visits the reserve about once a week, and the health nurse employed by the federal Department of National Health and Welfare who visits as often as the squalor and sickness require. If the band has any extra money, it provides the rest of the services itself; if no funds are available, they are not normally provided.

"Government" for the reserve is provided by the chief and council. Elections are held every two years, unless a by-election is necessary. One councillor represents every 100 band members, and each band must have at least two councillors and fewer than 12. Although many Indians move away from the reserve, they remain on the band list. Thus, a reserve with a band list population of 800 people will have eight councillors even if only 300 of those people actually reside on the reserve. Regulations governing band elections are made by the Indian Affairs department, although they conform generally to accepted voting practice. Ballots are secret.

A chief or councillor loses his office if he is convicted of an indictable offence or if he is removed by the Indian agent for absence from meetings or for corrupt practice. After six years, he may again run for office. A chief or councillor deposed by Indian Affairs has no right of appeal.

The government also sets down how band meetings are to be conducted, makes regulations about who shall preside at the meetings (usually the Indian agent), what notice shall be given, duties of the Indian agent at the meetings and the number of persons constituting a quorum. The agent can, and frequently does, rule that a quorum consists of himself and the chief. Most of the bylaws the council is authorized to make (all must be consistent with the Indian Act) simply enforce the regulations established by the government about noxious weeds, sanitation, etc. All bylaws, when passed by the council, must be forwarded to Ottawa for the approval of the Minister. If the Minister does not approve, the bylaw is invalid.

Almost all of the permissable bylaws are of a prohibitory character and have contributed to the construction of the invisible wall around each reserve. The council has authority for "the regulation of the conduct and activities of hawkers, peddlers or others who enter the reserve to buy, sell or otherwise deal in wares or merchandise." (This has a quaintly medieval ring which is curiously in keeping with the tone of the Act and life on Indian reserves.) The council has other duties which, obviously, the Minister considers too menial for his personal attention: "the regulation of bee keeping and poultry raising; the control and prohibition of public games, sports, races, athletic contests and other amusements; the construction and regulation of the use of public wells, cisterns, reservoirs and other water supplies."

When a band has, in the mind of the Governor General-in-Council, reached "an advanced stage of development" it can be given permission to levy taxes, hire civil servants, allow businesses to operate, pay its chief and councillors, and otherwise run its own financial affairs, assuming it can raise the money to do so. However, this authority can, at any time, be revoked by the Governor General-in-Council at his pleasure.

No Indian pays tax on his reserve property or on any personal property he has on a reserve. He pays no income tax on any money earned on the reserve, but is liable for tax on income from sources outside the reserve. This tax-free status is without doubt the strongest incentive an Indian has for staying on the reserve. It means he can live better than a white person in similar financial circumstances. Many Indians, when moving off the reserve, fail to take this tax factor into consideration and discover, when they have paid both income and property tax, that they are making less in the city than they did on the reserve. So they go back home.

Indians are not discouraged from drinking liquor. Since the government of Alberta capitulated in 1966, and issued a proclamation permitting Indians to use beer parlors and cocktail lounges, all provinces allow Indians equal drinking privileges with other citizens. However, many reserves still have regulations forbidding the sale or consumption of liquor within their boundaries. To permit liquor on a reserve, a majority of the electors have to vote in favor at a referendum. The discriminatory regulations are still, however, in the Act:

> *"93. A person who directly or indirectly by himself or by any other person on his behalf knowingly*
> *(a) sells, barters, supplies or gives an intoxicant to*
> *(i) any person on a reserve*
> *(ii) an Indian outside a reserve . . . is guilty of an offence . . .*
> *94. An Indian who*
> *(a) has intoxicants in his possession*
> *(b) is intoxicated*
> *(c) makes or manufactures intoxicants off a reserve is guilty of an offence . . . ."*

With its references to Indians in general, the Indian Act intrudes on provincial jurisdiction, since it legislates for Indians off reserves as well as on reserves. Yet if an Indian approaches Indian Affairs for financial or other help in establishing himself off the reserve, he is told that Indian Affairs has no authority over Indians once they have left the reservation. It can prevent him drinking; it can not assist him as the government might help other Canadians.

Freedom?

"109. A person with respect to whom an order for enfranchisement is made under this Act shall, from the date thereof ... be deemed not to be an Indian within the meaning of this Act or any other statute or law."

"en-fran-chise: 1. To set free; to liberate from slavery. 2. To endow with a franchise; to admit to citizenship."

Indians were given the federal vote in 1960. Enfranchise meant, and still means, to liberate from slavery. (John Diefenbaker, Prime Minister in 1960, comes from Prince Albert, Saskatchewan, a town with a large Indian population and centre of one of the heaviest concentrations of Indian-Metis population in Canada. The Indians of Prince Albert have a reputation as a hard-minded group. John Diefenbaker, with masterly political foresight, cast himself in the role of the liberator of Canada's Indians almost exactly one hundred years after Lincoln freed the Negro slaves in the United States.)

Enfranchise, in Canada, means, however, more than it did in the United States. It means, for an Indian, denying the fact that he is an Indian. Technically, the Indian is not being asked to deny his race, culture and personality, and is being asked only to deny his special legal status. But the wording of the Act, "deemed not to be an Indian," certainly has the implication of denying one's Indianness, especially since the Act could have read: "be deemed not to fall within the meaning of this Act."

A Ukrainian or a Frenchman or a Chinese accepting Canadian citizenship does not have to deny the fact that he is Ukrainian, French or Chinese. He simply renounces allegiance to his former nation and swears an oath of allegiance to Canada.

He exchanges one nationality for another, and the process has nothing to do with race. Theoretically, an Indian is being asked to deny allegiance to his treaty and to become a Canadian on an equal basis with other Canadians, but race and nationality become confused. The confusion can be traced to the signing of the treaties. The representatives of Her Majesty's Government pretended, and falsely led the Indians to believe, that they were negotiating with an independent foreign "nation" whereas they were simply making an agreement with an ethnic group of Her Majesty's subjects for the sale of some land. Indian nationality was nothing more than an elaborate government pretense. The government considered the Indians to be British subjects, and the Indians, themselves, considered themselves to be such (the term "Great Mother" was their name for Victoria, not the government's). By using the words "shall be deemed not to be an Indian . . . " in connection with enfranchisement, the Indian Act seemed to be asking the Indian to give up an allegiance to a foreign Indian nationality which was illusory and which he never at any time possessed. Since the Indian knew that he was already a British subject, he, correctly, interpreted "not to be an Indian" in racial terms. It meant, to his mind, that, in the process of becoming a Canadian, he would have to become a white man. From this perception has grown the agonizing debate over "assimilation vs. integration." How white do they have to get?

The expression "not to be an Indian" is deliberate and intentional. It means precisely what the Indians have interpreted it to mean—the Indian is to cease to live, act, think and exist *as an Indian*. It is a phrase aimed at exterminating his racial characteristics, or, more accurately, what the white government thought the characteristics of Indians were. The government wanted the Indian to become what it thought the ideal white man to be. Although the federal vote and the opening up of liquor rights to Indians have made enfranchisement an extinct formality, except for Indian women who automatically lose their Indian status when they marry a non-Indian, the phrasing of the Act remains as a demonstration of the attitudes which the government has had toward Indians. The attitude still remains to influence current policy.

> *108. On the report of the Minister that an Indian has applied for enfranchisement and that in his opinion the Indian*
> *(a) is of the full age of twenty-one years*
> *(b) is capable of assuming the duties and responsibilities of citizenship, and*
> *(c) when enfranchised, will be capable of supporting himself and his dependents, the Governor-in-Council may declare that the Indian and his wife and minor unmarried children are enfranchised.*

Even though enfranchisement is now obsolete, the practice is responsible for many aspects of situations in which Indians now find themselves. The only benefit from enfranchisement an Indian can get now is the ability to sell his reserve property to the band or receive compensation for it from the government. Or he can, if he wishes, retain his property which he possesses by Location Ticket and, for 10 years, rent it from the band. After 10 years, it becomes totally his own. Thus, through enfranchisement, an Indian can get a relatively small financial stake for a new life somewhere else. This cash grant has been a major incentive for enfranchisement. For many Indians, it was the only way they could get cash.

Few Indians take the land grant, because they not only have to pay rent for the land for 10 years, but they cannot farm it. The Indian would have no farm machinery of his own and no property as security for a loan to purchase machinery. Indian Affairs would not assist him when he is no longer an "Indian." So his land would be useless unless sold or rented to others.

Freedom was not always merely a technicality. Enfranchisement was, until very recently, encompassed with mystique and ritual, usually took years, and was fraught with anxiety. Rejection could come at any time and, once rejected, the Indian had no appeal. It was, in fact, induction into the white race. If accepted, the Indian would cease to be an Indian and become a white person "of Indian origin." In 1880, the process had a Victorian simplicity. The first step was the hardest. The Indian had to obtain the consent of the band council. Unless the Indian were disliked by his own people, the band would not likely look with favor on his opting out, and would probably refuse consent. If, however, consent were granted, someone approved by the government had to vouch for the Indian. This was in most cases a clergyman. If an Indian were not a baptized Christian, he would not be deemed civilized and therefore would automatically be refused. If he had more than one wife, or were living with a woman out of wedlock, he would be called immoral. Civilization was also usually taken to mean a certain ability to speak, read and write English and to do simple arithmetic. The English text would be the Bible so the Indian would have some Biblical knowledge as well. Otherwise, the Indian's qualifications would depend on the personality of the clergyman. If the clergyman were strictly a teetotaler, an Indian who drank whiskey at all would usually be refused. Sobriety in 1880, for Indians, usually meant abstinence. The model civilized Indian is of course the portrait of the stiff backed, stone-faced unsmiling Indian in a bowler hat with a rolled umbrella underneath his arm.

The adoption of the basic white customs was thus built in to the requirements for freedom. The Indian had to be Christian, moral, sober and reasonably literate in English. None of these requirements was demanded of the hordes of immigrants who poured into Canada to settle on the lands the Indians had surrendered. Many of these were illiterate, immoral, hard-drinking, quarrelsome, violent and unable to speak, read or write a word of English. They were, however, white, Christian and Canadian.

In 1880, the word "savage" was used interchangeably with the word "Indian." The word civilized, therefore, meant, to an Indian, "white." It was clear in the tone and the language of the Indian Act, as well as in the way it was carried out, that by becoming "free" and Canadian, the Indian was expected to deny all or part of himself. Even after becoming enfranchised he was required to serve a three-year term of probation. A sensitive Indian, therefore, not only rejected enfranchisement, as many did, but rejected civilization as well, which many have done. They were called savages; many became savages.

By 1906, the ritual of induction into the white race had taken on a majestic pomp. An Indian wishing freedom had to obtain a certificate signed *under oath before a justice of the peace* by a priest, clergyman or minister of the religious

denomination to which he belonged or by *two* justices of the
peace to the effect that "the applicant for enfranchisement is
and has been, for at least five years previously, a person of good
moral character, temperate in his or her habits and of sufficient
intelligence to be qualified to hold land in fee simple and
otherwise to exercise all the rights and privileges of an enfranchized person." The signed certificate was then submitted for
approval to the band council. A public hearing was held at
which anyone could come forward and give reasons why the
Indian should not be enfranchised. If he passed these tests, he
became a "probationary Indian" for three years and was
expected to show "exemplary good conduct" before getting
title to his land. (Any Indian who became a doctor, lawyer,
clergyman or holder of any university degree did not have to go
through all the steps but could petition the government directly.) The magic steps to enfranchisement are reminiscent of the
ritual duties medieval knights had to perform before they were
admitted to full knighthood. No wonder many Indians were
disillusioned when, after they had slain their last dragon, they
found they were no better off then they were before and white
men were just as strange and incomprehensible. The magic
chant "Integrity, Morality, Sobriety" did not open doors to a
vision of the Holy Grail.

Most Indians were not gullible enough to accept this
nonsense about civilization. Enfranchisement meant two things:
money and liquor. The enfranchised Indian was entitled not
only to his parcel of land or the proceeds from the sale of that
land, but to his per capita share of the band's capital fund. In
some cases, this amounted to a couple of a hundred dollars. As
a non-Indian, he could drink. Thousands of Indians have given
up their Indian status for that right to drink. It was worth the
five dollars a year treaty money they forfeited. The government
encouraged enfranchisement, not on any high-sounding grounds
of civilization, but because it saved money. The fewer Indians
the government had to look after, the less money Indians would
cost and the less trouble there would be for the Indian agent.
Indian agents were also justices of the peace on reserves, and it
was a simple matter for them to sign certificates for enfranchisement regardless of the Indian's sobriety or other virtues,
just to get rid of the responsibility for that particular Indian.

Often the most troublesome Indians were most readily enfranchised. Indians with a taste for liquor became enfranchised with absolutely no understanding of the meaning of the word other than "legal booze." Intemperance, rather than temperance, became the motivation and the qualification for freedom. Sober, hard-working Indians stayed Indians. The newly freed Indians seldom understood what they had forfeited because they had, in the first place, little or no knowledge of the Indian Act, and they certainly did not understand what Canadian citizenship meant.

The enfranchised Indians and their descendants now make up a sizable portion of the Canadian population, although they have not always been absorbed in Canadian society gracefully. They became "Metis" or "half-breeds" or "non-treaty Indians" or, in one word, Nobodies. After they had drunk up their share of the band fund in the town beer parlor, they found they had nowhere to go. They were not allowed back on the reserve. Towns and cities were unfamiliar. They looked and acted like Indians, and white people treated them like Indians. As far as whites were concerned, they still were Indians, and had a position similar to that of the United States Negro after liberation. They took the same alternatives, became migrant labor, and engaged in farming, pulp cutting, railway section gangs, or settled down on subsistence farms as "squatters." Those who did not become wanderers almost always settled down in a fringe belt around their former reserve, and now almost every reserve has such a fringe. They still thought of the reserve as home and their friends and relatives were still there. But they were estranged from their friends and relatives. They were shunned for having sold out. Called "white man" for having accepted white status, they were to the treaty Indian what fink is to the union organizer and stoolie is to the criminal. Their relatives tolerated them because of blood ties, but relations were strained.

A woman whose husband or father had become enfranchised could regain her Indian status by marrying back into the band. Many did. A man, however, could not re-Indianize himself. He found, moreover, that treaty Indian women were reluctant to marry him, because he was not an Indian and they would lose their own status and protection. Enfranchised men, therefore, married Metis or non-treaty women or white women. These enfranchised Indians in a few generations lose Indian racial characteristics as well as Indian legal status. The loss of the legal meaning of Indian led, eventually, to the loss of the racial meaning of Indian. Grandchildren or great-grandchildren would no longer be recognizably Indian. They would be white in every meaning of the word, racially, culturally, legally.

Although the white men did not force the Indian to accept their values or their race through enfranchisement, the Indians themselves made it an inevitable process. Most of these enfranchised Indian-Metis-white people disappeared, absorbed into Canadian society. They learned how to make money, hold a job, get credit, buy houses or farms, vote, hold public office. In other words, they learned the skills of capitalist society and became a part of it. A large and indeterminate number of the French Canadians in Manitoba and Saskatchewan are non-treaty-Indian-Metis-French who have lost most of their Indian features and prefer to identify themselves as French.

In the southern, well-populated areas of Canada, an enfranchised Indian had no choice but to become absorbed into white society, since there was no land for him to "squat" on. He could go north, where a non-treaty Indian could follow his customary occupations, hunting, fishing and trapping, and could live tax-free on a piece of bush-covered rock. He did not have his five dollars a year or his free medical care, but the provincial government educated his children and kept him alive on welfare when the going got rough. He lived a life almost identical to that of the Indian, in some ways freer, in some ways more helpless.

Chapter 7
My Country 'Tis of Thy People You're Dying

"Fort Pitt was free from smallpox, but it had gone through a fearful ordeal: more than one hundred Crees had perished close around its stockades. The unburied dead lay for days by the road-side, till the wolves, growing bold with the impunity which death among the hunters ever gives to the hunted, approached and fought over the decaying bodies. From a spot many marches to the south the Indians had come to the fort in midsummer, leaving behind them a long track of dead and dying men over the waste of distance. 'Give us help,' they cried, 'give us help, our medicine men can do nothing against this plague, from the white man we got it, and it is only the white man who can take it away from us.'

"But there was no help to be given, and day to day the wretched band grew less. Then came another idea into the red man's brain: 'If we can only give the disease to the white man and the trader in the fort,' thought they, ' we will cease to suffer from it ourselves,' so they came into the house dying and disfigured as they were, horrible beyond description to look at, and sat down at the entrances of the wooden houses, and stretched themselves on the floors and spat upon the door handles. It was no use, the fell disease held them in a grasp from which there was no escape, and just six weeks before my arrival the living remnant fled away in despair."

William Butler
The Great Lone Land, p. 250

In the late nineteenth century, aside from periodic visits from the medical superintendent and occasionally from a doctor, the Indians were without medical care. A few primitive operations were performed by teachers, missionaries and Bay managers. Basic drugs were dispensed by the same people. Many Indians were completely riddled with scrofula — TB of the lymph glands — and whole communities would suffer from it in some form. Frequently, however, the TB victims would be carried off by measles, influenza or some other epidemic before

TB caught up with them. Indian Affairs took extraordinarily punitive measures against sick Indians. Sickness was associated with dirt and dirt with sin; the campaign against illness was not only military in character but aimed at reforming the Indian's whole personality and way of life.

"Great effort has been made to introduce more sanitary conditions in the dwellings of the Indians. Unsanitary houses have been destroyed, and circulars containing instruction regarding ventilation, removal of rubbish and other precautions have been widely distributed . . .

In our residential schools special attention is given to all that pertains to healthy living. Calisthenics is practised and the benfits of fresh air and personal cleanliness are carefully impressed upon the children; the instruction which they thus received cannot fail to influence their later life upon the reserve."

Indian Affairs Report, 1916

Attempts to cure disease were futile so Indian Affairs aimed at prevention. Those that were not instructed at school received circulars listing 36 health rules, including:

Some Don'ts

1. Don't drink whisky. Whisky and allied drinks are the world's national curse.

2. Don't throw slop water near the house or near the well.

3. Don't neglect to call the medical doctor when seriously sick, and, when you do call him, co-operate with him.

4. Don't wear wet moccasins. They may be economical, but they are not healthy.

5. Don't allow dogs in the house. They bring filth into it.

6. Don't hunt for $100 a season if you can make $1,000 by farming. Learn farming.

7. Don't be filthy. Water is free where you live.

8. Keep the flies off your food. They carry disease.

9. Drink pure water only. Boiling makes water pure.

These circulars were described as being "designed easily to arouse the attention of the more primitive type of Indian mind."

1936: *"During the earlier part of the year, whooping cough was very common and measles somewhat less so. The widespread prevalence of these two diseases, apparent during the past three years, appears to have run its course, at least among Indians. There were many more than the usual number of outbreaks of scarlet fever, and diphtheria. Fortunately neither of these diseases gained headway enough to become epidemic. Influenza of a fairly mild type spread widely during the winter between Fort William and the Rocky Mountains. While the death rate from all these diseases does not appear to have been very high, a good deal of effort and expense was required to deal with them."*

Indian Affairs, Annual Report, 1936

The Indians were discovered to suffer severely from trachoma—inflamation and infection of the eyes—which often rendered victims wholly or partially blind.

The only people the government could reach to cure the disease were children in residential school.

The residential schools, congregating hundreds of children from different reserves with different diseases, were contagion centers. The children died by the dozens or contracted diseases which spread easily through the unsanitary buildings. When they went home, they took the diseases with them. The schools were frequently swept by epidemics.

Tuberculosis was out of control by 1936. The government did not know how many Indians had it, or how many died from it. Lack of money was the reason for lack of treatment:

"There are plenty of known cases on the reserves. The difficulty is to devise any means of isolating the affected persons at a cost within financial reach. The department has endeavoured in every way to co-operate in the general Government effort to limit the taxpayer's burden. Sanatorium treatment is costly, and home isolation not very effective. . ."

"Throughout the winter of 1937 influenza was prevalent among the Indians, scarcely any part of the country escaping. The epidemic, on the whole, was not of a severe

nature, but, like all widespread epidemics, was virulent in a few places. Influenza together with measles at one residential school and with whooping cough at another resulted in high mortality.

This was the first widespread epidemic in 10 years, and it is interesting to observe the change in the attitude of the Indians during that period of time toward such visitations and towards the measures taken to deal with them. In this respect at least, the Indian point of view has changed remarkably. He used to accept such afflictions and the resulting loss of life as inevitable, and to look upon the counsel of his medical and other supervisors as worthless, or at least not applicable to Indians. Whole groups have been known to die, not so much from the disease as from resignation to fate."

Indian Affairs, Annual Report, 1937,
Report on Health Services

In 1941, the death rate from TB among Indians was 10 times the rate for the white population. Only a small number —about 530—were able to receive hospital care. The war took most of the doctors from the Indian Health Service, leaving the Indians with the minimum of attention until 1946.

"Throughout the winter there was a wide-spread and severe epidemic of influenza which resulted in many deaths, particularly among remote bands. This also resulted in lighting up many latent cases of tuberculosis, causing a sharp increase in deaths from this disease. There were sporadic outbreaks of whooping cough, measles, chicken-pox, mumps, and scarlet fever. In every outbreak steps were taken to control the spread of the disease.

There were two serious epidemics of diphtheria. At hobbema, Indians concealed the death of a boy with the result that a widespread outbreak occurred. The Royal Canadian Mounted Police were called in to enforce quarantine and general inoculation with diphtheria toxoid was carried out. At Norway House, Manitoba, sporadic cases of diphtheria kept appearing among the Indians in the bush, until at one time there was a total of 42 cases.

Department of Indian Affairs

In 1941, a team of doctors, out of professional curiosity, began a scientific study of health conditions among the Indians of Northern Manitoba, particularly in Norway House, The Pas and Cross Lake. Indian Affairs contributed to their expenses. Their study lasted until 1944. The doctors were appalled:

> *"The majority of the Indians we saw, according to our present day medical standards, were sick. They were not sick according to lay opinion, but when we examined them carefully from the medical standpoint, they had so many obvious evidences of malnutrition that if you or I were in the same condition, we would demand hospitalization at once. We were struck, particularly in 1941, with the inertia, the lack of initiative, the indolence of these people. Physically, they shuffled about; they moved slowly. Even though we had to speak to many of them through an interpreter, it was obvious their mental processes were going on at a very slow pace. We found, in that particular band, the TB death rate was just fifty times the tuberculosis death rate among the white population of Manitoba. This raises a problem far beyond the Indians because there is a focus of infection which is of concern to you and me. We can never prevent tuberculosis among the white population of Canada when we have a focus of fifty times that among those Indians.*

> *"In trying to find out what was at the bottom of this situation we studied the food which the Indians had. We found, according to our present day standards, the Indians received a diet which could not possibly result in good health.*

> *"The Indian of today at Norway House is a smaller Indian than forty years ago. This statement is not based on guesswork, but on facts obtained from the post manager of the Hudson Bay post, Mr. Laramont, who happened to be there forty years ago. He says the Indian of today is buying a smaller sized shirt and smaller pants compared with those articles he bought forty years ago. From appearance the Indians are definitely smaller and not as well developed as they were forty years ago . . .*

> *"We found definite evidence that the Indian of today has not got the physical stamina which we would desire for*

*good health or the stamina he had forty years ago as was
evidenced from the records we obtained from many people in
that district."*

Dr. Frederick Tisdall,
Testimony before Senate-Commons
Committee on Indian Affairs, 1947,
vol. 1. p. 8.

"We Are Starving"

Starvation can be a long, slow, imperceptible process.
Malnutrition is shown in very little ways, and it is frequently
overlooked. Bad teeth, repeated pregnancy, alcoholism can all
lead to subtle malnutrition. All three factors are almost universal in the Indian population. Many Indian women are continually pregnant. They are toothless by their mid-twenties. Most
Indian women are anemic. Their blood count ranges from 50 to
60 while healthy blood is over 80 or 90.

A visitor to any reserve is struck immediately by the fact
that the people look different. The people's teeth, especially in
small children, are brown and rotted. Their hair is dry, dull and
scraggy. The women have extraordinarily thin, emaciated legs;
their skin is dry and they are wrinkled at 30. Healthy-looking
people are immediately noticeable.

Many Indians are deformed, bent, and twisted. The women
often support immense, obese bodies on their spindly legs.
Their eyes are dull, their faces scarred. Many teenagers and
small children show the same dullness and thinness.

The clinical description of starvation could almost be the
stereotype of the Indian:

*"Severe dietary inadequacies have made people angry,
submissive, listless, disease ridden and incapable of productive work, resistance or, finally, of continuing to live. Entire
population groups reduced to the listless stage have subsisted
for generations with chronic dietary inadequacies sufficient
to lower progressively their work output, which, with high
fecundity, results in a constantly diminishing food supply."*

Clinical Nutrition
Jolliffe, Tisdall and Cannon,
New York, Harper, 1950, p.4.

This is the history of the Indians of Canada since they were established on reserves. Any Indian agent, missionary or social worker can describe the Indian's apathy, inability to work, lack of concentration, depression.

Only recently have the young people begun to exhibit signs of average vitality and enthusiasm.

Reports that the Indians are starving occasionally come from reserves, especially in the North. The government sends in a crew of experts, who find that the Indians are not lying dead in the woods but are shuffling around as usual. They see that they have lots of flour and lard, so the reports are dismissed as sensationalism. The Indians have food; they are not starving.

In 1962, at Nelson House in northern Manitoba, 800 Indians were living on 100 per cent welfare. Forty miles away, a huge nickel mine was being built. Not one Indian was employed. Indians were not allowed in the company town. The Nelson House people were desperate for work. "We are starving," the chief told a newspaper reporter. He was speaking metaphorically: the Indians were dying mentally as well as physically.

Reports of starvation were carried in Toronto newspapers. The Salvation Army responded by flying in hundreds of pounds of potatoes. The plane dumped the potatoes on the ice. The potatoes lay there, frozen. "Well, aren't you going to carry your potatoes up to your homes? " demanded the Indian agent. "Pay us for our labor," said the Indians. The agent went away in disgust. In the spring, the potatoes were carried away when the ice went out.

The Indians of Fox Lake, Alberta were living almost entirely on bannock in February, 1966. A week before the welfare cheques came out, the whole community was virtually without food. Everyone was unemployed and on relief although there was a great deal of work in the area. In October, 1965, Indian Affairs handed out $7,000 in welfare; by February 1966, this sum had been cut to $1,800. By cutting off the rations, Indian Affairs was trying to provide an incentive for the people to work. They could get their money by laboring on Indian Affairs "make-work" projects—land clearing, fence building, wood cutting. The men made a pittance in wages. The land-clearing project employed ten men: wages totalled

$1,135—slightly over $100 a man. Six men fenced the school yard; their wages totalled $222, or $37 a man. Food prices in Fox Lake are 25 per cent higher than in Edmonton.

An investigator reported: "Many children have chubby cheeks—a sign of adequate food supply—and others seemed happy as they swatted mosquitoes and played in the dirt." Chubby cheeks can also be a sign of malnutrition.

"We're hungry but happy," said one band member. "The food is expensive—two pounds of beef sausage is $1.50 —and many times we run out of money and food before it's time for our next welfare cheque." Another Indian said he supports his family on $40 a month welfare. They eat bannock.

A newspaper reporter who spent one week in Oxford House, Manitoba in 1962 existed on the diet of local Indians—bannock, lard, watered vegetable soup from a tin can, a few scraps of whitefish, and tea. During that time, he walked up to 20 miles a day with the Indians, hauling wood to feed the stove. A medical examination when he returned to Winnipeg showed he was suffering from malnutrition. It took all the energy he possessed to keep walking and hauling wood in spite of severe hunger. The Indians have been doing it for generations in Oxford House.

"The Indian in the north certainly was not keen mentally. He was very slow in his mental reactions and gave no evidence of any initiative or desire to do things. There is no use in growing to be an adult, well developed and strong physically, mentally active, if you are susceptible to every disease or infection which comes along. We had evidence of many diseases, I will only mention tuberculosis, to which the Indian was susceptible. There were many other diseases which they contracted much more readily than would a white person or person who was better fed; and they died from those diseases where the other person would not have died. In the Cross Lake band the infant mortality for one year—that is, the number of babies who died under one year of age—reached a total of five hundred compared to the figure last year of approximately forty in the city of Toronto. It was over twelve times the infant mortality rate of a well regulated white district in Canada.

"We found, of course, poor hygienic conditions. The housing was not up to our standards nor was the sanitation. All this could be explained to a degree by the fact that these people were sick mentally and physically. We believed they were sick primarily because their food was not sufficient or not of the proper type to allow them to be healthy. They could not possibly be healthy. We obtained a record of the food they purchased. Incidentally, due to the fact that the hunting and fishing resources have been depleted to a considerable degree in that area, the Indian of today depends much more on the food which is brought in and which he purchases at various stores than he did in the past. In fact, the records of the Hudson's Bay Company show that forty years ago a certain sized family would start out a winter with one hundred pounds of flour but today the same sized family would start out with six hundred pounds. Thirty or forty years ago the Indians lived off the land to a considerable degree—that is, from fishing and hunting—but today their diet consists chiefly of the food they buy at the store in return for the sale of the pelts they catch.

"No less than 85 per cent of the calories they buy come from white flour, lard and sugar. Just stop and think about that for a moment; think what that means in the diet of these people. Eighty-five per cent of all the food they bought, from the actual records of the store which were kindly placed at our disposal by the Hudson's Bay Company, 85 per cent of the calories came from white flour, sugar and lard. These foods are almost entirely lacking in vitamins and are very deficient in minerals. In fact, when we started to analyse it we found that where they should receive 900 milligrams of calcium a day, they were only receiving about 100 in the food they bought. The Vitamin A consumption should be around 5,000 units, but they were getting only 235. Consumption of Thiamin, or one of the B vitamins, should have been around one and a half, but they got one-third of a milligram. As regards Vitamin C which we obtain from fresh fruits and vegetables and of which they should have received about 75, they were getting under 10. We also found that in the past the Indians used to eat the insides, the liver and other parts of the animals and fish. Now, imitating the white *man's custom, they clean the fish and throw away these articles of food which we know are rich in minerals and vitamins.*

"Perhaps I should say here that we found lots of physical evidence in the Indians of defects, changes in their eyes, changes in the gums and changes in the tongue as well as changes in their reflexes."

An Indian child born into these conditions at Norway House would, if it survived, be 27 years old today. It is these children which the government is so anxious to train, upgrade and integrate into Canadian society.

"The problem we encountered at Norway House was identical with the problem of all the bush Indians of which there are 65,000 in Canada. It is a typical problem and Norway House is exactly the same as elsewhere. The Indian is fundamentally a good Canadian and his reactions to his conditions are no different from what our reactions would be if we were living under his conditions.

"They are not fundamentally indolent and with a lack of initiative. They are sick." Dr. Tisdall.

Indians live about half as long as other Canadians, and the infant mortality rate is double the Canadian rate. And for every white child that dies before its second birthday, eight Indian children die. Most Indians die from diseases which are prevented in other Canadians. In the west, the situation is worse than the east: prairie Indian women bear twice as many children as other Canadian women, but the infant mortality rate is three times as high. The north is even worse: venereal disease is a greater problem than anywhere else in Canada, and alcoholism, not only in the north but generally among Indians, has reached the epidemic proportions associated with smallpox and TB in earlier years. Dental care for Indians is almost non-existent, and few children have their teeth filled. Indians' teeth are pulled.

Tuberculosis is still a threat to Indians, with most cases found in children and teenagers. A 1965 check of members of the Maple Creek band turned up 16 more active cases out of a band population of 104. Epidemics of measles still sweep through reserves and infectious hepatitis is extremely prevalent among Indians. Indians use hospitals twice as much as other Canadians.

"The average age of death in 1963 for Indian males was 33.31 years and for Indian females 34.71 years. However, if the deaths occurring in the first twelve months of life are excluded, the average age of death rises in the case of males to over 46 years and to just under 48 years for females. The national average age at death in 1963 was 60.5 years for males and 64.1 years for females.

"Three quarters of all Indian deaths each year are found to be due to five main causes. The five main causes are, first and most important, "colds" and pneumonia, second and nearly equal in importance, accidents, third and much less important, heart trouble and "strokes", fourth, infant diseases, and fifth, stomach and bowel disorders, mostly diarrhea. All the other causes of death, including tuberculosis, taken together hardly ever add up to quite a full quarter of all the deaths of Indians from all causes.

"The fact that Indians appear to die most from causes which are preventable suggests that living conditions and health habits are important factors in the picture. It is perhaps reasonable to assume, though difficult to establish statistically, that many Indians who do not die nevertheless are affected for the same reasons by debilitation and disability which in turn reduces their employability."

Indian Affairs Branch,
Statement for Federal-Provincial
Conference on Poverty, December, 1965,
mimeographed.

"The health of permanent or long term residents in the north presents some unique features and problems. Alcohol appears to be more abused than elsewhere. The incidence of venereal disease is significantly higher than elsewhere in Canada. The suicide rate is abnormally high. The accident mortality rate is high. The rate of mental breakdown is disturbing. The general death rate is above the Canadian rate, mainly as a result of high mortality amongst the relatively

high proportion of the population comprised of Indians and Eskimos. Pneumonia is the commonest cause of death, again reflecting the experience of the Indian and Eskimo population."

Annual Report, 1965,
Medical Services, Dept. 9
National Health and Welfare.

The White Plague

Ten times as many Indians as other Canadians die of tuberculosis today. The death rate is low — seven Indians died of TB in Manitoba, northwestern Ontario, and the eastern Arctic in 1966 — but it is stubborn. The Sanatorium Board of Manitoba uncovered 112 new cases of tuberculosis among Indians and Eskimos in 1965. Twenty-six of these were located in southern Manitoba. Fourteen were children under 12 from Roseau River reserve. Sioux Lookout, north of Kenora, was also a heavily diseased area, contributing 35 new cases. Most of the inmates of sanatoria are now Indian or Eskimo.

Tuberculosis is a disease of the young. Manitoba had 94 Indians and Eskimos hospitalized in 1965 and sixty-three were under 30 while 16 were under five years of age.

Until the 1940's only the most severely ill patients could be hospitalized because facilities were so limited. They were taken away to protect the community; there was no hope of a cure. The patients died — by the dozens and hundreds — in the hospitals.

Many Indians propounded the idea that the hospitals killed the Indians. It is possible that, removed from home, lonely and in a strange place, many Indians did actually go into a "decline" and die of depression rather than TB. The Indians had no idea what a hospital did and no patients came back to tell them.

When x-ray units, transported by boat and plane, began to come into the reserves in the 1930's, the Indians ran and hid in the bush. It was very difficult for the doctors to x-ray anyone. To combat the fear, doctors were forced to return Indian patients to their homes before they were completely cured simply to prove to the people it was possible to come back from the hospital. The patients usually relapsed and infected more people, but the process of cure was established and confidence gained.

Tuberculosis has been brought under control in the Indian population only since 1950. In 1950, the Indian death rate from TB was 43.8/100,000 population compared to 12.8/100,000 for the white population. By 1965, the Indian death rate had dropped to 28.6/100,000. The white death rate was 2.7/100,000. Sanatorium treatment for Indians was not authorized in Manitoba by Indian Affairs until 1938. In that year, the Indian death rate was 25 times the Canadian rate. One-third of the total TB deaths in Manitoba occurred among two per cent of the population.

The old Indian sanatoria have, for the most part, been closed. They were terrible places. All the patients were desperately sick and many died. The buildings were old and run-down, wards were crowded, and a new patient immediately filled a bed vacated by a corpse. In Manitoba, the Dynevor Indian hospital was set up in a nineteenth-century stone building.

Of sixty-seven patients admitted in 1940, 59 per cent had extremely advanced TB, and 42 per cent were children under 15. The hospital suffered from a shortage of beds and a shortage of nursing staff. "If more beds are not soon provided, the benefit of case findings will be dissipated," the hospital director wrote in 1946. Of 88 patients admitted in 1946, 90 per cent had advanced TB of the lungs, and 21 patients died that year.

Indians received segregated hospital treatment until the number of patients dwindled so markedly that the Indians could be fitted into the white people's sanatoria. These institutions have now become, in effect, Indian hospitals, and they have had a marked effect on the Indians who have been in them. Indians who have spent time in TB sanatoria say that it was like a dream. Their experience bore no relation to the world as they knew it on the reserve, nor to any modern world they were expected to enter.

They had lots of food, sleep, no work, clean clothes and attention. They lived like vegetables, lying by the hour, day after day, talking or listening to the radio. Their slightest wish was looked after; they had parties and gifts. Cooped up in the hospital with other sick people, the Indians felt no relationship to the "outside" at all. The environment of the hospital was much closer to that of the reserve than to a town or city. It is impossible to expect people habituated to being sick, dependent and passive to suddenly acquire the energy and courage to adopt a new way of life. Instead, the sanatorium mentality was taken back to the reserve.

Professional Patients

Indians have been chronically, desperately, sick for more than 100 years. Illness is built into their traditions and their emotional reactions. Cures have been militant and authoritarian. Police have frequently been called in to enforce quarantines. Reserves have, at times, been "death camps." The Indians were not allowed to leave; white people were not allowed to enter.

Chronic illness and debility have influenced the Indian's achievement in every field. He has been ridiculed and upbraided for his appearance and conduct; he has been called lazy and immoral. Sickness, and the moral opprobrium attached to it by white people who mistook his illness for evil, has influenced the Indian's self-image and personality.

One has the impression that many Indians would be glad to spend their lives in the hospital, as many try to spend them in jail. They spend more time in hospital than non-Indians and make greater use of health facilities. Nothing the doctors or hospitals do for them is right. They complain and criticize, pointing out weaknesses and injustices in medical care, complaining about the nursing station when it's open and when it shuts down. Health nurses try to teach nutrition and sanitation but to no avail, so they throw up their hands in dismay. Health authorities receive the minimum of co-operation from the Indians.

Illness can be psychosomatic; it can also be sociosomatic. The smallpox and TB which ravaged the Indians for so many years have been explained by the fact that the Indians had never been in contact with these illnesses and had no physical resistance. This argument is now used frequently to explain why Indians drink to excess: "They are not used to it;" "They do not know how to use alcohol." This argument is obviously fallacious. If Indians need three or four generations to get accustomed to liquor, presumably white Canadians go through a similar pattern. There is no vaccine against alcoholism and one doesn't acquire immunity by exposure or heredity. Alcoholism is a psychosomatic disease produced by stress. It is suicidal.

Within Indian society poverty has been legally enforced and a tradition of illness has been established, so that sickness becomes a habit, an instinctive response. For a helpless individual in an authoritarian system, or for a group of people faced by technological annihilation, sickness can become aggressive, used as a subtle means of establishing control. Sickness can, in some situations, be a healthy, adaptive response. A sick person—especially one who is flagrantly sick—forces other people to accede to his wishes. He reverts to childishness, becomes petulant, demanding, and gains power through his helplessness.

The Indian adopted the sick man role from his first contact with British imperialism. A stone age people who had not yet invented the wheel could not compete with Victorian England or with the Sun King of Versailles without running the almost certain risk of extinction. The Indians are probably alive as a race today because they became sick, but they have paid a high price for survival.

The progression of illnesses illustrates the subtle change in circumstances. Smallpox and TB were both "white man's diseases," and many Europeans died from them. The Indians' suffering was similar, but more severe and more widespread. The Indians, however, now have specifically Indian illnesses. A kind of segregation of disease has become established alongside present social segregation. The diseases are also mainly psychosomatic or sociosomatic. Through his illnesses the Indian stays in touch with Canadian society. As a patient he is important, a problem, so the advantages of disease operate to keep the Indians sick. If they became healthy, they might be expelled from the hospital and left to fend on their own in an alien world.

Chapter 8
The Mudlarks

"We all live off each other."

Mayor, The Pas

Black crows wheel overhead, swooping, circling, looking for garbage. In the winter stillness, dogs are barking faintly a mile away across the river on the Indian reserve. The crows are always there in The Pas, even in winter.

"I picked Virginia up on the street. She was heading for the foster home, falling and crawling. She didn't seem to realize how drunk she was. When she got in the car she began to cry and became very hysterical and self-destructive. She hates herself."

Probation Officer

Virginia is 15, a pretty Indian girl living in St. Faith's, a group foster home in The Pas which accommodates Indian and Metis girls from northern Manitoba. Most of the girls in the home are picked up drunk on the main street of The Pas.

The Gateway Hotel beer parlor is warm and cosy on a Saturday night in January. It is full of people with big smiles crowded around little tables. All the tables are laden with glasses of beer. Faces glow red. Occasionally an Indian is propelled by a waiter through the back door but the Indian comes back in a few minutes later, sobered by the cold. A fresh glass of beer is waiting for him, and his friends continue their conversation as if he had never left. Few Indians can afford to drink in the beer parlor. They cluster, black wasps clinging to the outside of a nest, around the front door. The hive hums and buzzes with shouts, curses, arguments. Every time the door opens, they all peer in wistfully, hoping to see a friend who will stake them to a drink. People shove out, others are sucked in. The whole mass pushes, jostles, staggers with their passage. There is a cacophony of noise—scraps of Cree, screams, belches, mutterings, profanity. People fall down, spit, vomit and hit; the mass weaves and wavers, while bottles of beer and wine are surreptitiously passed around. Indians of all ages collect in this pool of light around the Gateway Hotel door, obese middle-aged women in bright, long skirts and kerchiefs, young girls in black—black ski pants, black windbreakers, black kerchiefs.

They are the mudlarks. They linger on the fringe waiting, watching. If one of them is lucky, some man will come along, buy her a beer or two inside and take her to a flophouse around the corner for the night. She might stay with this man for a week or a year; she might be beaten and thrown out on the street in the morning. The mudlarks live on the streets of The Pas, scavenging what they can. They have no homes, their families have disintegrated or don't want them because they cost too much to feed.

These pathetic little dark girls are not seductive, bundled up against the cold in ski pants and ugly nylon jackets, shivering. They are hardly noticeable, all dressed in drab black, hiding in the shadows. Skinny and bony, their faces are hard and lined already, dry and dull-eyed. Their hair is lank, dirty, and their efforts at soliciting clumsy and childish. Many men, I think, take them in out of pity. Their sickness and hunger are real but much of their pathos is fake. They feel white people are more ready to pity them than to admire them. These little waifs show, under stress, an amazing toughness, calculation, aggressiveness and capacity for endurance, but this vitality is carefully hidden. It is not really accurate to call these women and girls prostitutes. There is so little money involved and they are so apologetic, unassuming, and unprofessional, they will go with a man for nothing, just on a gamble that something will turn up.

It was winter when Virginia was picked up by the probation officer. She had no coat and would have frozen to death very soon. In the jail, she shouted, swore and banged her head against the steel wall of her cell, crying "nobody wants me." She was judged to be a sexual delinquent and out of control. She had had venereal disease five times and had already spent two years in a detention home for drinking.

Virginia is in grade seven. She is of normal intelligence and gets good marks. A psychologist found her to be primitive, impulsive, amoral and pleasure-seeking. She seemed, he said, to lack insight, perseverance and energy. She is suspicious, evasive and fond of daydreaming. She says she hates men but continually runs away for sprees at the Gateway, after which she is pulled again, drunk, out of the gutter. She gets hysterical when taken back to the foster home. She says she hates it, accusing the people of snooping through her belongings. She shows no remorse for her conduct and encourages the other girls to follow. Although the psychologist found her timid, passive, dependent and unimaginative, she faked suicide to get attention and, when jailed for that, escaped by opening a window and scaling the high wire fence. She turned up at the foster home, demanding her clothes and saying she was going away. She was put back in jail. Occasionally Virginia's mother turns up, saying she is going to start life over with a new house and lots of money if Virginia will come to live with her. Her plans never materialize and she disappears again.

Mudlarks grow old. Many are women in their fifties with grown daughters who accompany them on their nightly junkets. Husbands and sons come along too, so all go to jail together. The women's jail frequently holds a mother and one or two of her daughters; the father will be joined in the men's quarters by his sons. All are there on liquor charges.

Lizzie is a legend in The Pas, matriarch of a Sophoclean family. She is about 55, bent, toothless, wizened. She has spent most of her life in jail, has nine children who also have spent their lives in and out of jail, as have their husbands, wives, aunts, uncles and cousins. "When looking at the family tree," a probation officer told me, "it is completely horrifying to realize the trouble that has arisen from direct or indirect offspring of this woman."

Lizzie was born on the Indian reserve at the Pas, one of 12 children. She married a Metis at 16, lost her Indian status, left him after one month, and then established a common-law relationship with another man. She reached grade six in residential school but is virtually illiterate. Lizzie and her husband have been drinking heavily for 30 years, and in the last 20 years, she has been in jail 32 times on charges ranging from drunkenness to contributing to the juvenile delinquency of her own daughters. "She's the best old soul who ever was here," says the matron. Her sentences have ranged from five days to two months, depending on the whim of the magistrate. In three years, from 1963 to 1966, she was sentenced 21 times for intoxication and spent 25 of the 36 months in jail. Lizzie misbehaved only once in jail; she slashed a screen and escaped to share a bottle of wine with her husband in the bush behind the jail. She was found, asleep, a few hours later. She swore and wept when returned to jail, then calmly ate her dinner. "Lizzie is lazy in many ways but agreeable," a supervisor said. "She comes when she is called for work." A couple of years ago Lizzie developed stomach pains. She is now in hospital, still under sentence.

Martha, Lizzie's youngest daughter, at the age of 18 had been found by the RCMP under a railway train in The Pas station on a bitter January night. Police thought she had been run over. When they dragged her out she screamed and fought; she had been sleeping off the liquor. She has a reputation as a fighter; she goes all limp so that it takes three constables to carry her into the squad car. Martha doesn't work; her education is grade three, and she mumbles when she talks. Lizzie was already in jail and Martha had scarcely arrived when her older sister, Maria, age 20, was brought in, infested with lice. Her hair was matted and she was covered with open sores. She had been arrested for drinking in a public place and had already run away from a juvenile detention home in Winnipeg seven times. She has spent eight years in school but is barely articulate. Joan and Caroline, age 30 and 29, had just left jail before their mother and sisters arrived. Joan was pregnant. She had had three children; one had died and one had been taken by the welfare department. Caroline is illiterate and unable to speak English. Both had been in several times for intoxication. Another daughter, Florence, age 24, was jailed before Martha left. She had had liquor on the reserve. Her six-month old baby died while she was in jail.

In jail, the mudlarks shuffle around in blue and green smocks, aimlessly sweeping. Most are brought in emaciated and exhausted. They sleep round the clock, eat, wash and are cured of VD. Jail is home.

Making a Mudlark

"There were some lions in big cages. I think one was hungry. I did not stay to watch when he opened his mouth. I like elephants. They look big and kind. Do all elephants sleep standing up? "

Linda, who wrote this story, is twelve. There is nothing remarkable about it aside from the fact that Linda, an Indian from The Pas reserve, had written it at all. In 1967, when I met her, she was in an ungraded class in an integrated school in the town of The Pas. Linda is a phenomenon. Very few ungraded children write anything at all and few even speak. Opasquia School had, in 1967, been integrated for three years with about one-third of its pupils Indian or Metis.

Linda is classed as educably retarded. Her IQ is lower than 80. She ought to be in grade six, but she is working on grade three and four texts. She seems intelligent, is alert and attentive in class, and responds quickly to words and gestures, following them with bright brown eyes and a wide grin. She is small for twelve, but husky, with sallow skin and stringy long brown hair. Her elbow sticks out through a hole in her old yellow cardigan sweater and she wears shapeless dark brown ski-pants several sizes too big. There is a general indeterminate griminess about her, as if you were looking at her through a smudged, dusty piece of glass.

Linda's class is one of seven ungraded classes in the school. More than 75 per cent of these ungraded pupils are Indian or Metis, and half of the 300 Indian and Metis children in the school are classed as retarded. Most of the other Indian children who remain in regular classes are one, two and even three years behind their proper grade and need special coaching.

All the children in Opasquia School were tested by a team of psychologists in 1965. Over 60 per cent of the Indian children were judged to be incapable of functioning in a normal graded school system, while only five per cent of the white children were so classed. The psychologists apologized that they did not mean that the Indian children were intellectually inferior; they were, it was suggested, culturally deprived, or emotionally disturbed—handicapped simply by being Indian. To the people of The Pas, and to the Indian children themselves, it meant just one thing—dumb.

The Indian children in the school sit staring sullenly at nothing. Many who have been in school three and four years can hardly print and are unable to read. They show no interest in or comprehension of history, geography or science. Linda's teacher spends most of her time playing simple nursery games with her class to encourage them to talk. "They were scared," she said, "scared stiff." At twelve and thirteen, they are still at the kindergarten level. A 15-year-old boy pores over a grade one reader. All these children have failed at least once, some as many as five times. It was the custom on the reserve school to either pass children automatically whether they had learned the grade or not, or fail them repeatedly until they quit at 16 in grade three. Thus, when integration came, many Indian children entered Opasquia School in grade five unable to read. Of 40 Indian children who started grade one at Opasquia School in 1964, 70 per cent failed. Almost all Indian children drop out by grade seven.

Most Indian children have retreated into total, stolid, passive resistance; their apathy is so complete they seem to be asleep, like rows of dormice, although their eyes are open. They remember nothing from one day's lesson to the next and the teacher in the main repeats one day's work all year. Rigid with hate and boredom, they endure the days, playing truant as often as they can. Those who are not passive amuse themselves with activity—they chatter, jump in and out of their seats, sharpen their pencils and pay absolutely no attention to the teacher. They have retreated into a play world. A few appear to be trying. With wrinkled foreheads, they puzzle over their readers, following words with a finger, glancing up anxiously every few seconds. The teacher asks them to read but they say nothing.

In the English language and the English-speaking life style, these children are illiterate. They come to school speaking Cree, and know only a few English colloquialisms if any at all. The teacher speaks only English so they miss almost everything she says. School is a formal, strange place full of hidden rules and punishments. They are scolded or strapped if they speak Cree in school so they say nothing. They are scolded if they misuse or mispronounce English; they say nothing. School becomes an incomprehensible babble loaded with emotional overtones of anger.

The six-year-old has a book put in front of him. It is full of colored drawings and black marks in rows. The black marks, he is told, make words. He is expected to read in a language he doesn't know. He has, moreover, no comprehension of what reading means because he comes from a culture which never invented reading or writing. He sees no purpose to it.

The Indian child is coaxed, wheedled and embarrassed into trying to make sense out of these hieroglyphs. His other skills, verbal, perceptive, manipulative, are totally ignored. His own knowledge is scorned, while he is forced into single concentration on an incomprehensible task. A book is a code he must decipher.

At first, most Indian children make a tremendous effort to succeed. They memorize the sounds the teacher makes and they memorize the readers. If the text is repeated often enough, they can remember the different combinations of sounds the letters make on each page. Just by looking at the picture, they know what noises to parrot. Pre-school children can do this without being able to read a word. It is relatively easy to do in the early grades when the readers are simple. A conscientious child can memorize a whole year's course. Printing letters is just making a series of little drawings. By grade three or four, this solution becomes impossible. The quantity and complexity of sounds and patterns of letters to be memorized overwhelms the child. It is extremely difficult to memorize a language as well as the ideas it expresses, and it takes most Indian children two or three years to do it. The effort becomes too great. They give up, becoming silently hostile to the school which has beaten them, or they drop out.

Everything these children learn has the quality of fiction. Language, instead of being a tool to understand reality, becomes a barrier blocking off reality. The world of Janet and John which they memorize in readers is identical with the same Canada they memorize in history books. Neither has any existence outside the book. Canada is just a word. Any Indian child finds himself living in a fictionalized universe. He is out of touch, unrelated to it. He never gets beyond the words to the concepts which they contain. He accepts each book, each picture or map, as a thing in itself. A picture of India is India; when the teacher puts it away, India ceases to exist. A map has no north and south but up and down; cities are just dots. History is a story which has no relationship to real life. The entire school curriculum is make-believe, to be deciphered and memorized but not experienced.

Failure is, for the Indian children, inevitable, for it is built in to the integrated school. Failure and fear of failure produce the tension and frustration which lead to emotional disturbances teachers and psychologists are quick to notice. One-third of the Indian children tested by psychologists in The Pas were found to be emotionally upset. Then segregation soon re-establishes itself within the integrated school. The Indian children are filtered out into their special classes, and the teachers do little more than baby-sit for them. They learn nothing more than they did at the reserve school.

"We never had any problems with retarded kids before the Indians came in. Their parents are all alcoholics anyway."
"The parents don't care, don't give a damn. They're in town drinking all the time. They don't want their kids to get ahead."

The Indian children caused Opasquia School to break down. Teachers with years of experience could neither teach nor control the classes. Dozens of children played hookey, the failure rate became embarrassing, and the school was incapable of educating one-third of its pupils. Teachers and townspeople in The Pas preferred to see this failure as the fault of the Indians, not of the school. The Indian children were labelled culturally deprived, and their parents were blamed for failing to give them the ability to cope with Opasquia School. It is an easy accusation to make. Teachers were shocked by the appearance and behavior of the children. They had never taught children who smelled of kerosene and smoke, whose clothes were rags, whose hair was stiff with dirt, who scratched and fidgeted, who had impetigo and running ears. The children were undisciplined and uncomprehending. Sometimes they fell asleep in class, frequently had no lunch, and had no respect for school. It was summed up for me by Linda's teacher: "They come from such horrible homes," she said. She had never been in an Indian home.

Teachers were given a questionnaire about the reasons for the Indian children's failure. They listed six reasons: poor homes, language barrier, alcoholism, poor attendance, poor lunch, cleanliness. Each one of these causes carefully avoids involving the teacher, curriculum or school in the breakdown. "Language problems" refers to the Indian child's inability to speak English, not to the school's inability to communicate. The difficulties are now seen as welfare problems. The children will continue to fail until their parents are reconstructed, so health nurses, truant officers and welfare workers are unleashed upon the reserve. The Indian homes are thoroughly inspected and roundly criticized for their lack of crayons, food, storybooks, running water, electric lights, scissors and paste and beds. Until the Indians cure themselves of their poverty, they are informed, their children will learn nothing. Because the children's problems are seen to be so insurmountable, no further effort is made to teach them. In school, they continue to sit, staring sullenly into space.

Garbage Collecting

"They sell more wine in The Pas liquor store than anywhere else in Manitoba."

The Pas magistrate

The people in The Pas know about Indian poverty and drunkenness because they create it. The Indian industry is the town's biggest employer and liquor is the biggest source of revenue. The profit from selling liquor pays the cost of education for the town. Every dollar an Indian has is spent in The Pas. The town has only 3,000 people and another 1,500 Indians and Metis from the hinterland shop there. Traffic between town and reserve is dense; the Indians are not just wandering around, but are buying food, clothes, country western records, radios, hunting gear. Grocery stores and beer parlors are the most thriving businesses in The Pas. And, since much of the Indians' money comes from welfare, family allowance and unemployment insurance, the Indians support a growing bureaucracy which forms a large proportion of The Pas' population. Indians are the best customers the businesses and agencies have.

Indians and Metis drink most of the liquor consumed in The Pas, and the continuance of their drinking is important to the town's economy. The disorganization and debility caused by drinking is also important to the large corps of white police, health officials, probation officers, welfare workers, truant officers and Indian agents who fatten on large salaries by mopping up Indians. The town has 22 taxi cabs which exist exclusively to ferry Indians back and forth across the five miles which separate the reserve from the town. Fare for a one-way trip is about $2: if an Indian is drunk and has money, it can be $5 or $10.

The town has found it can sell an Indian food and clothing, then take it back. Bootlegging and the black market thrive in the Pas. The highest profit is made on the poorest Indians, the welfare clients. The welfare department issues relief in vouchers or chits to store owners, rather than cash or cheque, to prevent the Indians spending their money on liquor. When the Indian claims his $30 of groceries at the store, he tells the storekeeper he'd like $5 in cash instead of food. The storekeeper obliges and he pockets an additional $5 as payment for his labor. The Indian spends his $5 in the beer parlor, and it goes fast so he takes his $20 of groceries to a taxi stand near the Gateway Hotel. A taxi driver offers him $5 for the bag. The Indian accepts, keeping out a carton of cigarettes. He goes back to the beer parlor. The taxi driver sells the food for $15. Too drunk to walk home when the pub closes, the Indian hires a cab. When they reach the reserve, he finds he has no money left. The driver accepts the carton of cigarettes and maybe the new jacket his customer bought the day before. Back in The Pas, he sells the items.

He finds his customers among the other transients the pubs attract to The Pas—the miners. The Pas is always full of single men going or coming from the big mines further north. They buy the loot cheap. These men come to The Pas to drink, and when they're drinking, they like to have women around. This is how the mudlarks make their living. The town obliges by providing not only taxis but several cheap flophouses just around the corner from the Gateway.

Occasionally, when a public outcry is raised against this trafficking, suggestions are made to close the all-night hangout where the Indians congregate after the pubs close and where most of the trading takes place.

> *"If the Nip House were closed no one would be on the street.—It draws them like a magnet.—Make some regulations.—It's the greatest curse in this town. All the rangytangs hang out there."*

More police are hired to clean up the Indian problem. Strong editorials appear in the local paper condemning the moral depravity of the main street, but nothing is done. Such periodic bursts of outrage are a ritual in The Pas, but the Nip House remains. Bootleg wine is sold at $5 a bottle, whiskey at $25. Taxis continue to prowl, the women flock around the Gateway and inside, waiters continue to place, unasked, a full glass of beer in front of each customer before the first is half-empty.

"The Indians have to have a hangout," protests the mayor. "They're not hurting anybody. We should defer to them a bit."

"People need somewhere to stop for coffee," says another councillor.

"When I came on council I suggested we make the Nip House close at 1 a.m.," one councillor told me. "It turned out that of the four councillors, one did the books for the Nip House, one sold the Indians cars and one did the insurance for the Nip House. The Nip House stayed open."

During the day, the people of The Pas bemoan the poverty and debauchery of the Indians while selling them over-priced food and second-rate clothes. At night, they steal the little bit of money and dignity the Indians have left. The Pas lives by scavenging from the Indians. The Pas is a mudlark.

Although the people of The Pas generally feel that Indians are lazy, dirty, immoral, drunken, irresponsible and primitive, they show a strong desire to educate them. "We have done everything in our power to mix with them, treat them as human," said the mayor. The people here do not discriminate;

they want to uplift them."* However, the decision to integrate the schools was not humanitarian. Indian Affairs offered the school board an attractive financial deal, in which the Indian children were bought at a fixed price per head.

Linda will drop out of school when she is 16, perhaps before. She might by then, have made it to grade five or six. Her classmates will quit with her. If she gets hungry enough, she'll be found around the Gateway. It's the only job for an Indian girl in The Pas. Some night she'll be picked up, angry and drunk, by a probation officer or by the police.

Observations of the Town

Indians were restricted to the left hand side of the movie theatre in The Pas. One day, an Indian arrived from the North, a stranger, and sat on the right. "Indians are supposed to sit on the other side," said the usher. "Go to hell, I'll sit where I please," said the Indian. All the Indians now sit where they please.

One night in June, Mrs. John Lesko, who lives near the outskirts of town, was awakened several times by cursing and shouting near her home. She told police she did not get up to look because this kind of ruckus is a common occurrence in that area. She thought it was a bunch of Indians, male and female. "They were shouting and using filthy language."

Next morning, the body of an Indian man, badly beaten, was found floating in the river. He had been drinking heavily. The Indian accused of killing him said: "Stripped him naked. Took wallet. Dragged him through the trees, broken glass, into the river. Waded into the river, pushing the body. Held head under water for five minutes. Went back to Nip House . . . "

---

*John Dallyn and Frazer Earle, "A Study of Attitudes Towards Indians and People of Indian Descent, The Pas Manitoba," Canadian Council of Christians and Jews, 1965. The study found that almost 75 per cent of the town's residents showed some prejudice against Indians and 10 per cent showed extreme prejudice. Nearly half the people agreed that "The homes of people of Indian descent offer nothing good to a child or elderly person," and "Most people of Indian descent show complete disregard for the common standards of personal decency." A majority of people also stated that Indians are shiftless, undependable, and illegitimate.

"The Nip House is valuable to the police. The accused return there after a crime. The plan is hatched there. People tell us. It makes it easier for the police."

R.C.M.P. corporal

"People think I'm too tough on Indians. There's a law for the rich and one for the poor on liquor cases; if a guy can't pay his fine, he's got to go to jail."

Magistrate Neil McPhee

Magistrate McPhee has initiated an interesting system to add variety to the daily liquor docket. Starting January 1, he gives everyone the minimum sentence—seven days. The next time they appear, it is 15 days. For each arrest, the sentence is doubled up to 60 days. At the end of the year, he wipes the slate clean and begins again. Sentences are uniform, regardless of the individual or his offense.

The men's jail is on the top floor of the ancient brick court building. The men are crammed in like mice in a nest, lying on bunks reading comics for the duration of their sentence. It's a club like the jail for women. Most are in from five to 10 times a year.

Criminal charges are laid primarily against Indian children, mostly for break and enter and petty theft.

"Indian kids don't seem to be taught why you don't do things. They don't know the difference between right and wrong. They're not psychopaths. They come from broken homes; often their parents are in jail. The reserve is a kind of no-man's land."

Probation Officer

"We got to get tough with the Indians. Sterilize them. Don't give them any money, just food. They're children. It's all the fault of welfare—too many do-gooders in this town. The problem is getting worse; it's up to the government."

The Pas businessman

"We have done everything in our power to mix with

them, to treat them as human. The people here do not discriminate. They want to uplift them. The Indians are shy of civilization. The federal government should take the initiative. Move them into town in housing developments.

"We don't go over there because we're so busy. They have their own business.

"They've advanced quite a bit, it used to be they wouldn't talk to you. They have responsible jobs; they seem to be capable of driving trucks.

"Indians can stand a lot of cold. It's their big salvation."

Mayor of The Pas.

The Indian agent was barricaded behind his desk by stacks and stacks of papers. Rows of other desks, each occupied by a busily writing clerk and more stacks of papers, protected him on either side. His back was to the wall, and he peered out from chinks between the piles of documents, nervously shuffling some papers, while clerks scurried in all directions. The agent passed his hand over his grey brushcut and stared at me, his eyes wild and round. "You can create chaos out of disorder," he said.

"The Pas smells different at night, when the Indians come in. We used to watch them. The men would stand close to the road, the women back by the buildings. We could distinguish six different stages of pregnancy, all in a row. They just stood there, looking. We didn't know what they were looking at. They just looked."

tourist

Looking at the White Man

"Indians are willing to help the white people. We find out they are humans. We have our own little world and they have theirs. The Indians see the town but the townspeople do not see the Indians."

Joe Ross, The Pas reserve

Most of the Indian population of The Pas is invisible. The Indians who irritate the townspeople represent only a few families, fewer than 100 individuals, and only about one-eighth of the reserve population. The rest of the Indians stay home. They are respectable, hard working, apathetic, self-centered and politically indifferent. Compared to other Indian communities in western Canada, The Pas reserve is organized and has few problems, with 65 per cent of the men employed and welfare the lowest of any reserve in Manitoba. The reserve, like the town, is governed by a small clique of elite families. These people are well-educated, articulate, energetic and politically active. They all bear the names of famous Hudson's Bay Company traders and represent, for the most part, the old church families which entered enthusiastically into the affairs of the Anglican Church during its heyday on the reserve 50 to 75 years ago. The church taught them English and gave them status. These people continue to live close together around the big white frame church on the bluff overlooking the river and the town. The townspeople do not see these Indians and do not know them. Infrequent contact between the people who run the town and those who run the reserve is formal and coldly businesslike. Normal political and social relationships have been short-circuited through Indian Affairs, since the townspeople deal with the Indian agent, not the Indians.

"They call our kids retarded—they are no more retarded than you or I. The teachers complain that the kids aren't interested, don't want to learn; they complain to the Indian Affairs office, not to me. Whose kids are they anyway? The principal should send notes home to the parents, not to the office. I asked Mr. Verigen, the Indian Affairs school supervisor, to come out to the reserve and tell us what is going on. Parents don't take an interest because no one tells them what's happening.

"My son was having trouble. He was failing. He is slow. Then he started to stay home, pretending he was sick. I went to see Mr. Verigen. I told him I wanted to talk to my boy's teacher 'You have no right to go in the school,' he told me. He pounded his fist on the desk. 'My son is not the only dropout you're going to have,' I told him. 'You'd better figure it out.'

"I can fight with him, but it's wrong to have to get angry with someone to get somewhere. The people have to fight for what they want."

Mrs. McGillivray

There is no Indian on the school board in The Pas. There are two superintendents, one for the town and one for Indians. The teachers' information about the "horrible homes" comes from the people who "know" Indians, the Indian Affairs people, missionaries, welfare workers. Indian agents deplore the extreme poverty of the Indians, poverty which the Indian agents themselves help to create. With an instinct for self-preservation, social workers perpetuate the dependency and despair they are hired to cure. The mayor of The Pas, in a self-fulfilling prophecy, predicted the failure of school integration before it began. He told council he had discussed the matter with teachers, missionaries, church officials and others who had spent 25 to 50 years with Indians. It was their opinion, he said, that the Indians were not ready. When integration did begin, the mayor and his advisors were forced to make integration fail in order to preserve their reputations.

"The Indian agent gets tough, threatens me, hollering at me. He trys to scare people. He can do all the screaming and shouting he wants—so can I. But he frightens a lot of people. He makes it hard for people to ask simple questions. You have to understand him; it's just the way he talks; you'd think he was angry. People are afraid to talk to him. If we had been given independence 20 years ago, things would be different today."

Mrs. McGillivray

What Do You Think of the White Man?

"There is not much difference in white and Indian. Although white men are bound to be more liars than an Indian."

Mrs. M. H.

"I do not think that the white man is the same as he was

long ago—he is very modern now. But I hope he will not look on us as in the USA, like Alabama. He is very good to us in helping the Indian with funds like the Family Allowance, for which the Indian is very grateful."

Mrs. S. M.

"This is very hard to answer as the average white man is an equal as an Indian—both sides have the same qualities."

Antoine

"The White Man thinks he is usually better than the Indian. He looks down on them. Since the Indian knows that the White Man has more education, he lets him or her go ahead with supervising. Even if the Indian has practical knowledge he is afraid—as the White Man in general thinks he is superior. And another thing is, he cannot take being criticized as well as an Indian."

Mrs. C. J.

"Indians have their own characters. They cannot make judgements on persons but only use their common sense. The white man is a copy person."

Albert

"Some white men are bad—conceited liars. Like the Indian, their personalities are equal. But an Indian will most always apologize if he makes a promise and can't keep it."

J. H.

"I think the White Man should look around more, and see what the Indian can do, not only look at them in town where everybody meets. As the White Man refers to the Indian, when he saw one or two drunks he classed all of them. But when the Indians sees the White Man drinking, he says that White Man is drinking, he does not mean the whole population in town. Because of the White Man's education, he thinks he has more authority over those who are less educated and this puts the Indian well below. Maybe the white thinks that the Indian cannot do such work. I have to show him most of the work or he might not understand me, I

*might as well do it myself,' he thinks. But if the Indian has
the material, or could afford such material, power and
equipment, he would surpise the Whites. The Indian could be
very good, or better than the White Man. And when the
White Man works with the Indian, the Indian says 'He
couldn't keep up with us, and sets us back. He is too slow
and not capable to do He-man work.' "*

Gordon

Listening to the Indian

The Pas reserve was run for 20 years by one man, Chief
Cornelius Bignell. Mr. Bignell was defeated a few years ago. "He
did too much without telling the council," one woman said.
Government on the reserve consisted of little chats between Mr.
Bignell and the agent, with Mr. Bignell usually saying "yes".
The best roads were built near Mr. Bignell's new government
house; he was the first to have electricity. His family had
miraculous success acquiring machinery, homes, furniture and
frequent trips to Ottawa. A tall, dignified, white-haired old
gentleman, he lives with his wife in a new bungalow near the
church. Now, no longer chief, he is still on the National Indian
Advisory Council and flies to Ottawa regularly. He has a big
brown cowhide briefcase full of documents.

Mr. Bignell recently received a letter from the Manitoba
government, congratulating him on his appointment to an
honorary centennial commission and inviting him to attend a
meeting of the cabinet in Winnipeg. Mr. Bignell was confused.

*"I don't know what this is about. I'll have to see
the Indian agent about it this afternoon. Nobody asked me. I
never accepted nothing. I don't know anything about it. I am
not qualified. I am no good at reading and writing; I only
have grade three."*

Mr. Bignell had other problems. As a member of the Indian
Advisory Board, he had received a letter instructing him to
contact every Indian band in Manitoba and get their opinions
about proposed changes in the Indian Act. He was given no
money to do this. He tells about his years as chief:

"They put in the town planning scheme on the reserve without telling me anything about it. I looked out one day and saw them cutting the survey lines. Indian Affairs drew up the plans. 'We're not going along with it,' I said. 'You should have told us.' They built the houses anyway. Didn't put any basements in because they might move the homes.

"We don't feel so good when Ottawa rejects our resolutions. It's happened quite a few times. We get discouraged. How is it that everything we ask for is always refused? It is our own money we're spending; we need it for the benefit of the band. We finally got a tractor after many years so we could make a road for ourselves. They never gave us any reason whatsoever for refusing us.

"If you have your own land, there's nobody going to take it away. A reserve is my home. Reserves should not be abolished. We have an advantage; we can make a living out of this place. We have a home to fall back to. We want to live like the rest of the people but we want to hold our land. We try to hang on to what little we have."

Little Cornelius Bignell, whose father was the bellringer at the Anglican Church, was sent out to school in 1907. A group of boys went up the Saskatchewan River by boat to North Battleford.

"I was scared. I thought they were battling all the time. All the kids on the boat started to cry when we left. I started to cry too. I went to school there three years. Then I came home for holidays. I'm still on my holidays. I find it difficult to talk in public. If I had a little education, I might be prime minister."

"The old people are difficult. They sit there at meetings for hours and hours and say the same thing. 'In the olden days it was better,' they say. Indians are beginning to realize they can do things. The government took the country and that's it. Accept it. People are always talking about the country being taken away, about their rights. 'You took our country away; how much are you going to give us for it?' They can't see anything else. They don't put it out of their minds."

Joe Ross, band council member, The Pas

"The kids say they are happy in school. They still stay in their little groups. There's no bad feeling with the other kids. The Indians don't have full confidence yet. They mispronounce words; they're aware of that. It embarrasses them to death. The teacher embarrasses them; that's why they don't go to school."

Crow

"I went to coffee after church, in the basement. Everyone was talking. I sat on the other side. Nobody came and talked to me. I sat there a long time and then I forced myself to go and talk to someone I knew. It is a hard thing to do. Our confidence was killed a long time ago. In cubs, at school, in sports, the Indian feels humble. He is always pushed back and pushed back."

Joe Ross

"We've lost Canada. The people feel robbed; they depend on the government for everything. They're satisfied with their lot—a roof over their heads, a few sticks of wood outside—that's all they need. People refuse to accept changes; they won't lease out reserve land, won't sell the gravel. 'You robbed us so we won't have anything to do with you' they say to the townspeople."

Philip Bignell

(The town of The Pas is built on former reserve land which was purchased from the Indians at $5 an acre.)

"Like me, I drank to exist. I felt in a trap. You're helpless; you don't know how to get out. I was kind of lost for a long time. Then I grew up, I just grew up."

Philip Bignell

"Why don't they translate the Indian Act into simple language so we can understand it?"

Unidentified woman

"I remember when I was too shy to stand up and read in class. I had to be punished."

Mrs. Wilson

"I am angry. When I applied to Indian Affairs for a job, they said 'Here's an axe; go cut some trees.' I had a grade eleven education. At the employment office, the Indians get the shovels."

Crow

"Indian Affairs should have left us alone. We had everything, all the resources. Maybe they were learning too; maybe they didn't know what they were doing. They should have educated us how to run things for ourselves. When I first went to council meetings, I didn't like it. The leaders were very childish. I told them they acted like children. The agent told them how things should be."

band council member

"My dream is to lease land in The Pas and build a big housing development. We used to be able to live off the land."

Philip Bignell

"Many Indians walk in the town's streets today who really look stupid enough and who look as if they never had any formal education. They are also unemployed. These people of the lower second class—if given an open opportunity—could just as well work behind polished desks in swivels. For good outward appearance they could be made to visit the barbershop, cut their hair, be washed and cleaned, attired in white shirts, business suits, fine shows. No doubt some could pass. The Indians are a quiet people if let alone. They mind their own business. They are modest and would rather avoid sensation and publicity. . . The white man could be more friendly with the Indian. Let it be said that the Indian never forgets a good word or kindness, but he does not forget easily what he thought to be wrong."

A. J. B.

The reserve is now run by young, active men. They have formed committees—recreation, health and welfare, sanitation, and a handicraft guild. They are full of ideas about education, economic development and real estate. They have picketed the

Indian health clinic in The Pas, a kind of segregated out-patient department, and succeeded in having some of the more objectionable staff members transferred. The younger leaders are also from the church families and have little contact with other people on the reserve. "I met a lot of people since being on the council." said one, "It's really been interesting, talking to people."

"We need to analyze all the things that have led up to the present situation," says Philip Bignell, the old chief's son. "Nobody is around to explain. The government says it wants to help us but it doesn't go all the way in the things it does. We suffer from a brain drain. All the people with a good education leave, get jobs outside. If someone could only explain what has happened to the Indian, what has made him the way he is, how it grew up. There is no situation that can't be solved. If you have money, you can make money. We know that. We need the spark. Nobody from the town ever comes to visit here. It will come to the point, however, where the town will *have* to meet with us. I don't know if the town council will see it this way."

One of the band's biggest achievements was to persuade the Indian agent to sit at the back of the hall during band council meetings.

"The white people think I'm against the white man. That's not so. The white man's just the hardest to get to see the point."

Crow

Chapter 9
Suicide

The Short Happy Life of Lorna Marcellais

"I never saw him until he ran into my lights. He came from the right hand side of the road and was running. I tried to miss him and I tried to put on the brakes but I hit him. My brakes aren't too good and you have to pump them four or five times before they stop."

"We were driving along the road when all of a sudden we heard a noise like a shot. I thought a tire blew."

"I parked my car about twenty feet from what appeared to be a body. I got out and walked over to see what it was. It turned out to be a human. All I could tell was that it was female."

"A flap of scalp was lifted at the back of the neck and the upper neck spine bones were isolated. In this region, there was much haemorrhage and there was a complete dislocation of the atlanto-occipital joint. That is, the first joint between the skull and upper neck spine bones. The fracture-dislocation of this joint was so severe that the upper cord had been completely divided. The cause of death therefore was a broken neck with complete division of the upper spinal cord."

Lorna Marcellais. Age 19. Of Indian extraction. Born May 12, 1946. Died October 30, 1965. Lived at Wanless, Man. Single. Cause of death: accidental.

Wilfred Christianson, a taxi driver for Reo Cab in The Pas was driving out the highway north of The Pas towards the Big

Eddy Indian settlement to pick up a passenger about ten minutes past seven in the evening, October 30, when he came across "what appeared to be a body" on the side of the road. When the police arrived, they found the body of a female on the extreme west side of the pavement, about two miles north of The Pas on Highway 10. On the east side was a 1958 Pontiac, licence 27M97, facing north, with extensive damage to the driver's side of the car. Six people, three men and three women, were standing beside the parked car.

> *"It was dark out. I was looking in the back seat of the car when it happened and I didn't see anything but I heard a loud crash and glass was flying all over. I couldn't recognize who it was."*

The driver was identified as Charlie Constant. The passengers were Blanche Constant, Leslie Cook, Helen Cook, Simon Ballantyne and Mary Jane Ballantyne. Constant had been drinking and admitted they had just come from the beer parlor. He and his wife had spent the afternoon in The Pas, getting groceries, getting the record player fixed, just driving around.

> *We went over to the Gateway Hotel about 5 p.m. We went into the beer parlor and met Leslie Cook, Helen Cook and the two Ballantynes. We sat and drank. I had about four jumbo glasses of beer. We all left about twenty minutes to seven. We drove to the liquor store and Mary Jane Ballentyne went in and bought two 12-bottle cases of beer. Then we started driving for home on The Pas Indian reserve. We drove down by the Friendship Centre and out over the bridge. I was travelling about 50 to 55 miles per hour. We were going down the long stretch at mile 2 when all of a sudden I saw somebody run out between the two cars. (There was a car ahead. I could only see his tail lights; I followed this car at a distance of about 500 feet.)*
>
> *"After I hit him I sort of lost control of the car and I went on up the road. I don't know how far. When I got it stopped, I backed it up to the body. Then I stopped the car and got out and went over to the body. I never touched it*

and neither did the others with me. We were all scared. One of us stopped a car and told them to go get the Mounties. I don't know who stopped the car. I didn't know or recognize the body. I don't know Lorna Marcellais."

Charlie Constant

"I was standing on the far side of the car and I was crying," was all Blanche Constant had to say. "We were busy talking in the back seat and never saw anything. All we heard was the noise. I told Charlie it sounded like he hit somebody. I didn't recognize it but I could see that it had been female."

Ross McLeod, who was driving a taxi full of passengers from Big Eddy reserve south to The Pas a few minutes after 7 p.m. was the last man to see Lorna Marcellais alive and the only one to recognize her.

Only a few moments before McLeod's taxi had passed her, another cab had passed, going in the same direction — towards The Pas. It was driven by John Lesko.

"As I rounded the corner a car was approaching from the south. I could not see too far ahead as the vision was bad. I had my headlights on dim until the car had passed. I saw a person about 100 to 150 feet ahead. I applied the brakes and I applied them fairly hard as I scared the other people in the car. I realized I might not be able to stop before I hit the person so I let off the brakes and went around the person. I had five other people in the car, and I felt the brakes wouldn't hold. This person was walking south towards town on the west side of the road four to five feet from the white line and staggering. I knew I was coming up to a drunk person and I felt it would be safe to dodge around him. I had to go over to the extreme left hand side of the road to miss him, but I missed him all right. I didn't recognize the person."

John Lesko

There were no skid marks leading from Constant's car back to the body. The car had gone 700 feet past, judging by a trail of water from the radiator. The brake pedal went right to the floor.

"Bilateral compound fractures of both lower legs . . . of the left wrist . . . the whole upper jaw . . . front upper teeth

were missing . . . the lower jaw was broken. The head was completely loose on the neck."

"I saw a girl about thirty-five feet in front of me at the west side of the road walking towards The Pas. This girl was most difficult to see due to the dark colored clothing she was wearing blending in with the surrounding colors of the road and due to the darkness of the evening. As I passed her I recognized her as Lorna Marcellais and I felt I'd been lucky not to hit her. She had been walking on the extreme west side of the pavement and as I passed her I noticed she moved farther over to the gravel shoulder of the road. When I saw her she seemed to be walking in a normal manner."

Ross McLeod

In 1963, when Lorna was sixteen years old, she was sent to the House of the Good Shepherd in Winnipeg as a result of her many appearnaces in Juvenile Court in The Pas on liquor charges. The social worker assigned to help her made the following appraisal:

"Lorna is temperamental and sneaky. She uses sickness as an excuse for not going to school or to employment. She is not a behaviour problem but could be if she is frustrated too much. Low frustration tolerance. She is a lone wolf. She distrusts adults. She is a very stubborn girl and latterly has been refusing to move and it requires almost force to move her from one room to another."

She was finally dismissed from the home as a case of "poor adjustment" and was arrested again on another liquor charge shortly after. The juvenile court psychiatrist made this assessment of her:

"Lorna seems to be the product of a very deprived and neglected upbringing, typical of her race and culture, and has failed to develop standards, direction or controls. She seems of passive temperament but her moral attitudes and lack of control do not give her much of a defence against delinquent influences. She would be submissive and easily led. I feel the

girl has made as much of an effort as she is capable of but the adjustment to our culture is beyond her capabilities. She has not benefitted from her committal."

"There is little anyone can do now," wrote her probation officer, when Lorna was seventeen.

Lorna was a very attractive girl, dark, slim and neat in her appearance. She was Metis and illegitimate. She had a grade five education and had never worked since quitting school. Her father had deserted his common-law wife and eight children and, since Lorna was twelve, her mother had spent most of her time in jail for liquor offences. The only family home was that of her older married sister. Jail was home for most of Lorna's brothers and sisters. For the most part, Lorna lived off the streets in The Pas. She was one of the "Edwards Avenue girls"—Indian and Metis girls who, for a couple of glasses of beer, a bottle of wine, a sweater, would go with any man as long as he wanted them. Usually, all the men wanted was an hour or two on the creaky springs of a bed in one of the flop houses off Edwards Ave., and the girls would be out on the streets again, drunk, tired, hungry, looking for another man. There wasn't anything special about Lorna. She was, in every way, typical.

In 1964, a year before the accident, when Lorna was eighteen, she and a couple of friends drank two bottles of wine in a back alley in The Pas. One of them suggested starting a fire to cause some excitement. The giggling girls set fire to some papers in an outhouse near a house. They started walking nonchalantly toward the Nip House, the local hangout. Looking back, they saw only smoke. They returned and started another fire in a wood box, then went to the Nip House. The fire was noticed and put out before it did any damage. "We did not expect the house to burn down," the girls told police when they were arrested. They had nothing against the occupant. Lorna was charged with arson and sentenced to three months in jail. Her mother and two of her brothers were in jail at the time and a younger brother had been placed in a foster home. "Lorna has never had a very stable home due to the fact that all family members have a problem with alcohol," said the probation officer. Her mother was "a very unstable person with a severe alcohol problem." Lorna herself was not "capable of very rational behavior under the influence of alcohol."

Lorna was out of jail only a little over three months before she was picked up in The Pas for disturbing the peace while intoxicated on March 6, 1965. She was sentenced to $100 fine or two months in jail. She was released April 22 after partial payment of her fine. She was in jail again on May 3 on an intoxication charge. She got out again May 26. August 14, 1965 Lorna was offered $60 fine or 22 days for being intoxicated. She was released September 1st and picked up again the following day, charged with consuming liquor under age and sentenced to two months in jail.

Lorna got out of jail on October 22, 1965, and was killed October 30. Her mother, who was in jail at the time of her death (having been in and out repeatedly since Lorna first arrived in 1946) went into a frenzy when she was told that Lorna was dead. She cried and wailed for hours. The matron of the jail took her to the funeral.

Lorna was typical. She lived on what she could scavenge in the way of warmth, nourishment and pleasure from the stream of free-spending sexually-hungry men that flows south through The Pas from the northern mining camps. The kind of "alcoholism en famille" of which Lorna was a part was extreme, but not unique or even remarkable in The Pas. Yet Lorna was exceptional. She had special qualities of passive resistance to be able to cause so much frustration to social workers and law enforcement officers, to make a probation officer give up the possibility of helping a seventeen-year-old girl. She was aggressively irresponsible, and seemed to know exactly what things would annoy people most—little things like playing sick and setting fire to a wood box. Lorna waged a kind of one-man underground resistance against the powerful people in The Pas. She never committed big crimes, just petty, irritating ones. Her incorrigibility was positive and ultimate.

Lorna's defiance was the strongest thing about her. She would deliberately disobey and irritate people, knowing that by angering them, she was harming her own chances of ever escaping from them. But the pleasure she experienced from defying them was worth the sacrifice of her own life. She conducted her civil disobedience on a small scale, but the picture of the good Sisters dragging her bodily from room to room is worthy of any civil rights demonstration. Lorna conducted a sit-in in the Home of the Good Shepherd. It worked; she was dismissed.

The people against whom she was waging her war did not realize what she was doing. That she was called "sneaky" was the closest anyone came to perceiving her guerilla tactics. Lorna, as far as the psychiatrist was concerned, was not "capable" of adjustment, but in fact she was not willing to adjust.

"Run Over By Three Vehicles"
"Fifty-nine year old Henry Nepinak of The Pas Reserve died instantly Friday night December 23rd on the No. 10 Highway near the Fairway Service.

Nepinak was run over by a bus and two other vehicles. His body was found in a decapitated condition. Coroner Neil Macphee has ordered an inquest."

The Pas Herald, Jan. 4, 1967

Henry Nepinak, wearing dark green coveralls and carrying a cardboard box in his left hand, was walking south towards The Pas on the west side of the road (the same side as Lorna had used) about four miles north of town when a Manitoba Transit bus smashed into him at 7:20 p.m. Two cars ran over him immediately after. The first went over him with a "bump" but the second, a taxi, skidded and pushed his body on to the shoulder of the road. His body was found 84 feet from the first sign of blood. The first blood was found five feet from the west shoulder and a stream ran from there to another pool 18 feet south. The entire upper half of Nepinak's body was crushed. His head was squashed, neck torn, both jugular veins and arteries torn, heart and lungs mashed, thorax squashed, ribs broken.

"The container in which he had been placed when brought from the scene of the accident smelled very strongly of alcohol and I should imagine he had imbibed a considerable amount prior to the accident," said the doctor.

There was a light fog that night and the road was covered with a thin layer of ice.

> *"As the west shoulder of the highway is a common foot path for numberous people travelling back and forth from The Pas to The Pas Indian Reserve, it was impossible to trace Nepinak's path in the snow."*

A bus and a car had gone past him earlier, the bus crossing over to the middle of the road to miss him. Nepinak "smelled strongly of liquor", said the accident report.

> *"Nepinak is well known for his drinking habits being quite commonly seen in the local police court for infractions of the Liquor Control Act. He is very hard of hearing and blind in one eye, being the victim of an accident in the same general area one and a half years ago. Nepinak is known to consume quantities of extract going into a complete drunken stupor."*

Nepinak had been seen in The Pas an hour before the accident and had bought a bottle. He did not appear drunk at the time.

> *"Once again, however, referring back to Nepinak's drinking habits it has been understood that he can hold large quantities of liquor very well without showing the effects until finally a saturation point is reached. With Nepinak being placed in The Pas one hour prior to the accident it would seem to contradict all statements stating he was walking south along PH No. 10 towards The Pas, however, it is strongly felt that he had been drinking during the course of the day and upon his way home to his residence in the area became confused when the full extent of the alcohol affected him and became, to a certain extent, completely immobile."*

No one will ever know whether Henry Nepinak was drunk or not the night he was killed but it seemed necessary to the police that he be drunk.

The same unsubstantiated over-emphasis on drunkenness can be seen in Lorna's case. The last man to see Lorna alive, taxi driver Ross McLeod, said that she was walking "in a normal manner" on the west side of the road, headed toward The Pas. As he passed, she moved over to the west shoulder, off the road. McLeod knew Lorna. He recognized her. He did not think she was drunk. Only minutes before, when John Lesko had driven his taxi past in the same direction, Lorna was in the middle of the road, four or five feet right of the white line and "staggering." All Lesko saw was a "drunk person." He thought it was male. To one man, Lorna was drunk; to another she was sober. Was John Lesko looking at an image in his own mind, or was Lorna really drunk when he saw her?

She was walking south along the footpath on the west side of the road, heading towards The Pas.

Charlie Constant's car was driving north, away from The Pas, on the east side of the road.

"I never saw him until he ran into my lights."

The driver's side of the car was damaged. A human tooth was found under the left front ornament.

Lorna Marcellais ran across the highway straight into the path of Constant's car. Constant had his headlights on. She must have seen the car coming. It was a "long straight stretch of road." The normal footpath was on the west, where Lorna had been walking. Why did she cross over suddenly? Why was she running? Why did she cross at that moment?

Lorna Marcellais committed suicide.

"Accidents"

"We know that suicide can be accomplished indirectly, that is, without the active, conscious participation of the individual. We know of people who seem to have accidental deaths which, we are convinced from our knowledge of the case, are unconsciously determined. I do not refer to actual suicides which the persons, out of pride, consideration for family, or greed try to make look accidental, but those cases in which the person would not purposely and consciously bring about his death and yet gives considerable evidence that he has unconsciously wished for it. I know of a man who had

had several disappointments and was quite depressed and in fact had tried several times to commit suicide, but was unsuccessful. A little later, however, he accidentally stepped in front of an automobile and was killed. There is no proof that this accident was unconsciously self-determined, but it is plain the man's own carelessness brought about the accident and to that extent he brought about his own death."

Karl Menninger
A Psychiatrist's World
New York, Viking, 1920, pp. 347-348

Indians have a penchant for dying under railway trains. Ted Burton, the Crown Prosecutor for the Kenora Ontario district, was quoted in a newspaper article in April, 1966 as saying that the deaths of numerous Indians under CNR trains seemed to be evidence of a growing suicide cult and a final protest against hopeless living conditions. Between 1961 and 1966, 15 Indians were killed by trains in that area. Four of these deaths occurred during the preceding ten months. Many more Indians had been maimed by trains. "Countless others have been pulled from the tracks," Mr. Burton was quoted as saying. All the accidents took place on one 70-mile stretch of track between Minaki and Quibell, Ontario. They did not happen on the CPR line farther south. Burton had written a letter to the provincial coroner about it two years earlier:

"I have it on my mind that there is a religious aspect to this type of death. These deaths are not suicide as we know it and do not fit any category to which the white man can attach a label. Neither Indians nor whites elsewhere seem to die in precisely this manner."

Burton's suggestion about a religious cult came, apparently, from a report by a train engineer that an Indian was on the tracks "on his knees" before being run over.

The suicide suggestion was vigorously denied in favor of other explanations: the Indians have to walk on the tracks because there are no roads; they are drunk on cheap wine and homebrew and unable to see or hear the trains coming. Similar explanations are, of course, also used in The Pas to explain the highway accidents. These reasons are plausible, but still it seems difficult to account for the sheer volume of accidents.

Pete Seymour, Kenora Indian leader, was quoted as stating that the suicide cult was "not true", but he went on to get close to the unconscious motivation: "Often the Indians are drunk when they are walking home along the tracks. They drink because of repressed feelings—a lot of things are working against the Indians—but these deaths are just accidents." Seymour said that where the Indians travel by boat and canoe, drownings are proportionately high. The local Indian agent was also quoted on the subject: "It has nothing to do with religion. There is nothing in their pagan beliefs which leads to suicide rites."

The local coroner told the newspapers that blood samples from 13 of the dead Indians had a high alcoholic content. One Indian had no blood left to analyze and the fifteenth was an old man over 80 years of age and almost blind.

> *"One of these forms of chronic self-destruction is alcoholism. Even the layman knows that people drink themselves to death. What he does not know is that the original difficulty in such cases is not the alcoholism but the underlying personality defect which creates the inner tensions and leads the individual to seek relief ... Physicians are familiar with patients who take relief-giving drugs such as barbital, as a means of suicide; so it is with the person who finds temporary relief in alcohol but eventually destroys himself by its excessive use."*
>
> Menninger, p. 349

A person can drink himself to death, and he can also use alcohol as a means of assisting himself to a more direct, quicker form of suicide. There is only a slight difference between a person who throws himself under a train and one who becomes so paralyzingly drunk in the middle of a railway track that he will be killed if a train comes along. Menninger calls this second type "indirect suicide." The individual does not take his life by a deliberate, aggressive act but by leaving himself vulnerable and reducing to almost zero his chances of survival. Indirect suicide shows a passive personality, he says. Individuals who lie down before or expose themselves to irrevocable force—trains, trucks, steam rollers—show an extreme form of passive, masochistic submission which has strong erotic overtones. It is also, as the crown prosecutor suggested, a form of social protest:

> " . . . *the act of suicide is an aggresssion against those who in some way may be related to the life of the person who kills himself. It may be taken as a reproach against certain individuals or against society as a whole and actually does serve in many instances as an embarrassment or humiliation.*"

Menninger, p. 334

Trains form a particularly effective tool for the potential suicide because, especially along this stretch of the CNR mainline, they are travelling very rapidly and are, unlike motor vehicles, unable to swerve to avoid the man. Death is fast.

Maiming—the compulsion to remove part of the body—is, according to Menninger, a form of partial indirect suicide. By losing an arm, a leg or a finger, an individual is able to feel that the guilt which has been oppressing him is expiated. Sometimes, maiming is not sufficient. Henry Nepinak lost his eye and his life in the same spot, a year apart.

Indirect suicide is, of course, impossible to prove. Scientists and psychologists are, therefore, hesitant to investigate the phenomenon. This disguised quality of indirect suicide is one reason why the individual unconsciously selects it. He needs to hide his intentions from himself and from the world. He camouflages his real purpose underneath an "accident."

Suicide is disguised murder.

The factor of embarrassment or humiliation for others—the hidden aggression of the indirect suicide of an Indian—is shown clearly in The Pas and in the railway deaths. Many white people driving cars that "accidentally" hit and kill Indians are not only afflicted with feelings of guilt and remorse for the rest of their lives, but are forced to go through the anguish and inconvenience of a police investigation, inquest and trial. When the unhappy driver is a civil servant or is driving a company vehicle, his problems are multiplied because the government or the corporation is also involved in the death. The driver is in danger of losing his job. Railway engineers are in a similar position because the incident involves unpleasantness for the company and for the passengers. The messy death of one Indian has many repercussions in the white world. Is it this world the Indian is trying to attack? By dying, an Indian achieves the power to haunt the imaginations of numerous people who, otherwise, would never know he existed.

This form of revenge is accepted by the white people in The Pas without complaint, almost as unconscious self-punishment. Lorna Marcellais was not the first Indian to die on Highway 10. There have been many after her and there will be many more. No month goes by in The Pas but at least one Indian is killed on that stretch of highway. The deaths are so commonplace they go virtually unnoticed. There is no public outcry. Many drivers have, like Charlie Constant, been drinking; they are driving unsafe cars sold to them by merchants in The Pas. Yet the police do not enforce the laws. Even those men unlucky enough to kill an Indian are not prosecuted for murder or manslaughter; they are given suspended sentences if they come to trial at all. Vehicle traffic is extremely heavy along the five mile stretch of highway between The Pas and the reserve and it reaches its peak at night. A steady stream of people makes a continual pilgrimage along the footpath at the side of the highway. But the speed limit is 60 mph, there are no lights and the road is seldom patrolled. The drunk drivers and the drunks on foot play a macabre nightly game of "chicken".

This form of hostile suicide by Indians is probably far more prevalent than is commonly believed. The deaths take place in very remote, out-of-the-way locations and it is a form of death of which the public takes little notice. If an intensive study were made, I imagine more highly "accident-prone" stretches of highway or railway tracks would be discovered near Indian communities.

"It was a great year for accidents and violence in 1965 and these deaths just escaped being number one in rank. Two infants smothered in bed which is bad enough but a great improvement over 1964 when 10 died in this manner. One other infant was asphyxiated by aspiration of vomitus and

another was killed in a car accident. Six youngsters in the 1 to 4 group had accidental deaths—1 in a fire, 2 in car accidents, 2 by drowning when a boat overturned and 1 when he fell into a tub of water. A five year old fell from a tree and fractured his skull. A second five year old was killed when the stove exploded at home. A third sliced open his head when he ran into a power saw. A seven year old child was killed when hit by a car as he stepped off a school bus. A ten year old was murdered—a teenager beat him to death. A twelve year old committed suicide by hanging.

"Heaviest loss from accidental death was in the 15—24 year group but there were some at every age. Altogether 20 were killed in car accidents, 12 were drowned, 10 were murdered by various methods, 10 died as a result of acute alcoholism and exposure, 5 committed suicide, 4 were burned to death. They choose methods which are quite final in their result."

1965 Annual Report,
Saskatchewan Region,
Indian Health Services

"They choose methods. . . ." wrote the doctor. In Saskatchewan, the 71 Indians who died accidental deaths in 1965 made up 25 per cent of the total death rate, and were exceeded in number only by deaths from respiratory diseases. Motor vehicle accidents were the major killer of the young adult population. In British Columbia and Manitoba, accidents were the *major* cause of death. British Columbia is a sea-coast province and the Indians live, for the most part, in coastal villages. *Yet, the leading cause of death for Indians in British Columbia in 1965 was motor vehicle accidents!* While 37 Indians in B.C. died in highway traffic accidents, only 36 died of heart disease, and all other causes of death were smaller in proportion. Drowning accidents accounted for 35 deaths. The incidence of highway traffic deaths is extraordinary, considering not only most Indians' geographical isolation and inaccessibility to roads, but the fact that only a small proportion owns cars. Most of the accidental deaths in British Columbia—there were 146 out of a total of 401 deaths (36 per cent)—can be related to forms of indirect suicide.

Motor vehicles	37
Drownings	35
Suicide	8
Murder	10
Acute Alcoholism	11
Fire	19
Falls	6
Exposure (Freezing)	6
Poisons	2
Shooting (accidental)	2
Suffocation	6
Other	4

The health service director attempts to explain the phenomenon by alcoholism, but alcoholism is, of course, caused in turn by something else:

"In Coqualeetza zone (around Vancouver) there were 23 deaths caused by motor vehicle accidents... This can partly be accounted for by greater density of population within that zone, better access to high-speed highways, and greater utilization of motor cars by Indians. One would normally expect more accidental deaths by drowning in the Nanaimo zone and Miller Bay zone... It is not possible to account for the number of deaths by assault or homicide, but one would suspect they are closely associated with alcohol. It is of interest to note that among the 10 assault cases, 6 were due to head injuries obtained in a brawl, 2 were homicide by firearms, 1 by a knife wound and 1 by strangulation.

"Alcohol may have been involved in drownings, motor vehicle accidents, death by fire and, perhaps, suicide. The number of suicide cases has markedly increased during this year. This cannot be fully explained, as normally within the Pacific Region, rarely more than 1 or 2 deaths per annum have been recorded as due to self-destruction.

"It is obvious . . . that health education programs will have to be directed towards accident prevention, particularly with regard to the use of alcohol, fire prevention, water safety and to driving habits . . ."

Accidents and violence led also in the central region— Manitoba, northwestern Ontario and Keewatin, a district of the Northwest Territories. Drownings were higher than motor vehicle accidents. Railway accidents make their appearance for the first time in the central region. Six Indians died on railway tracks in 1965; another six committed suicide; nine froze to death; 23 drowned; 13 were killed in highway accidents; eight burned to death; five suffocated in motor vehicles and two were murdered.

In 1966, accidents in the central region remained high in number and peculiar in nature. (Statistics for other regions were not available at time of writing.) Of 89 persons who died through accidents or violence, 33 drowned, and most of the drowning victims were Indians between the ages of 15 and 35. The majority of the victims were men. Accidents among children accounted for only 16 of the 89 fatalities; 51 of the victims were aged 15 to 40. Within this age group, 19 drowned, five were killed in car accidents, four froze to death, four were murdered, four died under railway trains, three were killed in hunting accidents, three suffocated, one died from burns and another was killed in an employment accident. Seven died from unspecified causes. There were 22 Indians over 40 who died accidentally. Drowning claimed seven; three died under trains, three were burned and three froze. Only one suicide is listed in the 89 fatalities.

Chapter 10
Twins

In the spring of 1966, twenty-five Indian children were expelled from school in Dominion City, Manitoba, after four years of integration. The school board gave financial and administrative problems as their reason. The newspapers said it was racial segregation. The people of Dominion City deeply resented the charge of racism. They did not see their action as segregation; segregation was something that happened on television to Negroes. All they had decided was that the Indian children were not doing well at their school. Before the expulsion and subsequent publicity, the school trustees felt confident they were doing the right thing. After the public outcry labelling them racial bigots, the people of the town withdrew, offended, into themselves. They became suspicious of strangers and reluctant to talk to outsiders. Their long ordeal began.

The motion to bar the Indian students from returning to the school in September 1966 was made by E.J. Hancox. He gave as his reason the fact that the Indian students were concentrated in the lower grades and there weren't sufficient numbers of white students to absorb the Indian students. "This is working the wrong way," said Mr. Hancox. "It is dragging white children down to the Indian level, rather than bringing the Indians up to the white level. White children are more advanced than Indian children, at least I like to think so."

There were no Indian children in high school. There were, in fact, only 25 Indians in the school. They were all in grades one to three. Next year, there would be more Indian children in grade one than town children. The Indians had been integrated for four years. School board chairman Lorne Ramsey said the board was worried about "integration in reverse." The white enrolment in grade one had used to be about 20 pupils. Now, it had slipped to seven or eight. The class would have 12 or 13 Indians.

"We are elected to look after our own children, not theirs. If we can help the Indians, fine, but we won't do it if it means dropping our standard to theirs."

Cleanliness was the biggest problem, said Mr. Ramsey. The School Act provisions sent Indian children home when they were dirty or infested with lice. The child had to return with a doctor's certificate. In 1965-6, five children were expelled from the school for uncleanliness. Mr. Ramsey said the situation was not exactly segregation because there was a concerted attempt at integration. He didn't know how the Indians would feel when the school doors are closed against them—"slighted, I guess . . . they're here and we have to live with them. I get along with the Indians but I don't think the people of Dominion City care one way or the other."

Mr. Hancox said the whole board was against the Indian students being top-heavy in the lower grades but "nobody wanted to wear the goat horns. I moved the resolution because someone had to do something."

"We don't want them concentrated in three grades," reporters quoted Mr. Hancox saying. He also saw the Indian children as a possible source of disease. "Some white children contracted skin diseases from them."

Mr. Hancox's views were supported by another trustee, farmer Bill Kyle. The newspapers quoted him too: "More Indians than whites would mean that the whites are going to have Indians' ways and that's not good." Mr. Kyle blamed the reserves for blocking integration: "They [the Indians] should be spread out and the sooner the better. The situation could boil over and become another Alabama."

It was not discrimination, said Mr. Hancox. It was simply a measure "to protect a way of life." Mr. Hancox felt the Indians would be better taking their education in an area far removed from the reserve, a place where there was no cause for friction between Indian and white. "They would be better received in Altona, for example, because Mennonites are more interested in mission work than Dominion City people."

He, also, blamed the reserve. "You can't take a group of 750 people, white or Indian, coop them up on a reserve, huddled together with nothing to do and expect much. What will the problem be in twenty years? "

The people huddled together were not happy. When the school board made up its mind on May 11, the Indians were living in abandoned RCAF barracks in Macdonald, Manitoba, 100 miles northwest of Dominion City, because the Red River had flooded their homes on the reserve. The reserve is at the junction of the Red River and Roseau River, five miles west of Dominion City, 50 miles south of Winnipeg. Chief Albert Henry said: "Ending the integrated classes in Dominion is a setback to our education which in turn is a setback to integration." The Indians didn't know about the board's decision until a Winnipeg *Free Press* reporter told them. "I'll have to get in touch with the Indian Affairs people," said Mr. Henry.

"We are striving to integrate our children. In the past Indians have been too close-knit and this is bad for the children when they start to grow up," Mr. Henry said. He denied that the children had been going to school dirty, sick and lousy. "There was the odd incident of that type. I think that is just an excuse on the part of prejudiced people who want something to kick about."

School principal Gabe Girard was on the side of the Indians. He used the phrase "racial segregation." "How else could it be interpreted?" All the teachers felt the move was unfortunate and retrograde, he said. "The field of education needs expansion and we are going in the opposite direction."

The Dominion City school board at first did not notify the Indians about its decision. Neither had it notified Indian Affairs, which had negotiated the integration four years previously and was paying a per capita rate for the students. Integration was not costing the board a penny.

May 12: Indian Affairs leaped in, suggesting that Dominion City wanted the Indians' money but not the Indians. That hurt. The official, the regional director of Indian Affairs, Robert Connolly, knew that most of the 500-odd Roseau Reserve residents spend their money in Dominion City. He knew because their money goes directly from his office to the Dominion City stores by way of welfare vouchers. "The Indians," said Mr. Connolly from his office in Winnipeg, "have never felt accepted in Dominion City." Dominion City, he said, was not the only trouble spot the branch had encountered.

A man who takes the Indians' money, Michael Sokolyk, proprietor of the United Stores in Dominion City, said he treats the Indians the same as anyone else in business and socially.

"We get along pretty fine," said Mr. Sokolyk, who estimates he gets about 100 per cent of the Indians' business. "There is no trouble in my store."

In Winnipeg newspapers, Robert Connolly admitted that the arrangement had not been working well in Dominion City. Indian children were playing hookey. "Some Indian parents are not as responsible as they should be in seeing their children get to school. And a number of the children feel discriminated against."

Another reason behind the ban was brought to light a week later, when the press quoted a number of Indians who believed that the reason for closing the school to Indians was the band council's decision not to renew leases of band land to white farmers. One farmer affected by this decision was a school board member, Bill Kyle, and his arrnagement was not a strictly legal lease. Kyle was leasing land from Chief Albert Henry without the approval of the band. Henry had been granted the reserve land under the Veteran's Land Act. He had farmed it for a few years, then given up. He and Kyle had made a private deal. When Indian Affairs discovered it, they forced Henry to cancel the lease.

Three other local farmers also leased reserve land. In return for the land, they gave the band one-third of the crop. Bill Kyle had invested a lot of money in improving the land and had taken only one crop off it when the lease was cancelled.

Chief Henry had been watching TV that winter, and suggested a boycott as a retaliatory measure against the school board's decision. The chief estimated that the Indians spent about $10,000 in the town every year. His calculations were about $90,000 or $100,000 short.

By this time, the residents of Dominion City were angry. They didn't know what the school board was doing any more than anyone else. Nobody in Dominion City attends school board meetings and interest in education is very low. Why should the whole town be blamed for the board's action? What is the board to them? the people asked.

"It doesn't make any difference to me," said the manager of the local hotel.

"I don't want to talk about it. I want no part of it," said another man. "This is a good town, and we treat the Indians good. Then all of a sudden this thing is splashed all over the paper. I won't talk."

The president of the Chamber of Commerce clammed up too about the effects of a possible boycott. Obviously, the businessmen were worried. Mr. Connolly of Indian Affairs evidently panicked at the thought that his comments connecting Indians and business might have suggested the boycott, and said that he did not feel it would be a good idea. "It would be a negative step." The Indians did not boycott. (All their money comes from Indian Affairs and if Indian Affairs didn't approve the boycott, it could cut off the cash altogether.)

The final jab was given by an Indian, Adam Cuthand, an Anglican clergyman, in an open letter to the Dominion City school board:

> *"The first approach to breaking the vicious circle of relief has been shut. It is education and integration that will enable the next generation of Indians and their children to earn their livelihood and so be self-supporting as other Canadians. It is you as taxpayers who are paying for this relief.*
>
> *"In the last war the highest percentage of any ethnic group to volunteer were the Indians of Canada. Many of them did not return. They gave their supreme sacrifice so that you may be free to express your opinions and actions. You were then free to ban the Indian children from your schools. Through your actions the Canadian politicians will be embarrassed to express their opinions concerning apartheid in South Africa, the black-white situation in Rhodesia, the color problem in the United States and other areas where there is racial discrimination."*

The Dominion City Chamber of Commerce rallied. By the end of May the Chamber had prepared a brief to be sent to Arthur Laing, then Minister of Northern Affairs and Natural Resources, requesting a royal commission on Indians. It took the attitude that the trouble was all the government's fault:

> *"The majority of people in our community favour improved relations with our Indian neighbours and the Chamber has in the past made every effort to improve such*

relations. We commend the efforts being made by the Indians themselves to become integrated into the framework of our society and we are prepared to assist in any program designed to accelerate this integration, and deplore any form of discrimination on the grounds of racial descent. However, both the Indians and people of our community must be assured that both the federal and provincial governments are sincerely interested in providing a program which takes into account the welfare of both communities. Only when there is evidence of sincere interest can there be mutual acceptance and agreement among us."

"Programs of integration should be planned without lowering or disturbing the educational standards of the public school system," said the brief.

Although the Chamber expressed interest in promoting integration, that integration was to be "systematic" and controlled. Dominion City was not aware of the fact that only a small number of the reserve's 325 school-age children went to school in Dominion City or Letellier. If complete integration came, Dominion city's 114 children might find themselves in an "Indian school".

Dominion City wanted an end to the reserve system. Incentives should be provided for the young people to leave, more treaty money, training bonuses, training programs. The concern was not without self-interest: "Industries should be established or encouraged in villages close to reserves. . . " Give Dominion City an industry, which it wants so badly, and Dominion City will integrate cheerfully.

The brief went on to deal with a problem at the root of the trouble about integration:

"Assistance should be provided in policing small towns and villages in the neighbourhood of reservations. In the case of Dominion City, which has a population slightly over 500, and is close to a reservation with a much larger population, the ratepayers assume the entire cost of policing [$250 a month for one skinny part-time policeman]. From October 1, 1965 to December 31, 1965, nineteen offences were recorded and of these, fifteen were committed by the residents of the Roseau River Indian Reservation. All these offences were

committed within the village boundaries and included liquor, traffic and more serious ones. We contend that it is unfair to burden a small village such as ours with full policing, jail and transportation costs when these offences are committed by Indians from reservations. The situation is leading to ill feeling between taxpayer and Indian and restricts integration and acceptance of the Indian."

When the Indians straggled back from Macdonald to their flood-damaged homes the following week, the school term was nearly over. The Indians departed for the sugar-beet fields to the west, taking the children with them as they always do.

School opened in September; the Indians were back playing hookey at the reserve schools and the Dominion City school all-white. Two new things had, however, happened. A kindergarten opened on the reserve for the pre-school children. A Community Development Officer arrived to help the two communities come together again. And Chief Henry was beaten up and run off the reserve by his own band.

In November, just as the Community Development Officer, Pat Dunphy, was on the verge of getting the Indians and school board to agree to a meeting on integration the *United Church Observer* hit the village once more with an article entitled "Everything's Lily White in Dominion City." It condemned the town much more thoroughly than had the Winnipeg newspapers.

It called all the reasons put forward by the board and the town "excuses," and again hammered out the parallel between Dominion City and the American South:

"Not that the school board members were unreasonable. No more unreasonable than white parents in the American south who fight school integration because they don't want white children swamped by Negroes. . .

"Gary Roberts, who is 12, has been going to the neat new school in Dominion City, Manitoba, for four years. He got along well in his classes last year and shone on the ball diamond at recess. Gary can't go back to school this year. They don't want him any more. Gary is an Indian and Dominion City's school is now lily white. . .

"They said it was 'an administrative decision.' But Gary's mother and the other Indian parents also heard the other things some of them said about Gary not being clean enough, or smart enough, to go to school with the whites."

Dominion City became a bad word. Throughout the province and the country, moral, liberal people had sneered and pointed the finger. Criticism was helped by the fact that Dominion City is in the Canadian "South"—a kind of agricultural backwoods, populated, in the minds of many people, by hicks and rednecks who are presumed capable of any bigotry.

But Dominion City people considered themselves to be just like other Canadians. They didn't like being branded with a word which has become one of the strongest labels of evil in our society—prejudice. "But we don't hate Indians! " they said. "Some of them are real nice people."

ROSEAU RESERVE

Tools

Leonard sat at the kitchen table, cap on the back of his head, his face sleepy, or hung over. Half-naked children ran back and forth between his chair and a group of women in the next room who were watching Mickey Mouse cartoons on television.

"You still owe the department store $50 for those two chain saws you bought, Leonard," said the social worker.

"Yup, I guess," said Leonard. A long pause. "Ain't got no chain saws nomore." He grinned. He glanced out the window at the snow-covered yard. "One's broke," he said. "A guy borrowed the other one. I didn't need it. Was going to go to Ontario to cut pulp but didn't go. Never seen it since he took it."

"You still owe the store $50."

Leonard was unconvinced. "No money."

"Or you could return the chain saws to the store and tell them you'll pay them later."

"They can take the saws back," said Leonard. "I got no more need of them. I'm going to go to school. That's why I never went to cut pulp. Changed my mind to go to school instead."

"Why do you want to go to school, Leonard? "
"Gotta make some money to pay off the $50."
"What are you living on in the meantime? "
"Bark." He smiled broadly.

The Indian Band

Perhaps it is the bush which makes Roseau reserve look so dark. Turning down towards it on a narrow road off the sun-blinded saffron prairie, I was suddenly engulfed by trees. The reserve, like Dominion City, has its back to the road. One has to penetrate inside, near the river, to find its centre. Wild grass and weeds grow high in the open places around the houses. In the summer, it is green and lush. The Roseau River joins the Red River nearby, and the land is damp and low-lying. In winter, the willow branches show up red and yellow against the snow. It is a beautiful place, loud with the hum of mosquitoes in June.

I felt that I was going downhill as I entered the reserve. Roseau, like many reserves, is situated on a swamp so the land is actually lower than the surrounding area. The illusion is intensified by the bush, the drab grey houses, the dark faces. All three narrow roads leading into the reserve end about half a mile in. There is an open field, a rudimentary central square, which contains, scattered haphazardly, two deserted white missions, a United Church school, a cream-colored house used by the teacher, a band hall and an office for the Community Development Officer and vocational counsellor who comes down once a week. A single road stretches off beyond, towards the northern end of the reserve. The houses are strung out along this road and along the three which join the highway. The red Roman Catholic school is also out on the north road, about half a mile from the central square.

The teacher at the United Church School (neither school has any other name) is the only white person living on the reserve.

"I was terrified. My husband brought me a week before school started, in order to get the place cleaned up. I stayed by myself. All day long the cars full of men and boys would chug past outside the front door, moving slowly while they

all hung out the window and stared. They all came just to look at me. The caretaker's eyes popped out of his head when I told him I was going to stay here by myself for a week. At two a.m. one night there was a loud pounding on my door. I lay there and shook. The banging got worse. I got up and went to the door. A flashlight shone right in my eyes. I was blinded. It was the R.C.M.P. 'Did you hear a woman screaming? ' they said. 'No,' I said. I could have killed them. No one had told them I was there — they thought the place was deserted. I guess someone had said there was a woman in the teacherage. That was the only incident that happened. I went out and talked to the people that came by; the kids aren't reticent."

The reserve has the ugly monotony of most reserves. Four eras of Roseau's history are clearly visible in the houses, like strata in a rock. There are old, abandoned log huts in the bush. Most of the homes are second era—cheap frame one-room shacks covered with grey asphalt siding which look like the houses children draw, square, peaked-roof, two windows and a single door in the middle, with a curl of smoke coming out the chimney on top. Each is heated by a wood stove, and a big pile of split wood stands by the door. The ground around the door has, even in winter, been trampled into a black mud mixed with toys, garbage and tin cans. Some homes have electricity but some do not. Some have outhouses; other families use the bush. The third era shows in the boxcar red bunkhouses clustered along the most open road, the last before coming to Dominion City. Indian Affairs encouraged the people to move out of the bush by building new homes in groups close to the highway. If the family wanted the house, it had to live where Indian Affairs wanted. Most recent are the few new summer cottages Indian Affairs has erected, thin shells of plywood to which the people have added little and have, in fact, scarred and dirtied. Although a few are painted and well-kept, in many cases the Indians sold the paint they were given to people in Dominion City. As more and more of the new houses are built close to the highway the people of Roseau are becoming more visible. Every spring, flood-watching is a tourist attraction. Hundreds of cars ply the roads of the reserve, the occupants gawping at the Indians. "You think we're animals in a zoo? " says the chief.

All the children and teenagers dress exactly alike. Standard dress, for boys and girls both (they wear their clothes interchangeably) is black or light blue nylon quilted windbreakers, black or blue pants (stretch for the girls). In winter, the standard jacket is black fleecy material with a red and white "V" down the back. The clothing is almost a uniform, looking like government issue, and is, in fact, almost that. The clothing is bought with vouchers supplied by the Indian Affairs department. (The agent won't give cash for fear it will be spent for drink.) The voucher gives the name of the store where the clothes are to be purchased, and the price to be charged for them. The mother dutifully presents her voucher at the store and receives her allotment of parkas, pants and shoes. The storekeeper is paid by Indian Affairs. All the vouchers are issued on one store, because it is easier for Indian Affairs to pay one big bill than a lot of little ones. Since most of the reserve is on welfare, all the clothes are bought at the same store. The store owner knows he has a captive market and knows exactly how much he will get for his goods. He buys in bulk, and gets the cheapest stuff he can. The Indians wear black and pale blue windbreakers and parkas with a red "V" on the back because that is all that the store has in stock.

The band has a registered population just over 600. Of them, 330 are children under 16. Four hundred of the residents are under 20. To be 20 is to be old in Roseau. The band has only 22 people older than 55 and only ten over 65. The population balance is exactly the reverse of Dominion City. About 100 band members have moved away from the reserve, leaving the resident population exactly equal to Dominion City's. The reserve seems deserted. Only 95 families live there. People seem to materialize out of nowhere, appearing suddenly from the bush or from a car, and fading away as rapidly behind a rise in the land. The homes are scattered and hidden in the trees.

Roseau has only 55 homes: these are houses and shacks, and 40 families are without shelter altogether. People are forced to double-up and sometimes triple-up with relatives and friends. A house inadequate for a family of five holds 15 people in Roseau. The shacks are uninhabitable—no insulation, no floor, no furniture, often no windows—but people live in them because nothing else is available. A shack which, at best, could contain three or four people, holds seven or ten.

Walk into a home in Roseau—into a wall of people. The homes are fetid, suffocating, den-like, full of humanity. Dark, silent shapes occupy the corners, squat on the floor, sprawl and clamber over beds, chairs, chesterfields, stoves. The rooms are dark because the people, eyes glinting in the gloom, are watching television. The flickering white glare fills the cave. A door opens only to reveal another squalid room full of people. Over everything is a slimy trail: mud, spilled water, food, soot, grease. Smoke from the wood stove has covered the walls and floor of even the newest homes with a grey, gritty haze. Every square foot of available floor space has a person or a dog sitting on it. Children scurry from room to room in the twilight.

The houses have too many people for furniture. There is room for no more than two or three beds, a table, a couple of chairs. Mattresses are spread on the floor. Most of the inhabitants sleep, eat and watch television on the floor. They sleep in their clothes, wearing coats and parkas in the winter to keep warm. They huddle together, three and four to a mattress, often just on the bare boards. More subtle forms of animal life—mice and lice—share the garbage and the human feast. The Indians can do nothing about the situation except put up with it. They find tents too cold in the winter now, and this is much preferable to tents, the only comparison they know.

Sixteen families have moved away. Of the remaining families, 23 are married couples, 34 are common-law, and 15 are unwed mothers. Illicit, semi-permanent unions form the majority of the relationships. In addition, six are widows with children or grandchildren. Most of the reserve's children are illegitimate. Families of six to ten children are normal, even for unmarried women who are not living common-law. Names are confusing: a child will be known by his mother's last name, his father's last name, and his "step-father's" last name. All these names are in English and Saulteaux both.

Almost half the income is relief. Indian Affairs invests

about $40,000 a year for food and clothing by both cash and voucher. The relief is spread over all twelve months of the year and seldom falls under $1,500 in a month. Spring and fall, when the children need clothes, it goes to $4,000 and $4,500 a month. In 1964, the welfare rates were doubled. In 1963, $17,835 went into Roseau from Indian Affairs; in 1965 the same number of people received $37,724. The result is no appreciable improvement in living standards and a big increase in drinking. Most of the rest of the money comes from the government too. Family Allowance contributes about $20,000 a year and various pensions add another $15,000. Whatever else the people have, they earn themselves. This earned income ranges from zero in many cases to $500 or $1,000. There are many opportunities for seasonal and part-time work: sugar beets in the summer, pulp cutting in Ontario, manual labor, construction, and, most recently, chicken-plucking. If a man could take his children out of school, put his family in a trailer and move from one job to another, he could make a respectable income. This is impossible because the children must attend school, or so the government claims.

Every year, 25 babies are born to the Roseau band—one quarter of the women are always pregnant—and about five people die. A couple of those who die will be babies, one or two children, one a young person and maybe an elderly man. Between 1960 and 1965, the population of the band increased by 105, with 130 births and 25 deaths. The reserve has an increase of about 20 people every year although the building rate for new homes is only about one a year.

Like almost all Indian bands in Canada, the Roseau band is slowly going broke. It began operating in 1884, ten years after the settlers first arrived and four years after Dominion City was named. The band started with $357.22 in the bank—more than the settlers had. The band, again like all others, sold its land out from under itself between 1909 and 1921, at the instigation of the Indian agents. By 1921, sales of reserve land had accumulated $76,036 in the trust fund in Ottawa. Until 1955, this capital remained virtually intact (nothing happened on the reserve). Between 1955 and 1965, it dwindled to $47,000. Since the band has almost no more land to sell and there is no likelihood of oil, it has no source of capital income. At this pace, it will be broke in ten years, at which time the band will number over 800 people. The money was not invested: it was frittered away. In 1955, $1,590 went to "buy off" enfranchised band members who were entitled to their per capita share of the capital fund when they left the band. (Bands tend to lose a lot of members directly after a big land sale.) In 1961, another $1,000 was spent for enfranchisement. Housing cost the band $5,000 in 1957 and another $8,000 in 1962. (Houses may be "free" to the individual owners but they are charged to the band.) Also in 1962, $6,000 was spent to install a water system which did not function. The following year, $4,816 was spent on horses and equipment. (I have yet to see a horse on the Roseau reserve.) In 1964, $3,486 was spent to purchase a water truck to replace the useless water system. Each year, the band gets a pittance to spend on road upkeep, repairs to the band hall, etc. The annual revenue is spent strictly on public works. It barely covers the cost of light bulbs and a load of gravel for the roads every five years.

The Roseau Indians are sick. Eight members of the Roseau band were admitted to hospital with tuberculosis in 1965. Roseau people always provide at least one-quarter of the area agency's TB cases. A 1965 health survey showed that no Roseau baby under one year old was immunized. The infant mortality rate for the reserve is 272.2/1000, the highest in the Clandeboye Agency and one of the highest of any community in Canada. Between 70 per cent and 98 per cent of the pre-school children are not innoculated against any disease, including smallpox. The nurse managed better with the school children. Vaccinations for children six to sixteen ranged from 89 per cent for some vaccines down to 9.7 per cent for others. Only 11 per cent of the adults were inoculated. Although every band member is supposed to get a chest x-ray before getting his treaty money every year, the x-ray does not reach more than a quarter of the population. (Presumably these 125-odd people produced the eight TB cases in 1965. No one knows whether the other 375 band members have TB or not.) Pneumonia, bronchitis, colds, sinus trouble and intestinal infections are chronic and general on Roseau Reserve, the unavoidable result of cheap, badly heated homes, overcrowding, bad food and poor sanitation.

Children are badly infected with skin diseases. Many are

disfigured with impetigo and scabies and similar skin infections. These diseases and acne later leave them scarred by the time they are 20. They are also prey to the usual contagious viruses of childhood which reach epidemic proportions on the reserve— measles, mumps, chicken pox. This mass illness is not for want of medical attention. The Roseau people get much more intensive treatment than the average Canadian. Indian Health Services, local doctors and hospitals take good care of them. The health nurse averages twenty home visits a month. Doctors' bills, paid by Indian Health, averaged $30 *per capita* in 1965—a total of $18,000 for the reserve. The band is served by four doctors—in Dominion City, Emerson, and Morris, Manitoba.

The Roseau people spend an extraordinary amount of time in the hospital. (Driving people back and forth to hospital absorbs much of the time of the men on the reserve.) The Emerson hospital has an average of three or four Roseau patients every day of the year. The Morris hospital has anywhere from two to eleven Indian patients every day. This does not include out-patients, Indian people who are examined and treated at the hospital without being admitted.

"It is amazing that these people are not sicker than they are," said one physician. "The reason must be their use of the hospital."

The situation is a result of a combination of dirt and indifference. The people do nothing at all to prevent illness. Nurses and doctors find the people apathetic and indifferent.

Slimy Things

"We have had no water for two days," said the woman. "The water delivery man has been out on a bender. I don't know when he'll come. Sometimes he doesn't show up for about a week. We've been melting snow to drink but I wanted to wash all the clothes before we moved to Winnipeg."

The Roseau Indians used to dip their water out of the river in pails. The Roseau River is now polluted. When the $6,000 water system didn't work, the band bought a water truck and employed a man to haul the water from Dominion City. The driver, who is paid $100 a month, is unreliable and alcoholic. He would be hard put to service the whole reserve even if he worked eight-hour days. He usually spends the eight hours in the Queen's Hotel beer parlor. The water truck operates primarily as a taxi service. Men from the reserve hitch rides in the cab into Dominion City; and they pay in beer for the rides.

The water is pure when the people get it, but it does not stay that way long in the homes, especially in summer. It is dumped into dirty, leaky containers left uncovered and open to cats and dust, flies and germs. It soon develops a scum and slimy things with legs. The people get stomach cramps, dysentery, and diarrhea. When the people do not have enough water to drink, they do not take baths or wash very much. It also becomes difficult to wash clothes for a family of ten. The outhouses are primitive and many families have none, so that children and adults alike use the bush, walls, and the river. The hordes of flies and mosquitoes that breed in the area carry germs from the offal in outhouses and bush into the homes. Similarly, Roseau has no garbage disposal, so that garbage too collects in the bush behind the homes or is tossed into the river. The more primitive families heave it out the front door where it is consumed by dogs or rots away.

Man in the Blue Jacket

"A two year old boy, Russell George Atkinson of the Roseau River Indian Reserve was killed early Sunday when fire destroyed his home.

RCMP in Winnipeg, who believe the fire was started by a candle, said Alex Laroque and four other children escaped. All live on the reserve. No inquest will be held,"

Winnipeg Tribune
Feb. 27, 1967

Russell's mother lived in a shack on the reserve, and was away from home drinking at a party. The shack had no electricity—only the candle—and rumor had it that there was drinking in the home too at the time the candle was upset.

The snow is damp and soggy; a faint dripping sound is heard from somewhere. Other than that, the reserve is silent. It is early afternoon but no people seem to be about. Near a clump of bush stands the United Church school, with its bare light bulb burning day and night over the door. It is plain white, pre-fab, one-room and matches the blank snow. So do the twin outhouses set next to the bush about 25 yards from the school. Beyond is the old white wooden church, boarded up, blinded.

Two tiny women suddenly appear to rise out of the ground to the right of the deserted church. Dark and small as toys in the distance they make their way, walking slowly, towards the church in single file. A man follows . . . then some children . . . another woman . . . a whole line walks like gnomes, out of the earth, in single file. They walk in a straight line—20 or 25 of them—into the front door of the church. At the same time, two cars drive up. Some more people get out. A second procession makes its way from the cars to the church and disappears again. The women are wearing their red and blue kerchiefs, brown parkas, black boots. Some have slacks; others wear print skirts. The men wear their windbreakers, black parkas and cloth caps. They have come on a footpath through a gully behind the church, emerging suddenly just beside it.

One of the cars, full of men, does not stop but goes past the school, a few yards further to the band hall, a cream-colored quonset hut. All the people disappear. In a few minutes, the men re-emerge from the hall. One carries a pine box about three feet long over his shoulder. He handles it nonchalantly, slinging it on his back with one arm as if it were empty. One man carries a hammer, another a shovel. The group—everyone dressed in work clothes—climbs back in the car and returns to the church. In the snow-covered yard outside, a cluster of men and small boys gathers around while a couple of men fuss with the box, kneeling on the ground. They appear to be having trouble fastening the lid down. Finally, they are done. The men squatting by the box stand up.

The man in the old blue sports windbreaker again slings up the box, balances it on his shoulder and walks, with the other men still grouped around, back into the gully. As if by a secret cue, the women and children straggle out of the church and follow the man with the box. There is no minister.

They stop about 15 yards from the church, half-hidden in the gully. The man in the blue jacket slips the box off his back and others help him place it in a shallow grave which has been dug in the frozen earth. Earth is shovelled quickly over the box and tamped down. A small bunch of flowers is placed on the top. The people disperse in twos and threes, heading off in several directions. The men return the shovel and hammer to the band hall and the cars drive off. It took about 15 minutes. Everything is as still and silent as it was.

Town Planning

The economist from Winnipeg has his back against the wall. He has brought all his charts and his diagrams in four colors and his briefcase full of notes. The diagrams are four feet by three feet and nicely covered with plastic so that dirty fingers won't soil them. He has them all spread out on a table in front of him. There isn't much room left in the office. The chief and six members of the Roseau River band council are crammed in on the opposite side of the table. They are not small men. Two are over six feet and about 220 pounds each. Stan Nelson, the band constable, is here too and he is the biggest of them all, taking a whole corner, looking expressionlessly at the economist from under the peak of his red baseball cap. The council members are here to be shown the new townsite Indian Affairs has planned for the reserve. Several slightly different choices have been drawn up; the council may choose one.

The townsite—new houses, roads, street lights, running water and sewage, parks, "industrial complex" and "commercial area," dikes and school—will be built free by Indian Affairs. The idea for a townsite for Roseau River reserve was discussed originally with the previous chief and council. The present council members have had no idea of what it involves until today. They look skeptical. One of the council members, an elderly man in sunglasses, crosses one leg over the other and smokes. He speaks only Saulteaux, so that the economist's remarks will have to be translated for him later. The economist sweats. It is hot and the Indians are not impressed. The econo- mist is a young man. His face is pale, his light brown hair brushed straight back off his forehead. He wears glasses, a pin-stripe shirt and a conservative dark blue suit. As he speaks, he points with a pen to the diagram. A gold ring on one finger glitters. A couple of the council members chew gum and stare into space. It is up to the chief. Besides, he is the only one able to see properly.

The diagrams are beautiful, with roads neatly marked out and lined with squiggly marks representing trees. The houses, now scattered helter-skelter in the bush, are in neat, straight rows, side by side, along the roads. They are colored yellow. The industrial site is colored red. The commercial area has been left white. The park, colored green, is along the river and a dike protects the reserve. The sewage lagoon has been located discreetly on the other side of the highway.

The plans differ only in the number and location of the roads: do the people want to be able to drive to their homes, or would they prefer to leave their cars in a central area and walk to their homes, which would be in a park-like area? It is a momentous question. The chief ponders. Do they want three roads or one? It is difficult for the chief. He is in a tough spot, since he doesn't live on this reserve. He lives at the Roseau Rapids reserve, a second parcel of land owned by the band, 16 miles east. How can he decide for these people? When he was elected chief he didn't even know a townsite was being planned.

The council is under *no obligation* to make up its mind now, says the economist. The study has been paid for by Indian Affairs. About $4,500 for an economic study will, however, come out of the band's capital fund . . . (he coughs) . . . if they would just be so kind as to sign this authorization.

"What authorization?" said John James, the chief. "We never asked for this plan. We never made any authorization to spend band money. Maybe we don't want to spend our money on this. What's this authorization? "

"Ahem," said the economist. "The authority for the study was given more than a year ago by the previous council. They signed the paper. However, it unfortunately was lost by Indian Affairs in Ottawa and therefore we would like you to just sign . . . "

"I think our treaty rights got lost in Ottawa too," quipped John James with a grin at the council. They nodded in unison.

"I'd like to discuss this with my council before I sign anything," he said.

"Fine, *fine*," said the economist, looking crestfallen. "Of course," he continued, trying to pacify and persuade the chief, "the council is under no obligation to accept *any* plan. You can turn the whole idea down. And," he continued as another bright idea struck him, "even if the townsite is built *no one* will be obligated to move there. No one will be forced to live in it if they don't want to. No one will be moved against his will." The economist beamed. Freedom.

The chief had gained courage from the success of his initial foray against the economist. "We might take a while to teach the people what a townsite is," he said. "Maybe they won't want to live in it." The council nodded again. "I don't want to be the only one living on the townsite," grinned the chief again, looking at the economist.

The economist blanched again. Imagine, a townsite with one house in it! Imagine all the Indians still living back in the bush. "Well, of course the townsite will have running water and *sewage*," he replied confidently. There was an unbeatable argument. Who could reject sewage?

"Do all the houses *have* to be close together like that, in rows? " asked the chief, pointing to the houses diagrammed cheek-by-jowl. "We have lots of room here. The people don't like to live that close. They like to have privacy. Can't we get new houses and keep them on the lots we have? "

The economist looked amazed. "But you can only have water and *sewage* if the houses are in a townsite," he explained patiently. "Otherwise it's too expensive unless the houses are close together." He also implied that Indian Affairs would not be generous with new homes unless they were in a townsite and equipped with toilets and taps. The chief was silent.

"I notice you have here a large area set aside for industry," piped up the Community Development Officer. "What exactly do you have in mind as industry? "

The economist now blushed. "Well, that is a problem," he said. "The economic study is being done by Indian Affairs and it has not been completed yet. As I've explained, the documents were lost... At any rate, we have had to go ahead with the townsite plan although we have no idea of the economic potential of the area. You'll have to ask the regional superintendent about the economic study. We were just hired to do the plan."

"Do you," continued the CDO, "have any idea of what

will be going into the commercial area here? It seems odd to set up more stores when there are already stores in Dominion City and Letellier."

"You will have to ask Indian Affairs," said the economist patiently. "As I explained, we were just hired to do . . . "

"But what if there is *no* economic base to the reserve? " persisted the CDO. "Why bother setting up a town? Shouldn't the people move away? "

"As I said before," said the economist, "we were just hired . . . you'll have to ask . . ." He hadn't expected this white man to be there asking embarrassing questions.

"Ahem, excuse me," said Stan Nelson from his corner.

"Yes," said the economist, looking up brightly.

"Is that a sewage lagoon, you said, on the other side of the highway? "

"Yes," said the economist brightly.

"Hmmm," said Stan. "That little dot over there. That's my house. You've got your sewage lagoon right next to my house."

The chief and council guffawed uproariously.

In order not to send the economist away feeling sad, the chief selected one of his designs, more or less at random, and requested that a small scale model be made.

The model, like the town itself, was free. It would keep the economist busy for a few months and keep him out of the council's hair. After the model was made, it would be on display for the people to see.

"I don't think the people will accept the townsite," said one of the councillors later. "They don't like to live close like that. I'm not too keen on it myself. Even if we do get water and sewage and lights and stuff, where are we going to get the money to maintain them and fix the watermains when they break down? We have no money now."

Let's Build a Ghetto

The people of Roseau River will probably reject the townsite. When they do turn it down, Indian Affairs will moan that the people are backward, primitive, and prefer living in a slum.

But this project isn't Roseau's own. Nobody from the reserve had planned for it, saved for it, or even wants it. If they accept the town, it will be because it's free and because they want to keep Indian Affairs happy. Nobody from the reserve was asked to help make a plan, nor was the council involved in discussions about what kind of community the Indians want. Stan Nelson was not asked if he objected to the sewage lagoon being located at his back door. The Indian people have contributed nothing toward this townsite, not even ideas, comments, or suggestions. The economist flew in, his rolls of designs under his arm and said "Here you are folks—your new town." The town looks pretty on the plan. But it was conceived with no relation to reality. Not only was the plan drawn before an economic study had determined the resources of the proposed community, its financial base and its potential, but it was drawn in complete contradiction to existing Indian Affairs policy on the reserve.

In 1966, Indian Affairs entered into an agreement with four Indian men to farm the reserve land, slowly taking over more land as their operation grew. The men have formed a corporation. The reserve has enough farm land to give them a bare living. The reserve has 94 families. What are the other 90 families supposed to do for a living? How can they continue to live on the reserve if it provides a livelihood for only four families? Obviously, by turning over reserve property to four band members, Indian Affairs was suggesting that the rest of the people would be wise to move off. There is nothing to do around Roseau except farm. The townsite project contradicts this. If it goes ahead, the people will stay, and they will remain unemployed and on welfare.

As part of their agreement with Indian Affairs, the four farmers have agreed to turn over part of their annual profits to the band revenue. They are, in fact, taxpayers. If the rest of the band remains, these four hard-working men will be expected to support, with their profits, a population of indigents. It is their money, the money from the farm, which will go to pay for upkeep on the water mains and sewage pipes, repair the streets, fix the lights after the kids knock them out with stones. The only conceivable economic activity at Roseau, farming, which neither needs nor can support a town, would be saddled with one.

In Roseau, Indian Affairs faces formidable problems in trying to make its incorrigible Indians into nice, clean, sewage-

disposing white people. Roseau people do not cite lack of
running water and flush toilets as major problems. Drunkenness
and violence are their obsessive concerns. How are water,
sewage and parks going to cure drinking, fighting, murder,
vandalism? By herding the people into a townsite, Indian
Affairs would intensify the crime and alcoholism, something
which has already happened in Camp 10, Churchill. The only
protection, (and it is very meagre), the Roseau people have now
against attack, irritation and obnoxiousness from their neighbors is distance. Families can (and some do) lock themselves in
the house, turn out the lights and hide from the gangs of drunks
and wild youths that roam around the reserve. They do not hear
the parties a mile away. Protected by a screen of bush, they can,
if they choose, keep much to themselves. As far as many people
on the reserve are concerned, they live too close together as it
is. They don't like each other much. The reserve is split into
clans and factions which war with each other.

Roseau people have evolved a style of life which makes
living in a townsite impossible. Accustomed to living at a
distance from others, they have not developed the codes and
defences which can protect them from their neighbors in close
quarters. They lack community organization because they have
never had a need for it. The only organization the people have
known in the last one hundred years has been on the reserve. It
too was imposed from without. What reason does Indian Affairs
have to believe that doubling this imposition would not double
the disaster?

Roseau is currently working its own way out of the reserve
prison by destroying it from within. Tensions within the
community are driving the people away. They want to leave to
avoid the violence, theft and drinking. The community is, in its
own peculiar way, trying to right itself after being thrown off
balance by the reserve system. It is disbanding itself.

A Boy Called David

David Seenie had black prickly hair that stuck up all over
his head like porcupine quills. His eyes were black and slanty,

almost Chinese. He wasn't handsome, for a 12 year old. His head was too long, his ears stuck out and his mouth was big and thick-lipped. David had a heart defect which wasn't discovered until he was nine. He was a treaty Indian and lived in the bush on the Roseau Reserve. Most of the Indians had moved from that part of the reserve to the section of the reserve close to Dominion City and the main highway to Winnipeg, but a few families, including David's, remained.

When nine-year-old David Seenie was brought into a Winnipeg hospital for heart surgery in 1963, he could barely speak English and had no schooling. Indian and Eskimo children are made pets in city hospitals and David was no exception. The nurses grew very fond of him during his six months in the hospital. One of the nurses, Mrs. Cooney, who had a boy two years younger than David, took David home with her when he was discharged.

David started grade one in Winnipeg when he was ten years old and barely spoke English. In two and a half years, he was promoted to grade five. He joined the Boy Scouts and won a trophy for scouting when he was eleven. He, Brian Cooney and a neighbour, Simon Knight, were called the "Three Musketeers" in the neighbourhood.

David rode his bicycle over to the school August 21, 1966. Three hours later he was dead. The funeral was held on the Roseau Reserve.

The Cooneys had loved David and were proud of him: "He won a junior scout trophy last year—he was very proud of being an Indian once he found out he was an Indian." He could do things with his hands and he loved Scouts. There were more than fifty Scouts at the funeral.

"Once we asked him what he wanted most in the world. We thought he would want to go back to the reserve. But he wanted an education for his younger brother. That's the kind of kid he was."

The roads are narrow on the Roseau Indian reserve and the drifts pile high in December.

The transport truck carrying the gifts for the people of

Roseau reserve got stuck. It was about 7 p.m., already dark and very cold. There are few street lights on the reserve. The truck driver wasn't sure exactly where to go and had wandered onto a little-used side road. Two carloads of people from Winnipeg were stopped behind the truck.

The people of Roseau sat patiently in the band hall about two hundred yards away, waiting while the men dug the truck out. Most of the people had been sitting there on the hard benches in rows against the wall since 4 p.m. that afternoon. Another half-hour or hour wouldn't hurt. They had come at 4 p.m.—clusters of women with little children making black dots on the white snow—because that was the time they had been told the truck from Winnipeg would arrive. The hall was silent with breathing, silence broken only by the scurrying and yelping of children, as the truck's engine roared and labored to get out of the snow.

The women sat silently, slouched with their backs against the wooden wall, holding their children against bellies swollen with too many pregnancies, shapeless in sagging flowered skirts and parkas. They were waiting. Christmas was coming. The truck was coming.

They had come on a gamble. There must have been about thirty women and seventy children in the little wooden hall built of rough lumber in a quonset shape with a sloping, rounded roof. The hall is heated by an oil stove and lit with bare electric bulbs. The benches are the only furniture. There are no windows.

Rumor had gone around the reserve that afternoon that presents and toys for the children were being sent from Winnipeg and that a party was planned. But this wasn't going to be a happy party. There was talk of it being a religious service, a memorial ceremony with toys and candies. It was said the dead boy had come from the Roseau reserve but no one knew him.

It was the first time the hall had been opened up and used for anything in a long time. The unclaimed sacks of flour that each band member gets as his treaty right had been stored there and it had been locked up. It made them think of the dances and parties that had been held there years ago, more than fifteen years ago, before the drinking got so bad. The woman sat and dozed. When the children got rowdy they were shushed with "The truck is coming, the truck is coming."

It was Monday, December 19, 1966—David Seenie Night on the Roseau Reserve. No one on the reserve had heard anything about the memorial party until that morning, when the Community Development man had driven over, red in the face and waving a copy of a newspaper story from Saturday's paper.

The Story of a Boy Called David"

"David Seenie was 12 years old when he died last August. But he knew Christmas only three times. For David, who had a heart defect, spent his first nine years on the Roseau Indian Reserve, 60 miles south of Winnipeg. And there his family did not celebrate Christmas.

"For 2 1/2 years David lived with the Cooneys and enjoyed three Christmases with them. The neighbours grew to love the bright youngster. So much so that now the area's residents have started a drive to bring Christmas to the Indians on David's home reserve.

"Mrs. Cooney . . . and Mrs. R.S. Knight were gathered at the home of Mrs. R.I. Drayson — depot for the drive in David's memory. Half the Draysons' basement is full of donated gifts and a large truck will be needed to transport the gifts to the reserve.

"Mrs. Knight, Simon's mother, picked up the story. 'We were away at the time David died. Simon nearly broke his heart and we felt we wanted to do something David would have liked.

'We know David wanted to help his people so we started to collect gifts from along the road to send to the reserve.

'It's not charity. The whole thing is being done out of respect for David. It's to let David's people know how much we loved him.'

"Mrs. Drayson thinks there is more than $2,000 in gifts in her basement, most wrapped and many with tags reading 'From a Friend of David.'

"Said Mrs. Knight. 'It's not a charity drive. It's a David Seenie Drive. This is instead of flowers.' "

David's people had been through a number of charity drives but they had never been on the receiving end of a David Seenie Drive before. Word began to spread around the reserve that the children were not to go home after school. One of the teachers took his whole school full of children over to the band hall after class. Four o'clock came and the truck did not. But Mary Jane of the Children's Aid Society came from Winnipeg.

"Four o'clock? " she said. "Whoever said four o'clock? Why, that's impossible. They'll just start loading the truck at four. Then it will take an hour to drive down. It will be at least six or seven before the truck is here."

Mary Jane perched brightly on the extreme edge of one of Steve Seenie's broken-down kitchen chairs. Steve Seenie is welfare officer for the reserve and at that time, acting chief.

"The people in Winnipeg are not missionaries. They are not interested in meeting people," Mary Jane announced.

Steve Seenie thought that over for a while. "Was anybody coming down with the truck? " asked Steve.

Mary Jane didn't know. She didn't think anyone would come. They were all very busy people. Mrs. Cooney was pregnant. She had sort of been given responsibility for getting the truckload of stuff to the reserve, because she was the Children's Aid worker. That's why she had come to see Steve. She looked at him. Steve looked back at her.

Mary Jane was young, pale and thin. Her brown eyes opened very wide and she blinked very fast.

"They are out of contact with the people on the reserve," Mary Jane explained. "They thought that this is what David would want. They're doing it out of love for David. It's a memorial. They don't want to establish any relations with people on the reserve. They are doing this for David."

Steve said that after he had been shown the newspaper story he had gone ahead and lit a fire in the stove in the band hall with the idea that it would be the best place to distribute the gifts or hold the service.

"Oh no," said Mary Jane. "We didn't think it should be distributed in the band hall. This isn't charity, you know! " After a pause, she asked: "What do you *do* at a band hall? "

She said she thought it would be better to just store the
stuff in the hall and distribute it quietly the next day in the
schools.

Well, Steve laughed drily, there were 100 people sitting
over there in the hall waiting for the truck to come.

Mary Jane blanched, paused, then brightened again.

"I'll leave it all up to you," she said to Steve, and got up to
go. "This isn't organized, you know," she added.

Steve's good-natured nervous laugh became hysterical.
"No! No! " he said, and raised his hands unconsciously to
shield his face.

"I guess I'll have to make a speech then," said Mary Jane,
sitting down and making a face. She immediately went into a
trance trying to compose what she was going to say.

Why, she asked, was everything so disorganized? She had
told the white school teacher to tell everyone else, and no one
had been told! Or they had been told the wrong things.

The people in Winnipeg wanted this to be a quiet thing
with no fuss, she said. They didn't want the Indian people to
know.

With this, Mary Jane produced a framed copy of the
newspaper story about the David Seenie Drive (with photo) and
handed it reverently to Steve. The Cooneys had never known
David's parents, she said. They didn't know where they were
now. If Steve found them, he was to give them the picture; if
not, he could do with it as he pleased. Hanging in on the wall of
the band hall might be a nice idea. And Mary Jane left.

As the truck labored and groaned in the snowdrift, people
began to materialize out of the darkness and head for the band
hall. The men had been sceptical but now that the truck
actually did exist, they came by foot and in old jalopies.
Teenagers came too — jammed into the battered old cars,
peering out through their thatches of black hair. The men
lounged against the walls inside looking as if they had just
dropped in by chance, or ran in and out pretending they had
some reason other than curiosity or greed to be there. A steady
procession passed in and out the front door between the
warmth of the stove and the case of beer stashed in the shadows

outside. The band hall quickly filled — imperceptibly as if the people had been sucked in through the walls. A dozen more men and boys stood around in the darkness just outside the single puddle of light from the glaring bare bulb over the door.

The noise and excitement increased with the heat and beer. The air in the hall smelled of wood and leather and oil. Children began to shout and run around.

Suddenly a bunch of strange white people walked in. The Cooneys had come and so had other people from Winnipeg. The transport had made it out and was at the door. The Cooneys were dressed in slacks and casual clothes. They looked lost and dazed, standing there in the middle of the hall with all those Indians staring at them. The men, glad of something to do, quickly unloaded all the boxes from the truck. The boxes were hauled in one after the other and piled on the stage. The mob of pushing, yelling children surged up to the base of the platform. The Cooneys, Mary Jane and the school teachers took refuge on the stage. One of the teachers had brought a record player and Marion Anderson wailed Christmas laments over the din. The white people smiled broadly. The Indians looked glum.

Mrs. Cooney had brought a wreath of plastic lilies in a cellophane bag. She hesitantly approached a couple of women asking them if they knew David or his parents. The women made noncommittal clucking noises of sympathy and said nothing. Mrs. Cooney eventually gave the wreath to Steve Seenie's wife who promised to place it on the grave.

The children were distracted temporarily from the boxes which appeared from the labels to be full of toilet tissue when Mrs. Cooney produced some color snapshots of the dead boy and went about the room showing them to one group of women after another. The children would dart up briefly, peek and zoom back to make another grab at the boxes.

"This was a picture of David. Did they know David? Had anyone ever known him? David had lived with us. We had loved him. He had died." Mrs. Cooney spoke very slowly and in simplified English — leaving out all the in-between words. But no one knew David. They shook their heads in sympathy. Not a word or a glance of recognition. Nice photographs. Mrs. Cooney seemed close to tears.

Mr. Cooney shouted a short speech over the din:

> *"Not long ago we had a very warm opportunity to have the friendship of a young boy whom my wife and I grew to love very closely . . . As he lived with us, as he grew to be one of the boys in the community, one of the most popular boys in school, one of the smartest, he was a great honor to himself and to the people of Roseau River. . . ."*

The attempt was drowned out by lustful cries of the children after the gifts fended off with curses and shouts by the older boys who were guarding the hoard. The boxes were opened and the presents thrown in the seething mob: dolls, skates, books, trucks pelted through the air in a steady rain.

The toy rifles caused a sensation. "Gimme, gimme! " "Me! Me! Me! " "I want one! I want one! " The teachers heaved them out, box after box, while Mary Jane smiled.

The children panted with exhaustion. They staggered, arms laden, back to their parents. Everyone suddenly and quietly disappeared. They melted back out through the walls. It was very quiet outside in the dark and very cold.

A letter of thanks to all the people who helped the "drive" appeared in the Saturday paper in Winnipeg. It was signed by the David Seenie Canvassers.

> *"The high glee and complete joy on the faces of the children, when the toys were given out last Monday was enough to gladden any heart."*

The David Seenie Canvassers would be shocked if they were told that David's people were unhappy with their memorial. They had to wait three and a half hours. The toys were second-hand and battered. Most were not wrapped. None of the children got what they wanted or anything that was appropriate for them. The little ones got nothing. The people had money. They could buy clothes and presents for their children. David's people had been bought and they knew it.

David had told the Cooneys what he wanted. He wanted an education for his younger brother. But no one listened. No one tried to locate his younger brother or, instead, provide a scholarship or assistance for some other young boy from the Roseau Reserve.

I doubt that David's friends in Winnipeg would consider themselves prejudiced. Yet they never got past the initial fact that David was an Indian. "He was very proud of being an Indian once he found out he was an Indian." David probably had his Indianness pointed out to him in subtle ways a dozen times a day. It was always his "differentness" that was noticed —his inability to speak English, his poverty. People seemed surprised to discover he was normally intelligent and popular with children. David was a victim of reverse racism. The white people had to emphasize repeatedly their love for him because they were afraid of showing dislike or contempt. Skills of an average twelve-year-old were considered especially wonderful because David was Indian.

His Indianness was always noticed and commented on, but the qualities he was praised for were those of white middle class culture—popularity, success at school, winning. By praising David his friends could praise themselves. It was as if they were building their memorial—a wall of cardboard boxes full of toys which they could hide behind, peering out as they lobbed presents at the Indian children, while the children fired their toy rifles back.

Hear No Evil; See No Evil . . .

Raymond Hayden of the Roseau reserve beat his wife to death on Hallowe'en, 1966. The remarkable thing about Alice Hayden was that she didn't die immediately. The coroner later estimated that she could have lived 20 minutes; actually, she lived for 36 hours. During that time, several people on the reserve, including her own brother, knew she was desperately ill. No one did anything to help her.

The reserve has, of course, no doctor. The nearest one is five miles away in Dominion City. There is no nurse and the rudimentary first aid kit is locked up in the band hall. There was, at that time, no police officer on the reserve. In fact, the chief himself had just been beaten up and run off, and was recuperating at some distance from a broken leg and lesser injuries. The band had put forward the name of a potential police officer but the Indian agent had objected because he had a criminal record, so the matter was stalled.

Raymond and his wife had enjoyed a mobile party Saturday afternoon. With Alex Tait and his wife, they had driven (in Alex's car) into Emerson. Hayden bought some groceries and two bottles of wine. The four of them drank the two bottles in the car driving back to the reserve. They picked up Rosie French and drove north into Morris where Hayden bought some more wine. All told, seven bottles of wine were consumed by the five of them in a few hours. About 5:30 p.m., Tait had let Raymond and his wife off in front of Lena Boubard's home on the reserve. The Haydens were living in a shack behind her house across a little gully. The shack had no furniture, and it was heated only by a wood stove. Raymond and Alice had lunch at Lena's, while they got into a vicious fight. They left and headed for their own little shack, their small daughter in tow. In a few minutes, they returned.

Lena:

"I locked the door and when they came to the door I didn't open it. They were knocking and asking for matches. They wanted to make some fire."

"You didn't give them any, did you?"

"No. A little while after I went outside. Then I looked at their house. I seen Raymond fighting with Alice. I was standing and watching Raymond hitting and kicking and jumping on top of Alice. He was hitting with a big stick. I seen him twice. I went inside right away. After a while again I came out. There was nobody around. I didn't hear any noise. I went inside."

No one else saw Raymond or Alice until Sunday afternoon:

Harriet Hayden:

"*I was driving around. I was riding. He was waiting on the road. He waved for me to stop. He asked me to take him to town. In Dominion City, he wanted to see a doctor. There's only one doctor, Dr. Artes. He told me he had to go to see a doctor about his wife. Because she might have a broken back, she couldn't make it to a doctor's. He told me not to tell anyone. He seemed kind of worried.*"

Q. "*When he came out of the doctor's, did he bring anything with him?*"

A. "*I thought he had a little pink box.*"

Q. "*Did you see him the next day?*"

A. "*In the morning. He came in the house. He said his wife died. I didn't hear the rest. I went in the other room.*"

James Smith: (Alice's brother)

"*I happened to pass by. I went inside and asked the little girl for a sandwich. It was in the cupboard so I took it and ate it up.*"

Q. "*Did you see Alice Hayden?*"

A. "*She was laying down, sleeping.*"

Q. "*Was she covered or uncovered?*"

A. "*She was covered.*"

Q. "*By what?*"

A. "*A blanket.*"

.Q. "*How high was the blanket on her?*"

A. "*Over her head.*"

Q. "*Did you talk to her at all?*"

A. "*She talked to me. She asked where Raymond was. I said I didn't know. I just ate the sandwich and I left.*"

Three people had, in the course of two days, good reason to believe that Alice Hayden was in trouble. They all walked away. The next time anyone reported seeing Raymond was a day later.

Lena:

"*I saw him Monday morning. 7:30 a.m. He asked me if he could leave the little girl inside the house. I said 'Why?' He didn't tell me. He said 'Alice, something wrong with her. I've got to get a car.' Then he went out.*"

Clarence Henry:

"He came, asked to phone for an ambulance. He said 'Phone for an ambulance.' I asked him why and he said 'My wife is . . . I can't wake up my wife. She's cold and stiff.' I called the doctor first. I called the R.C.M.P.' He says, 'Call an ambulance and call the R.C.M.P.' He says, 'I'll go back and get my kiddies and bring them to the neighbours.' That's the last I seen of him."

Dorothy Hayden:

"He sat down and I offered him some breakfast. He didn't talk but he seemed troubled. He didn't eat. He just sat down for a while and then he got up and walked around a little ways. He said he was troubled and didn't know what to do. I tried to ask him what it was. I asked him, did he want somebody to take him to the hospital or take him to town? I asked him in my own language. Sometimes he used to come to our place for that before, in other years. He wanted to be taken to town for groceries, you know. He used to come to our place to get a ride in.

"He said he wanted to get a phone and we told him we had no phone . . . we told him to go to Bouchard's and he said that he had called an ambulance and he asked us if we had seen the ambulance pass. I told him that I didn't.

"He said he didn't know about . . . about what they were doing . . . he didn't know what they would be doing to him in the future like he said that . . . that he might do away with himself or go to prison for life.

"He said that his wife was to be picked up then, and he had called the ambulance and that his wife was home lying . . . he tried to get her up, tried to lift her arm but it was stiff and cold he said, 'At last I've done it, I was so mean to her.' He said in our own language he had done away with his wife at last.

"I told him that he always kept so far from me, like, you know, that he feels much closer to me than he was. I could easily have given him advice on what bothered him, I did before, because he used to come to my place before. I used to tell him to be . . . I used to tell him how to go around with his wife. How to treat her. I tried to be nice to him."

Raymond:

"We were drinking Saturday and we bought some wine. That is all we drank, just some wine. Then I guess we went home. I don't remember doing that to her. I just don't remember anything. I got up around 2 a.m. and lit a match. I seen her laying there covered up. I was looking around for the groceries I bought and I couldn't find them. It was Alex Tait that gave us a ride home so I went to his place to see if the groceries were over there. He said we took off with the groceries but he didn't know where.

"Then I left and went to Rosie's to see if the groceries were there but they weren't in there. Then I went back again to the little house. When I woke her up she told me I had left the groceries at Lena's. I went to Lena's and asked for the groceries. She had them. Then I went back to the little house with the groceries and me and my little girl ate.

"I lit some kind of a candle. I seen there was blood on the pillow case. I thought it was just a nosebleed or something. The light wasn't very bright. After we ate we went to sleep. I got up in the morning and that is when I saw how she looked.

"I asked her what happened and she told me I fought her but I don't remember fighting her. I asked her if she wanted to go to the hospital and she didn't say anything at first. I went out and tried to hire a car. I couldn't find nobody. Everybody said they were low on gas. I walked to Dominion City and went and got some aspirins and tape. Then I came back and tried to fix her up. I washed her face and everything. She was all right. She was standing up and moving around. That evening I tried to hire a car again. I was trying to hire Edwin Klippenstein. I walked around until 12 o'clock trying to find someone to take us to the hospital.

"I got tired of walking around. I stayed up most of the night making fire. I was trying to tend her. When she needed water I used to give her. Then I asked her if she could hold out until morning until I could get a car and she said she could. I finally went to sleep with her. I slept beside her to keep her warm. When I got up in the morning I tried to talk to her but she wouldn't answer. I started to listen to her to see if she was still breathing. I tried to shake her. She just

made a noise. I was still shaking her. Then I ran out right away. I went to Clarence's right away and I told him. Then I went back and could hardly believe it. Sometimes I didn't know where I was going. That is all. I just went back to that little shack."

Q. *"What injuries did you see on your wife?"*

A. *"I seen she had a cut over her right eye. I tried to look at the back of her head but I couldn't."*

Q. *"What was wrong with the back of her head?"*

A. *"I put a sweater on her and a little while after I looked and it was wet on her sweater"*

Q. *"What time was it when you asked her if she wanted to go to the hospital?"*

A. *"Sunday. About 10 o'clock."*

Q. *"Was she still in bed?"*

A. *"Yes."*

Q. *"What did you do then?"*

A. *"I borrowed an axe to cut some wood."*

Q. *"Did you try to hire a car at this time?"*

A. *"After dinner I asked her if she wanted to go and she said 'Yeah' and then I looked for a car. I asked Alex Tait."*

Q. *"What did he say?"*

A. *"He said he was low on gas and besides he didn't want to go no place."*

Q. *"Did you tell him Alice was hurt?"*

A. *"Yeah"*

Q. *"He still wouldn't take you?"*

A. *"No, he figured she wasn't hurt bad."*

Q. *"Did you know she was hurt bad?"*

A. *"Yeah. She told me after dinner. She told me she had sore hips."*

Q. *"Did she say anything about her face?"*

A. *"No."*

Q. *"Who else did you ask for a car?"*

A. *"I asked one of them Seenie boys, Richard Seenie. I asked him if he had enough gas to go any place and he said no."*

"Did you tell him why you wanted a car?"

A. *"No."*

Q. *"Did you ask anyone else?"*

A. *"I tried to ask James Martin but he was drunk."*

Q. *"You said you asked Edwin Klippenstein. Did you?"*

A. *"I didn't actually ask him. I went there and he was having a service so I figured I would ask him later. I was going to go there but he was driving off. I tried to wave but I guess he didn't see me."*

Q. *"Did you walk to Dominion City?"*

A. *"Yes."*

Q. *,"Where did you go?"*

A. *"To the doctor. I told him my wife had a sore head and I asked for some pain killers and some tape. I seen one of my cousins and she gave me a ride back."*

Q. *"Did you tell her what had happened to Alice?"*

A. *"No."*

Q. *"When you came back from Dominion City, did you go right back to your wife?"*

A. *"Yeah. She was sitting up when I got there. She asked me where I went and I told her. I told her I couldn't get no car. I gave her one pill . I made fire and tried to keep the house warm so she wouldn't get cold. She didn't say nothing at all until towards evening. She told me to wash her up and go hire a car. I walked around until 12 trying to hire a car but there were no cars passing by to stop."*

Q. *"Did you try to telephone anybody?"*

A. *"No. Clarence and them were in bed already. I hardly remember anything from there because I didn't know how I felt. The doctor told me I was sick in the head. Everyone on the reserve knows I go that way—out of my head sometimes. I don't know how to control myself. I shake all over. My wife knew that too. Lots of them took me into the hospital because of that but I just used to get needles. I was supposed to stay in Morris but I didn't want to."*

Alice Hayden, age 22, had lodged a complaint with the R.C.M.P. in Emerson exactly a week prior to the night she was killed. A warrant was out for Raymond's arrest on a charge of assault. Alice had been beaten up regularly.

Raymond was 24 when he was convicted of manslaughter. He received a lecture from the judge and five years in jail.

It's a strange pantomime, the murder of Alice Hayden. People drift in and out as she bleeds to death; her husband tries to treat her with headache pills or rushes aimlessly around the reserve trying vainly to find a car. The Roseau people seem content to ignore what was happening, asking no questions. Perhaps there are reasons for this. Alice Hayden's death was the third murder on the reserve in a matter of weeks. People were frightened, frightened not only of being attacked themselves but also of the lengthy police investigations.

The death rate on the Roseau reserve has been rising. The number of people dying is still small—four, six, eight a year—but it is steadily increasing. Before World War Two, the Indians boasted they had never had a murder on the reserve. Now, there is one or more every year. Alice Hayden had been used to being beaten up, and the Indians were used to seeing her beaten up. Perhaps no one thought she would die this time since her suffering was not unusual enough to be remarked. "He's always fighting his wife," Lena Boubard told the court.

Some of the motives for ignoring Raymond Hayden were probably more selfish than merely avoiding trouble. Very few people on the reserve have cars, and most of these are operated as taxis. People who ride in them are expected to pay. Raymond Hayden had no money—it had all been spent on wine and groceries. Alex Tait claimed at the trial that Hayden had cheated him. He had not paid for his joy ride on Saturday and had stolen wine. Tait felt no obligation to help Hayden out of a spot. Probably, one of the reasons Hayden was shunned by most of the reserve population was that he had a reputation for being psychotic, untrustworthy. The fact that he and Alice were living off in the bush in a cold, wretched shack indicates that their status in the community was low. Hayden had been in trouble on the reserve most of his life and had caused trouble for others.

Maybe Hayden lied, and maybe all his stories about looking for rides and being turned down were false. If Harriet's story is true, he did find a ride on Sunday, but he did not ask to have Alice taken to the hospital. He did not tell the doctor that his wife was seriously hurt.

If he had told the truth, he knew someone would call the police. There was a warrant out for his arrest, and he would have gone to jail. Raymond Hayden didn't try very hard to get help for his wife. As soon as she arrived in hospital, the cause of her injuries would have been discovered and Hayden arrested. Hayden gambled that she would get better, as she always had in the past.

Alice Hayden was killed by fear, apathy and moral paralysis. No one would help Raymond Hayden; no one would harm him either. No one would call the police. Life on the Roseau Reserve produces this kind of withdrawal.

"Please sir, may I have some more? "

About 3 a.m. one May morning, a medium-sized Indian boy disappeared through a back window into a service station garage. Two more, looking once over their shoulders, went in after him. Two stood guard in the darkness. Those inside scurried around like mice while the boys watching urged them to hurry up. They located the flashlights. They saw the soft-drink machine next to the counter. A couple of minutes later they started handing the stuff out the window—four flashlights, twenty flashlight batteries, five cartons of soft drinks and twelve dozen plastic ball point pens—and crawled out after it. The haul was worth $15. Three of them started off walking home with the loot. But the coast was still clear so the other two—two brothers—went across the street. They broke into a grocery store and took eight packages of cigarettes and three packages of cookies. They met up with the other three about half-way home to the reserve. They ate the food, smoked the cigarettes and threw the flashlights, batteries and pens in the bush. The two eldest were 15; the youngest was 12. The youngest did most of the stealing.

This was not the first time Barnabe's Garage in Letellier had been broken into. From May to November, the garage is plundered an average of once a week. The other garage in town, the Co-op, is hit about the same number of times. Letellier is a two-garage town, two miles down a gravel road from the Roseau Reserve. Dominion City is five miles in the other direction from the reserve. It is also a two-grocery store town. The one that was broken into that night is the Red and White. It is the chief target because it has more desirable loot than any other building around. The other store, a little green one across the street, is never broken into because the owner and his wife live upstairs.

The owners of the store and the garage don't get upset any more. They almost expect when they unlock the door in the morning to find that the place has been pillaged. They call the police and tidy up. This recurring theft has been going on for years and it is, in fact, now in its second generation. The fathers of the present thieves were breaking into the stores when they were young boys. "You can always tell if it's been Indians," says the owner. "They mess the place up a lot but they don't take much—just little things like drinks, cigarettes, cookies and batteries. A lotta junk." The kids don't steal money, or anything which could be re-sold or, if they do, they discard it. Food is not taken in order to stock the family larder at home. Luxury items are taken, things every little boy craves. To an adult this is "junk" but to a young boy it is treasure. The thieves split the loot and have a feast in the middle of the night, their cigarettes making little points of light in the dark while they stuff down dozens of cookies and fistfuls of candy. Everything is consumed. Nothing is saved, and what cannot be eaten is thrown into the river or the bush. Utility is the logic: bicycles are to ride; if they are broken they are thrown away. Houses are to be entered, food is to be eaten, beer is drunk; knives are to cut things with. Everything is disposable.

A very elaborate game of Cops and Robbers is played in the area around Roseau Reserve, Dominion City and Letellier. Everyone plays, and everyone sticks to the rules. The whole community—white and Indian, kids, police, court, parents, businessmen, farmers—is united in playing this game which keeps them together. The Indian parents supply the children. Families of eight, ten and twelve children are common, although many are smaller. Because the children are so close in age, gangs are almost inevitable. A 12-year-old boy will be responsible for looking after his 11 and 10-year-old brothers so he takes them with him wherever he goes, morning, noon or night. It is common for six and seven-year-olds to be reported at the scene of a crime. Parents generally ignore their sons' misdemeanors. They will not accept stolen goods in the home and, if they find out their boy has been stealing, they will chastize him. They will express regret and mortification over the incident, but will not co-operate in any way with the police or the court. If they are informed by the police of their son's delinquency, they will frequently deny it. A mother will warn her boy that the police car is approaching the house and he will take off into the bush. When confronted with this, she will deny her son was in the house. The parents who do express regret and shame make little or no effort to punish or control the child. He is allowed to run as free as ever, and the mothers and fathers appear to be completely helpless, throwing up their hands and saying, "I just don't know what to do." They do nothing, and by their neutrality, the parents sanction the children's acts.

The store which the boys raid at night is the store where their parents shop the next morning. The kids know where everything is on the shelves because they've been in so often. Every Indian family has a big bill at the store. If they run short of money before the next cheque from the government or the next payday on sugar beets, they still have to eat, so the storekeeper gives them credit. When the money comes, it usually goes to pay off groceries purchased a month before. The Indians are always in debt. The credit depends on the goodwill of the storekeeper. The Indian parents are afraid that their credit will be cut off if they admit responsibility for their son's theft the night before. If they can pretend that the boy is completely out of control, the storekeeper might feel sorry for them and they will continue to get credit. Unless the parents admit responsibility, there is no hope of stopping the break-ins.

The situation is even more complex. Because the family is in debt to the storekeeper and has, perhaps, even borrowed money at interest from him, they resent him. They hate being in debt and dislike the man who is responsible for it. They begin to believe that they are being robbed, that his prices are exorbitant. They come, very soon, to the conviction the man is a crook and shyster. By robbing him, the kids are only claiming what they think the storekeeper has gypped the family out of. They are evening the score, getting their money back. The same principle applies to the garages. The fathers buy gas there and may even purchase one of the old cars from the owner. If the car is rotten and falls apart after a week, the Indian has to have it repaired at the garage, and he blames the garage for selling him a bad car. To the parents, the garage man and storekeeper are criminal; the children are not.

Why do the store owners and garage managers take no precautions against theft? How is it that a garage owner can know that his building is being entered night after night through the same window and he does not lock it? Or put up wire grills? Or install lights? Or a burglar alarm? He doesn't want to antagonize his customers. The stores and garages of Letellier stay alive on Indian business. Letellier is the post office for Roseau Reserve. The post office is where the cheques come from Winnipeg. Much of the money, funnelled directly into the store or the beer parlor or the garage, never leaves town. There are about 400 people living on the Roseau Reserve. The population of Letellier is only about 250. That money, and there is a lot of it, is vital to the townspeople. The storekeeper does not take precautions or prosecute the children because he is afraid the parents will no longer cash and spend their cheques at his store but will drive the seven miles to Dominion City. Small Indian boys also have big Indian fathers, many of whom have criminal records. The storekeeper doesn't want his face pushed in or his store blown up. He offers a twenty-four hour service to the people of Roseau—credit during the day and free cookies at night. His losses are small. The damage estimates given to the police are seldom more than $15 or $20, and even then are exaggerated. The loot is offered as a kind of bonus to induce the Indians to come to his store. The loss can be made up from the parents by hiking the prices a little and over-charging a bit. Because it all goes on the tab anyway the parents hardly notice a few extra pennies missing here and there.

School Phobia

In the autumn of 1966, a twelve-year-old Roseau Indian girl wrote a letter to her brother in reform school:

"How's the world treating you these days? For us it is just fine. You know what? Alice and me broke into the school last Saturday night. Guess too much wine and beer, eh? But Steve and Fred were chicken out to break in. We mess everything and tipped all the desks even the teacher's desk. But they don't know who did it. Well, brother, guess I

have to close here cause there isn't any news around this place. So good bye for now."

All incoming mail is read and censored before it is given to the boys. Her brother never received this letter.

Her brother was then fifteen. When he was his sister's age, twelve, he too had broken into the school and messed it up. That was one reason why he was in reform school. And his older brother had done it before him. No, breaking into the reserve school is not news. It is, as a matter of fact, almost a monthly occurrence and has been for about seven years. The school—it is the Roman Catholic school (there is also a Protestant school on the reserve which has never been touched)—has been wrecked and looted countless times. Sometimes the desks are broken and the windows smashed. Other times, school supplies are taken and strewn about the yard. The damage is always done by children from the reserve who attend the school. They succeed in bringing classes to a halt and getting a vacation which lasts from one day to a couple of weeks.

"I hate school, I hate the teacher," is sometimes the explanation. It is, at any rate, mass retaliatory school phobia which has by now become a habitual pattern, a ritual, on the reserve. School exists to be smashed. As a result, most of the children on the reserve are still in grade five or six when they drop out at sixteen. Destruction and not theft is the motive behind the break-ins.

The school is an ugly, two-room wooden building covered with red artificial-brick asphalt siding. One half used to be living quarters for the teacher but has now been made into a kindergarten. In addition to the regular expense of hiring a teacher, supplying textbooks and equipment, heating and hiring a janitor, it costs Indian Affairs about $2,000 a year to make repairs and replace supplies. An annex building with another classroom is located about thirty feet away.

In 1965, the school was virtually demolished by three boys under fourteen. They threw rocks through every window, tipped over or broke all the desks and threw all the equipment, papers and books around the room. It looked as if a hurricane had hit it. "I don't like school," said one of the boys. It cost Indian Affairs $1,500 to fix it up. They replaced all the windows but took the precaution of covering them with plywood. The children now learned by electric light in a school where it was always night. The theory was that the plywood would come off when the children stopped wrecking the school. The plywood came off:

> *"Yesterday, I was playing with my brother and some other kids. We were playing by the school. We decided to go into the school. Arnold pulled the plyboard from the window and broke the window. Then Arnold climbed in and opened the back door and we all went in. We broke windows, knocked the desks over, scattered the paper and books, spilt the water tank. I carried a chair outside. Arnold carried out a mirror.*
>
> *"Then we went over to the other school (the annex). Arnold pulled the plyboard off again and climbed in and opened the back door so we could all enter.*
>
> *"We broke some windows, knocked over some desks, emptied the cupboards and threw the books and papers all over the floor. We broke some lights and scattered the paper cups all over."*

The damage was another $1,200. The girl who gave the above report was eleven. She was the eldest. With her were younger sisters and brothers and a couple of their friends. Two were ten years old; two were age eight and two were seven years old.

Damage is at this point being committed often by children who are too young to be sentenced by the court. They are not considered capable of understanding what the court process means. The alternatives are to leave them alone or have them apprehended by the Children's Aid. Both are unpleasant. To the children, it's a lark. One of the seven-year-olds involved in ripping off the plywood thought it was the most exciting thing that had ever happened to him. Says the court worker who talked to him:

> *"He was pressed into the service of this group of children and his involvement with them is regarded with some delight and humor. He is pleased to be allowed to*

associate with a group of older boys. There is little personal attention in the home and he may even be subjected to abuse by older persons during drinking bouts in his home."

This boy is an illegitimate child—one of several born to a woman on the reserve. His father is unknown.

The break-ins and damage probably have very little to do with the religious denomination of the school and even little connection with school itself. The Protestant school probably is untouched because it is less isolated. The teacher lives across the road, the band hall is next to it and it is on the main intersection in full view of ten houses. The Catholic school is down a lonely road with no houses nearby. The Catholic school also used to have a teacher who was disliked by the Indians. She would not associate with them and spied and tattled to the police.

> *"On Saturday night at about 10 p.m. we broke into the RC school on the reserve. J.S. broke a window on the north side and we all went in that way. We left by the back door. We scattered everything all over the place. They broke into the school because they didn't get anything for Christmas. I got some candy, peanuts and an orange. I attend school there but they don't. Also, they broke in as they didn't like the teacher because she wouldn't permit them to do as they liked. B.T. watched to see that no one was coming.*
>
> *"Then we came home and went to bed. It was about 11 p.m. I guess. I didn't tell this at first because I don't want to go to reform school. I am afraid of J.T. and P.B."*

Wrecking the school after Christmas gave the children an extra week of holidays.

Paranoia

One day late in February, 1967, two students from the University of Manitoba drove on to the reserve. The Community Development office was locked, so they headed for the only other institution they could see—the school. They told the teachers they were studying sociology and were interested in the Indian way of life. Could they watch the teachers instruct the classes and talk to them about their problems? One of the boys carried a camera and took pictures.

The boys were pleasant and interested. The teachers talked freely. Besides, the teachers were frustrated at having to teach, by artificial light, a lot of students who didn't come to class very frequently. A week later, the student newspaper, *The Manitoban* carried a big story about appalling educational conditions on the Roseau reserve. The story omitted no embarrassing details:

> "... *The reserve schools consist of three thirty-five year old wooden structures with an overhead heating system that keeps the upper air stifling hot and dry and makes the floor cold and drafty.*
>
> *"The windows are covered with huge sheets of plywood. 'Otherwise,' said the only male teacher, 'the school would be broken into almost every night.' Cracked lighting fixtures and dented heating pipes showed what he meant. One school has no latrine. When students must 'go to the wash room' they make use of a single enamel pot located in the entrance hall.*
>
> *"Three white women and a Negro man teach the eighty-five Indian children. One teacher boasted she uses Eaton's catalogues to show the children what are the 'better things in life'.*
>
> *"Two schools are Roman Catholic, the other is United. Such slogans as 'Work and prayer equal success' and 'God bless our reserve' are carved into the walls. What do these slogans mean to the students? 'Nothing,' according to the Negro teacher-principal, 'They were put there by the nun teachers ten years ago and it's difficult to scrape them off the walls.'*
>
> *"The young Indian children seemed bright, healthy and eager to learn. They were asked what they wanted to be when they grow up—doctors, pilots, nurses, engineers, headed the list. 'We give them something to be enthusiastic about at school,' said one teacher, 'but when they go home they see the real condition of things and lose their spirit.' 'The biggest problem is at home,' said another. 'There is no real motivation to keep the students' aspirations high.'"*

The story was well illustrated with photographs—boarded-up windows, children at their desks, a large photo of the white enamel pot in the hallway. The students neglected to mention that there is an alternative "washroom"—two outhouses, 20 yards behind the school. The children have difficulty running the 20 yards and peeling off their clothes in time, especially when it's 30 below. Indian children are so poorly clothed that in wintertime they must wear several layers of pants and shirts to keep warm. Unable to struggle through all this, the child wets his pants. His clothes freeze stiff as he struggles back to the school.

Officials, both in Indian Affairs and on the reserve, reacted adversely to the article, and their concern was increased by the article's report of actions to be taken:

> "The parents are not anxious to see conditions change. In a recent election for chief, three candidates were nominated. According to one resident, the best-educated, most progressive candidate was rejected by the Indian electors. A conservative chief with no significant platform was elected. 'He has close ties with most of the Indians so he was elected.'

> "A group of dedicated students are anxious to bridge the gap. Sponsored by private organizations across the country, these students are going into communities to live and work with the Indians. One of the lucid members of this group is John Stringham, in Law at the University of Manitoba. 'What we're trying to do is help the Indian help himself. By promoting his understanding of our society he can more successfully cope with problems within our society.'

> " 'We don't want to do this ostentatiously,' said Mr. Stringham. 'We simply want to become one of the members of the community. We have no specific aims or goals. Just by being in contact with the Indians in their homes, on their jobs, they will come to know us better and we can come to know them better.' "

I arrived on the reserve unannounced, uninvited, on impulse, about a week after the students' story appeared. I knew nothing about it. It had created no stir in Winnipeg whatsoever, for neither of the daily papers had picked it up. As I walked into the CDO's office, he turned pale. One of the teachers was there and she seemed worried. It was 11 a.m. When I asked her, by way of making conversation, why she wasn't in school and whether it was a holiday, she replied: "Well, I might as well be here for all the good I'm doing over there." I was told about The Article. You'd think it had been a picture spread in *Life*. Both fumed and raved about the "bad publicity" although they could not point out any serious inaccuracies in the story. It was, in fact, quite truthful. The chief, I was told, was in a rage. He wasn't too sure whether I should be allowed to come onto the reserve. The Roseau Indians got too much bad publicity, he had said. He was suspicious of reporters. I was going to have to ask the chief and council for permission to visit the reserve.

I waited for the chief for an hour. Finally, I went out to the outhouse next to the front door of the band hall. While I was inside, I heard a couple of cars drive up to the hall, and men got out, talking and laughing, passing within five feet of the outhouse. I was too embarrassed to emerge, until they disappeared inside. I poked my head out and scurried back to the CDO's office, and there was the chief. He was seated on the chesterfield playing solitaire as if his life depended on it. He looked at me askance out of the corner of one eye, and said nothing. I told him who I was and why I was there. He jumped and fidgeted, pacing around the room, slapping the cards down, glancing at me. When I remarked that I hadn't met him before because he hadn't been chief very long, he immediately stated that he had been chief before, twelve years ago (and a very good chief too, I think he added under his breath) and had been on the council since elections first came in.

"I can't talk to you without consulting my council," he said, and bolted for the door. He headed over to the band hall to consult with the council. (He had, of course, been told some time ago that I was waiting for him in the office. He took so long to arrive because he had to round up the council and hide them in the band hall. Little did they know that I was hiding in the outhouse.)

I waited for him and he was back in about five minutes, about three or four councillors peering in the door behind him looking me over. A couple of them I had, luckily, met on my earlier trips. We grinned and nodded. "Come back tomorrow," said the chief. "We're having a meeting tomorrow. You can tell us what you want and we'll let you know our decision."

"Do I have your permission to talk to any people on the reserve today? " I asked.

"No, you *can't* talk to any people here today," said the chief, and stomped out the door.

I had them over a barrel, of course. The chief was more upset about the article's reflections on his own ability than he was about the school. He had complained bitterly that nobody ever came and talked to the Indians before they wrote their stories.

I said the next day, when the council was gathered in judgment, that I was there to talk to the Indians. I would listen to anything they had to tell me. The chief and council welcomed me with big smiles. They were very friendly and have been ever since. There was never much doubt I would be accepted on the reserve and I had the feeling they were only too glad to have interested visitors. They had been angered and frightened by the condescending student, Mr. Stringham, and his group of "dedicated" followers who had decided they were going to become "members of the community" at Roseau without the slightest acquaintance with the place or the people. The chief had been bitterly insulted by the unjustified criticism of his ability (he proved himself an extraordinarily able and progressive chief) and the council was embarrassed that their school and their people should be criticized.

I had much less success with the teachers. Two spoke to me freely and two ignored me. When I asked the Negro teacher at the red school if I might talk to him for a few minutes, he fled. My difficulty might have been enhanced by the fact that on the day I arrived at the red school, the children were being dismissed at 9:20 a.m. because the oil stove, the one near the door, was emitting noxious fumes which made the air unbreathable and the school a fire trap. Maybe some kid had plugged the chimney. But another teacher on the reserve had many comments on what was going on in the school:

"The children are tired. They're tired and they're sick. They need to do work at home, but they can't get any help at home. Their parents are illiterate. The parents want them

to learn and the children want to too. These people are being run by a machine. We are teaching them to be little machines and then we say 'Why are you machines?' Each individual is scared by an overpowering force. Nobody can agree how to overcome it.

"Boarded up windows don't make any difference if the educational system is good. The trouble doesn't lie with the school facilities—you can teach anywhere if what you're teaching is exciting to the students. The trouble is with the system. The science textbook says that television is a recent and rudimentary invention—good grief, these kids have watched television all their lives; they get most of their learning from it!

"I'm so sick of the 'Nina, the Pinta and the Santa Maria.' What about the space program? Aren't they supposed to know about it? Some of my students are women with babies. The only use for Columbus is to help them understand Indian jokes.

"Why can't we be permitted to cut the crap in the educational system and adapt the program to the children? They need good arithmetic; they need to learn how to gather information on their own. What kid is interested in reading about Uncle Funny Bunny at twelve? I tell them I am working for them and they can make their own rules.

"When I first came they deliberately gave wrong answers. They knew the answer was wrong. I could say anything—the blackboard is white—and they would not correct me. Now they will say 'You're wrong.' If they are slapped down, they are reticent. We discovered a mistake in a textbook. It was terrific—gave the kids a real lift.

"The kids couldn't cram in all the stuff that's in these books. They need to know how to find things out—they're more interested in a little crawly, fuzzy worm than in all these books. It's so easy to give money. These people have had so much equipment and so little knowledge about how to use it.

"They can't learn if they're scared. By the time you've gained their confidence, you're gone."

The teachers are as dissatisfied with the Roseau schools as

are the students. But the teachers do not have the courage to stay home or quit. The nondescript little article in *The Manitoban*, by describing the obvious, by printing out loud what was said only in whispers, by describing the reserve as it looked to a visitor, performed a valuable service for the people. And by berating the paper and the students, the people were, for the first time, able to talk about educational problems. The rocks of the children became verbal stones thrown at the paper. By talking about the story the people were, in a peculiar round-about way, able to talk about the school. The air was cleared and pent-up anger was expressed. By castigating the story everyone was able to castigate the school. "Bad publicity" was the cry; nobody defended the school, they simply regretted the fact that all its evils had to be advertised to the world. By deploring the publicity, they recognized the evils. The chief was, in addition, motivated to improve his public image and was determined to be as progressive as he could be to prove the students wrong. The council stuck together to do something about the school and to keep dedicated students away. The students, in their two or three hours on the reserve, saw and expressed something which desperately needed expressing. They made vocal the abhorrence that the children expressed inarticulately and unconsciously. Their little story was helpful and positive because it touched a real concern in an utterly truthful way. The results would be shown a few months later.

Out of Control

Pat Dunphy was sent as a community development officer to Roseau reserve and Dominion City three months after the Indian children had been expelled from the town school. He found the townspeople highly organized, bitter and apathetic. The Indians were also apathetic but totally disorganized except for bitter clan feuds. In September, 1966, he had this to say:

"There is a definite lack of communication among people on the reserve especially on matters affecting the band as a whole. At the moment there is very little evidence of power structure although I have found that there are sub-

power structures that appear to be at odds with each other. The official power—chief and council—while it exists on paper, in actual fact is ineffective. The band council does not meet as a council. The only outside agency in the reserve is the school system . . .

"Because of the religious connotations of the naming of the two schools there has been a certain lack of communication among teachers on the reserve in the past. This has also led to a split among the people which is a pity because none of the people, or very few, on the reserve practice religion of any sort. Protestant and Catholic are just names, yet this division of the churches has led to a division of the reserve itself.

"Attendance at the schools has been very poor over the last three years. . . The teachers asked me to help them form a parent-teachers association on the reserve. We held two meetings, one of which was attended by a half dozen parents. Since then, no parents have been to meetings. . .

"Several individuals have expressed concern about the violence and vandalism on the reserve. Most list lack of recreation as a cause. There is nothing for the adults or youngsters to do. Some have stated they used to enjoy the dances and card parties they used to hold ten years and more ago. When I asked why they were discontinued I was told drunkenness was the main cause."

Pat Dunphy

Eleven different agencies serve the people of Roseau—Indian Affairs, public health, provincial welfare, probational service, police, Children's Aid, two ministers . . . It works out to about one government employee for every family in this multi-problem community. Never a day goes by that one or two of these helpers doesn't arrive on the reserve. The Roseau people are hard pressed to keep a sharp eye out for cars and to decide whether they are going to run and hide, co-operate, pretend to be drunk, speak no English that day or refuse to answer all questions. Agency people are intensely disliked—the Indian agent never gives enough relief; Children's Aid and the probation service steal the children; the police send people to jail. A large percentage of the reserve's young men are always away in jail, either on 30-day drinking charges or on longer sentences for assault, rape and similar offences. If one adds together the total number of children, teenagers and men in institutions or foster homes, plus people away in hospital, plus those off seeking seasonal employment, the actual number of people living on the reserve falls to about 350 or less.

Charlie arrived in the agency office in Selkirk, Manitoba one morning in October, pleading for food. Family Allowance had been cut off, he said, and they had nothing to eat. He had been fired from his job (paying $16.50 a day) and didn't get paid from his new job for a week. "My kids have nothing to wear," he told the agent with an expression of extreme distress. A clothing order for $100 had been issued to him a month before but he had ten children. The agent gave Charlie $50 for groceries and $40 for clothes. The R.C.M.P. called two days later. Charlie had deserted his wife and run off with Mabel T. Mabel's husband had taken his nine children and six of Charlie's and had abandoned them in the main street of Letellier. The children had found their way to a relative's home. Indian Affairs of course provided for the children until their parents wandered back home a week or so later, sobered up and contrite.

Welfare is often issued to avoid a scene. (Threats of physical violence against agency personnel—probation officers, vocational counsellors—are common but seldom carried out, although rumor says the Indian Affairs superintendent for the Clandeboye area Agency was once chased off the reserve.) Many of the reserve's registered population of 400-odd children and teenagers are not there because they have been taken into custody by various agencies. About 40 children are away in residential school; another 40 have been placed in foster homes by the Children's Aid because of parental neglect. A lot of the older boys are in reform school, the younger ones in foster homes under probation. Although the people resist and fail to co-operate with the agencies by pretending to be deaf, dumb, blind and retarded, they do make maximum use of the institutional facilities available, especially hospitals and jail. The money spent by the government to keep the Roseau people in these institutions compensates for the lack of money coming into the reserve. Unhappily, people like Alice Hayden are murdered before others are institutionalized.

Jimmie S. has a habit of beating up his wife. They all got drunk on Treaty Day, and Jimmie's wife and her girl friend thought they would give Jimmie a taste of his own medicine. They beat him to a pulp with sticks and broken bottles until he lay still on the floor. Jimmie's wife was stricken with remorse when she saw his lifeless body. She ran and told a neighbour she had killed her husband. Stan Nelson, band constable, was called in and he called the R.C.M.P. By the time the police arrived, Jimmie had disappeared. When the women saw the corpse had left, their rage returned. They held three R.C.M.P. detachments at bay with broken beer bottles until one of the policemen threw a tub of water over them. After his wife had been taken away, Jimmie staggered, bruised and bloody, out of the bush. "Jeez," he said. "Those women! I had to play dead."

Roseau looks like a den of pirates. Many men are badly scarred as a result of these fights. It is common to see men with cuts and bandages, women with black eyes and bruises walking on the roads. One man has a scar making an "X" mark from one side of his face to the other. It was inflicted with a broken bottle by his brother. Another man has a scar looping across his nose and over one cheek. Other men are lame. Many people showing the effects of TB and other illnesses are thin, stooped, wrinkled and walk with the shuffle of an invalid. The Roseau people are extraordinarily good natured, quipping and laughing, and even their fights and beatings seem almost horseplay which gets out of control. Even the most upright and respectable members of the Roseau community have criminal records.

Roseau is a state of continual blood feud. The band is divided into warring factions each of which is violently hostile to the other. The fights usually take place between members of rival families or clans. The police, by interfering, contribute indirectly to the warfare. When a man is arrested and imprisoned, his family is left unprotected and vulnerable to the retaliation of his enemy. His wife or relations will be attacked and he, when released, is forced to take revenge again. This escalation is prevented only by incarcerating large numbers of the offenders at the same time, which is what the police try to do. If a man moves his family away from the reserve for a time, revenge will be taken against his belongings, and his house will have its windows broken; it will be entered, and the interior destroyed. A disliked family will be forced off the reserve by this kind of continual rock-throwing and vandalism.

The only peculiar thing about this Corsican mentality is that the fights, break-ins and assaults take place in a state of drunken euphoria. Both attacker and victim are stupefyingly drunk. Since a large proportion of the reserve population is frequently drunk and wild parties are common, fights are very frequent, and most are never reported to the police. Only the worst—those which end in death or hospitalization—come to court. The police wait. According to the law of averages, a certain number of fights will produce a serious one and they will be informed. Roseau is in a state of anarchy, out of control. No one is in authority and even the chief knows he has no power over his people. Normal social controls have become paralyzed so that people scurry like rats to lock themselves in their houses at the first sign of trouble. The strong do as they please; the reserve has regressed to the rule of the bludgeon. The people live more primitively now than they did a hundred years ago.

DOMINION CITY

The Village

"What we need around here is a lot of poor farmers."

I had stopped to buy some gas from the principal garage in Dominion City. It still bears the name—L.O. Baskerville—of the former owner, who went bankrupt. It is now owned by Bill Shroeder, who is also president of the Dominion City Chamber of Commerce, and he was describing the economic plight of the town:

> *"We need farmers who are poor enough to settle for buying trade-in machinery. We garage men and the farm implement dealers get stuck with a whole lot full of used equipment because everybody's rich and wants new stuff. We can't sell this second-hand machinery. We lose money. The farmers always want the latest model. They can shop around,*

find the place that will give them the best deal. It's the big companies, the ones that have a big turnover and can unload the old stuff that give them a good trade-in. Dominion City can't compete. Rich farmers get good cars. They travel around a lot, and spend their money all over the place. A lot of them go to California in the winter—takes business away.

"Take Bill Kyle's new Chrysler, now. Bill Kyle bought his new Chrysler in Winnipeg because he couldn't get a good deal here. No dealer in Dominion City would be able to sell his old Chrysler. The Winnipeg dealer gave him a real good trade-in. Kyle's a local man. There's business, good business, going right out of the town. Not because we couldn't provide what he wanted but we couldn't get rid of his old car. Just useless around here."

Forty of Dominion City's 500 residents are widows, and the only new industry planned for the town is an old folks' home. Dominion City is not a city or even a town, but a village. It has only a handful of teenagers and no people in their twenties. Almost no one has come to live there since 1950, while dozens of families have left. The ugly yellow grain elevator of Dominion City can be seen about five miles out. It's the color of fresh unpainted lumber and, up close, the elevator is a ramshackle thing which looks as if it's continually in the process of being built. It has been in that state for years.

Dominion City is not on a main highway. The turn-off comes about 50 miles south of Winnipeg on Highway 75, the main road leading due south into the United States. Dominion City is seven miles east of Highway 75 along a gravel road. All in all, it is little more than an hour's drive from Winnipeg. Off Highway 75 is Letellier, the little village at the junction. A one-elevator town, it has only about 200 people who are all French Canadian and Roman Catholic. It has two garages, two stores, a hotel (beer parlor), a school and a church (Catholic). French is spoken.

The road now crosses over the CNR railway line which goes south to Minneapolis. Two miles past Letellier, a steep old narrow bridge crosses the Red River. The river banks are heavily treed. A house painted white and blue is on the right side of the road directly across the bridge and beside it is a quonset roof with tractors and other farm machinery under it. This is Stan Nelson's house, band constable, truant officer and head farmer on the Roseau River Indian Reserve. To the left, three narrow roads—so narrow they are almost paths, lead off the gravel road. Along these roads, in the bush, are the Indians' homes. Those near the main road are small, white-painted bungalows, and farther back, along the third road, the homes, painted CPR boxcar red, look like railway bunkhouses. One house, across the road from Stan Nelson's, has a picture window with curtains. It belongs to Don Nelson, Stan's 25-year-old brother.

Five miles of blank, flat prairie separate the reserve from Dominion City. Here, just past the reserve, the yellow grain elevator shoots up. Dominion City is a two-elevator village. A white one stands along the railway track beside the yellow.

Now I cross the CPR tracks, running north and south parallel to the CNR line, just before reaching turn-off into Dominion City. A green and white highway department sign— the kind that marks the location of every settlement in Manitoba—points the way left and north—'Dominion City'. I leave the washboardy gravel for the potholed, weaving mud road that connects Dominion City with the world. A battered weatherbeaten white board says 'Welcome to Dominion City' in hand-painted letters. The paint is peeling off and it sags at an angle. Another white sign says 'One Mile' but I am already on the outskirts and the main street isn't more than 500 yards ahead.

At the junction where the mud road leaves the gravel road, the new brick and glass split-level home of Garnet Kyle stands on a little knoll beside a tree-filled gully. Kyle is a farmer like his brother Bill and his father before him. He is vice-president of the Manitoba Progressive Conservative Party and a political force in the village. (Dominion City has gone Conservative federally since 1957, the Diefenbaker year, and votes Conservative provincially.) Bill Kyle, Garnet's brother (and the instigator of the Chrysler crisis for Bill Shroeder) is a die-hard Liberal. Bill, 15 years older than Garnet who is still in his thirties, farms five miles north of Dominion City.

The railway tracks run parallel to the road and over a black iron bridge which crosses the Roseau River. The Roseau is a small, pretty stream which runs east and west, flowing into the Red near Letellier. Dominion City is built on the banks of the Roseau. The tracks cut the town in two. To the west, towards Letellier and the reserve, is the main residential area of town—streets of neat, old, white-painted bungalows. On the east is the business section with a couple more streets of homes. The tumbledown, decaying CPR station, a wooden shelter with overhanging eaves, painted the same dirty red as the homes on the reserve, is the dividing line. The grain elevators are next to the station.

I have to find my way into Dominion City. In most prairie towns, the road into town is also the main street, but Dominion City isn't like that. The mud road into town runs into the river—at least it ends at a house on the river bank. As I drive in, several more mud roads lead off to the right, but none of them seems to be the main one. Dominion City is laid out exactly like the Roseau reserve. Three roads lead into the reserve from the gravel highway; similarly, three roads lead into the centre of Dominion City from this entrance road. Take your pick. All the streets are dead ends.

The main street is the mud track with the hotel on the corner. The hotel is two storeys with grey-white shingles. It too has a hand-painted sign 'Queen's Hotel' in stark, upright black sans-serif letters. The proprietor would probably be flabbergasted if anyone ever asked for a room. His business is the beer parlor, and that is a good business. The interior of the lobby and beer parlor has a shiny, institutional look, like a bus depot: beige tile and light plywood, walls and floor coated with varnish. On the opposite corner from the hotel is Pete's cafe. Pete sells groceries too, but doesn't deal with Indians. None go in there, and in fact, I have never seen anyone go in or out of Pete's, although I presume people do. His white stucco store-cafe is the second most impressive commercial building in Dominion City.

Bill Shroeder's garage is next to the hotel along Main St. Two old pumps stand out front of the rambling white wooden structure with a litter of farm machinery and used cars in back. It sags, like all the buildings in Dominion City, and the windows are hard to see through. Next door, in a tiny annex, C.C.

Baskerville runs the Wawanesa Insurance outlet. A small white sign in the window says that the lawyers come every Tuesday. This little office also houses the secretary of the school board, C.C. Baskerville. The school board meets here once a month. Next door is a weedy vacant lot and past that, M. Sokolyk's United Stores, a square, false-front building covered in grey artificial-brick asphalt. Beyond, Main Street dribbles away past the new Co-op store and a little brand new brick post-office flying the maple leaf flag. Across the street, the Legion Hall, Lutheran Church, arena and community hall are all covered with the same grey siding like big wooden battleships. The municipality of Franklin has a dilapidated stucco office opposite the Co-op store and near it, hidden behind scraggy evergreens, is the dark shed in which lives the one forlorn Manitoba Telephone System girl who operates the exchange.

Directly across from Shroeder's garage, is Solnes Cafe, a cobwebby Dickensian building with the name hand-painted on the panes of glass in the big front windows. Solnes Cafe, with its oak pews, long wooden counter with chocolate under the glass and enamel-top metal mortuary tables, is the only restaurant in Dominion City. It has a dusty, homey antique charm. The floor is bare boards; meals are what the owner has on hand, and Mrs. Solnes does the cooking, waiting on tables and provides the entertainment—gossip. People tromp in and out, and the building is so small that everyone is crowded together. In the course of a day in Solnes' one can meet the entire population of Dominion City and half the reserve.

The gaps between the big wooden buildings on Main Street are filled up by littler and even older wooden buildings, made hideous by coats of fresh paint—manure brown, chartreuse, peony pink. One of these old wooden shacks has been gutted by fire; another houses the plumber and another Bernice's Style Shop. All the buildings on Main Street look as if they are about to disappear into the mud of the road. The mud creeps up the walls, pulling and tugging the buildings out of shape so that they look as if they would suddenly collapse in a heap of dust.

The men of Dominion City can't get their hair cut in town—no barber. The nearest drugstore is 15 miles away in Emerson, and there is no bakery in town. Main Street is dark at night with no neon signs and there are only a few ludicrous

colored Christmas lights strung across the street in the winter.
The fanciest signs are the new plastic ones—big yellow Shells, a
black, red and white International Harvester. The bright shiny
plastic creaking on rusty metal poles only makes the buildings
behind look shabby and cheap. Dominion City is a frontier
town—two rows of low, wooden buildings facing each other
across an expanse of mud-plain, no frills, serviceable. Many of
the buildings still have bravado false fronts to hide their meagr-
eness. Dominion City provides the essentials—food, gas, beer.
No entertainment. No movie theatre. Clusters of little white
bungalows fan out from the village's core and beyond, to the
north and west, hundreds and hundreds of square miles of the
flat prairie farm land of the Red River Valley. To the east of
Dominion City, the farm country gives way suddenly to stoney,
scrubby marginal country and then to bush.

Dominion City is, or was, a church-going community.
Nearly every street has its tiny pioneer church tucked away
behind old pine trees, a little, steepled white or red wooden
structure big enough to heat with a wood stove and seat a
congregation of fifty souls. Most of these churches, Presbyterian, Lutheran, Anglican, Baptist, Jehovah's Witnesses are, like
the identical little white frame mission churches on the Roseau
reserve, boarded up and deserted. Dominion City is served by
itinerant preachers, usually theology students, who come in
every Sunday for the service. The yellow stone United Church,
the biggest, newest and most expensive building in Dominion
City, is a tribute to the village's Presbyterian founders.

In spite of the age and decrepitude of its buildings, most of
which have been there since the city was founded in 1880,
Dominion City gives the impression of being unfinished. The
village is full of vacant lots and many of the business establishments are half-finished, as if 60 or 70 years ago, the contrac-
tor suddenly ran out of money, or died. The streets are in a
state of constant upheaval. The first time I went to Dominion
City, in the summer of 1964, they had been ripped up and huge
ditches dug to lay the water works. My car lurched through ruts
and potholes up to the axles. In the winter of 1966-67, they
were in exactly the same condition—snow-covered mounds of
mud filled the main streets, big holes were mysteriously dug in
front of the business establishments overnight, and the ruts and

potholes were as bad. The sewer was going in.

The village is little more than a big service station, gasoline the main item for sale, and with it, farm machinery and old cars. From the signs, one would think the name of the village is Shell, Manitoba. Not only does the owner of one Shell garage head the Chamber of Commerce, but the chairman of the school board drives the Shell Oil delivery truck. Dominion City is a watering hole for farmers within a ten-mile radius, and farm business is a large part of its business. The clientele is transient, coming into town for two or three hours to buy groceries, gas and beer, and only a small fraction comes from the town itself. The clientele includes the Indians.

Early in the morning, right at 9 a.m., the cars and pickup trucks start to arrive in town, coming from all directions. High in the old trucks, battered, dirty green with the unpronounceable name in shakey white hand-printing on the door, sit wizened, kerchiefed peasant women who seem never to have left the Ukraine. The younger farmers, still tanned in the wintertime, drive into town in late model Chevys, Ford and Pontiacs. The Indians can be heard coming a mile away—Chugchugchug... Bang! . . . VRROOOOMMM . . . ROAR . . . Splutter . . . Chuggg — as they coax the last wheeze out of the 1949 $100 bomb bought with last summer's sugar beet money. Fenders dragging, licence plates dangling by one screw, bumpers clanging, they lurch to a stop in front of the first building on Main St.—the hotel.

> *"At sugar beet time, right after the first week's pay, the Indians buy up all the old cars in the garage lots. The dealers don't even push their cars—they just wait until beet time. Wham, the car lots are cleaned out—not a car left for miles around. Don't last a year. Next year, the Indians come and buy another one."*
>
> Dominion City man

Social relationships function on the turtle principle—everyone is recognized and evaluated by the car he drives, his shell and identification. Every day, the cars are lined up on both sides of Main St. pointing in towards the buildings like suckling piglets. A quick glance can tell who is in town, where he is, who he is talking to and what kind of business he is doing.

If a man wants to be secretive, he has to leave his car at home or park it down the street and make his way deviously to where he wants to go. The people are, by habit and long training, inveterate car watchers.

Dominion City is not a white collar town—few towns in western Canada are. The farmers wear plaid sports shirts open at the neck, cloth caps, slacks, overalls or denim trousers and parkas in the winter. White shirts and ties are for Sunday church (for those who still go to church). At meetings, men will wear suits but with sports shirts underneath the jacket. The Indians wear the same kind of clothes as farmers and businessmen except older, cheaper, shabbier and darker-colored. The people are cheerful, prosperous, contented. Although the streets are poor and the businesses run-down, the homes are spic and span, well landscaped and carefully tended. Dominion City is not a slum; its decay is that of old age, not corruption. There is no garbage in the streets, no stray dogs, no filth and litter around the homes, houses and fences are mended and patched as best they can be. It's a dry, clean death—a dignified genteel decline into senility.

Settlers

Dominion City was named late one night in 1880 when the citizens, who had called a town meeting expressly for this purpose, couldn't think of anything better to call it. The village has never lived up to its pretentious label. It is now smaller, less prosperous and less hopeful than it was in 1880. Its horizon has narrowed, and a feeling of failure has set in. Everyone laughs at Dominion City, a scrubby hick town with mud streets. The Dominion Citizenry resent this ridicule; they are sensitive about their town's public image. They take a suspicious, pugnacious stance towards strangers and are quick to list the town's faults to forestall criticism from outside.

Dominion City's first resident arrived in 1874 via paddle-boat from Minneapolis. A Scot from Ontario, Duncan McKercher prospered. He soon owned a post office, a general store, a hotel, a rooming house and almost all the land for miles around, which he leased out at healthy prices to new settlers. The wagon trail from Red River to Pembina, North Dakota crossed the Roseau River at Dominion City and McKercher's business was brisk. When McKercher arrived, the settlement had one log house belonging to two brothers named Sullivan and a handful of French Metis who homesteaded in the area. The only other inhabitants were the Indians—a Saulteaux band which hunted and fished, roaming at will over the prairie. Sometimes, the stories go, the sturgeon ran so thick in the Roseau you could almost walk across on their backs. On the wall of the Dominion City beer parlor hangs a framed photo of a six-foot long sturgeon caught in 1910. Settlers hunted too, living off deer, grouse, rabbits, turtle and duck eggs and wild fruit.

The white paddlewheeler plied the river bringing boatloads of immigrant homesteaders and after the railway went through to Winnipeg, they came that way too, clattering in the old wooden gaslit coaches, eyes staring out of sooty faces. Mennonites, Scots, Ukrainians, Russians, English, French, Catholic, Presbyterian, Greek Orthodox, Lutheran, they poured in, dressed in black homespun. Ignorant, illiterate, they built their sod and log houses, put the pigs, chickens and cows in the barn attached to the house and made themselves at home. They stuck close to friends and relatives, and for protection built their churches with the triple cross and dome, with the Virgin and steeple, square, sparsely furnished white boxes where they congregated once a week to give thanks to God and Clifford Sifton. The Presbyterian Church arrived in Dominion City the year the village was named. "I was raised on the Shorter Catechism," says Jim Waddell, a grandson of McKercher. So was most of Dominion City.

Dominion City and Roseau were each unique. Other ethnic groups settled in clusters of villages while Dominion City was the only Anglo-Saxon enclave in the whole area. Roseau was the only band of Indians for fifty miles. The Indians traded at the Dominion City stores, as did everyone else in the area. Their drums occasionally kept the settlers awake at night, but the bell on the Methodist church woke the Indians up early on Sunday mornings. The Indians had, in those days, a reputation for scrupulous honesty but storekeepers were not trusting:

"Nate Bagshaw, he liked trading with the Indians, and

*had a weakness for the squaws. The Indians all called him
'Buckshot.' The Indians used to come into his place to drink
tea on the way back from Emerson. While they were drinking
and enjoying their tea, Bagshaw put his hand into his watch
pocket to take it out and see the time and discovered his
watch was gone. He straightway accused the Indians of
stealing it. In those days of the old Indians, they were very
honest and proud. When Buckshot accused them of taking his
watch they did not like it and in a huff got up from the table
leaving their cups of tea unfinished and walked out the door
and drove off, madder than hell. It was a year before they
came back. Later, Buckshot found the watch under his pillow
where he had put it the night before.*

Jim Waddell

Life was raw around Dominion City eighty years ago.
Wrote the town's doctor: "Some of the new immigrants only
needed a few swigs of homebrew to make the journey back to
the cave. A lot of the parties and dances in the district came to
a roaring climax with somebody murdered, raped, or badly
carved up . . ." In those days, the Roseau Indians were models
of decorum. Epidemics of smallpox, measles, whooping caugh,
typhoid and diphtheria swept through the population every
year, somtimes claiming half the children. TB was prevalent,
and everyone had lice. Infant mortality was high and many
women died in childbirth. Everyone has forgotten now except
the Indians. For the handful of the wealthy landlords, life was
rich and gay. They lived in gingerbread houses with indoor
plumbing. The women wore silk dresses and entertained at tea;
the men fancied horses and rode the hounds after coyotes. Life
was, for lords and serfs, much as they had left it in the old
country.

Dominion City's heyday also produced its first scandal. A
dozen of the leading men of the town, the pillars of respectability, were arrested and tried for keeping a "chain gang" of
girls in the town. The girls were kept in various establishments
and passed around the members of the clique. Manitoba was
aghast. "That sinful town! " people said when speaking of
Dominion City. The name, and the odor, have stuck.

Many of the original Anglo-Saxon homesteaders sold out and moved to Winnipeg or farther west. Their place was taken by others:

"My father was German originally but he came here from Russia—only the name was German. He homesteaded close by here . . . My father couldn't read or write; he had no concept of what was going on in government, elections. The storekeeper would put his thumb on the ballot opposite the name of the Liberal candidate and say 'You vote here.' and my father would mark his 'X'. Most people voted that way— the storekeepers pretty well controlled the whole thing.

"My father encountered tremendous prejudice, although he had some friends among the Anglo-Saxons. The prejudice peaked during the First World War; it was worse than with the Japanese later. Even to say the word 'German' would get you into a fight.

"Dad was a proud man; instead of leaving things alone he would stick up for his homeland. A lot of the Dominion City boys were being killed by Germans. Feelings were strong. My father was loud and outspoken. He had very strong opinions. I think he could have avoided a lot of trouble if he had just kept quiet and hadn't talked so much.

"I used to be embarrassed when I was a kid at some of his statements; we'd go to the store and the first thing you know he'd be hollerin' away. Soon everybody else would be yellin' too. I think my father asked for a lot of the trouble.

"There were a lot of little things that used to happen. People stole the yokes and neck-trees from our horses while we were threshing. We couldn't do a thing. Later, we'd find them burned. One day our dog disappeared. We found him partly skinned alive. Never had any proof of who did it. My father lost a quarter section of land. Somebody told him to sign a document so he made his 'x'. Later, it turned out he had signed over his land.

Garnet Kyle

Because the immigrants established themselves in little ghetto communities, racial and religious rivalry turned into inter-town feuding. Dominion City is one of dozens of identical little villages located about 10 miles apart. Each hates its neighbors and takes vicious delight in destroying reputations. Telephones ring with news of the latest scandal. Racial bigotry sublimated into local boosterism is a recent development. People used to know only one town, their town, the town that was closest to the farm. A trip to another town was an adventure and Winnipeg a magical land. Since the farmers have been driving faster cars, invidious comparisons have been made between the towns and the townspeople have become entrenched in their dogmatic isolationism; it is aggressive provincialism. Competition is intensified by struggle for the dwindling dollars. Every town used to have steady customers and a steady income, and it geared itself to that income level. Farmers now shop around, particularly in Winnipeg. The villages are in trouble; they have to modernize to attract business, but they have no capital to invest. The small shopkeepers grow to hate fancy new stores, and become more conservative and stauncher in their respectable poverty. Dominion City is, moreover, on the western fringe of a large poverty stricken area of bush and marginal farms where the tax base is low and most of the money comes from Dominion City pockets. Even more than they resent Indians, Dominion City people resent people with money. Specifically, they mean Mennonites. "One Mennonite store has the sign 'God Before Prices' stuck up outside . . . Ha! " observed one woman to me. Indians are only resented because they cost money. Dominion City people express far more strongly prejudiced attitudes about Mennonites than they do about Indians. If, like the Indians, the Mennonites spent money in the village, they'd be more lovable.

Time, for most settlers, stopped short the minute they set foot on the boat for Canada. Rural Manitoba now contains a nineteenth-century Europe-in-miniature, a social structure which has vanished from most of Europe itself. It exists primarily in the minds of wizened old ladies in high green pickup trucks on Dominion City's main street. Racially, it is as divided as Europe itself.

The ideas about government which the peasants brought and preserved were, naturally, autocratic. Each little town was an empire and had an absolute monarch who ruled by divine right and total control of the financial resources. He was usually the storekeeper. The storekeeper owned a lot of land, controlled jobs, and dominated the supply of food, especially during lean months of drought, hail and flood when everyone lived on credit. People had a financial obligation to vote as the storekeeper suggested. In return for producing the votes, the storekeeper would be allowed to put his hand in the party pork barrel and pull out more jobs, more land, more money. He expanded his enterprises, opened garages, businesses, hotels, and his power over the people increased. Many of these towns, Dominion City included, became the private estates of one family or a family compact. Power was centered around the general store, where people bought politics with the flour.

Settlers were handicapped. Uneducated, speaking little or no English, most of them had not lived under any system remotely resembling the Canadian. Moreover they were too busy staying alive. Political power became quite naturally associated with wealth and social prestige. Party affiliation was passed down from father to son like the Ten Commandments and Liberalism came with the Shorter Catechism.

"My father was a Liberal before me," said Jim Waddell as an explanation of his political convictions. People were expected to vote in lumps, along ethnic lines. The people developed a passionate, irrational attachment to a political party regardless of its policies, because it was a symbol of their right to be in Canada. In Dominion City, political affiliations are flaunted, campaigning is unscrupulous and political opposition interpreted as a personal insult.

Psychologically, the autocratic system is still basically the same in Dominion City as it was in 1880; the people, helpless in their inertia, look imploringly at the government, rattling their tin cups for an old folks' home. The people have no idea how to organize themselves to accomplish what they want and lack the financial resources which would make this easy. Without money, they say, we can do nothing, and they expect the government to give them money, invest it for them and run the business. The people will live off the dividends. The Chamber of Commerce spends most of its time writing letters to cabinet ministers asking for help. Each minister receives dozens of these missives from equally desperate little towns each day. Which town he chooses depends very much on how close the town is to the ear of the minister. The pork barrel may now be potato chip factories but the principle is the same—the state gives, the people receive. Because the people are so dependent on this pipeline into the government, the man who sits on it is the most influential man in the community. He brings in the votes, his town gets the industry. He acts as a governor, providing the ideas, energy, organization and connections. The rest of the people agree or disagree with his ideas, but if they disagree, he goes ahead anyway. Bill and Garnet Kyle occupy this important position in Dominion City, Bill when the Liberals are in power, Garnet for the Conservatives.

"No"

Dominion City is governed by silence. It has 31 organizations, committees or councils, from the local council down to the group that organizes bingo. No more than half a dozen are visibly functioning. The same 10 or 15 people make up the membership on all committees, and the most successful groups are those which organize entertainment and sports. Public meetings are tedious formalities in which the people participate only to ask how much money it's going to cost them.

The village is governed by a three-man council which has about $5,500 to spend each year. The village is not incorporated; the people rejected that in a 1964 referendum because it would cost too much money. The income the village gets is its share from the surrounding Municipality of Franklin, which is neither wealthy nor progressive. The only perceptible government offered by the council is the perpetual gnawing at the streets. The single notable thing the municipality has done for the village has been to withhold its annual budget in 1964. The $5,500 had, apparently, disappeared. Dominion City charged the municipality with graft and corruption; the municipality produced the money belatedly and settled out of court. Between 1964 and 1966, Dominion City had a scandal a year.

When Community Development Officer Pat Dunphy arrived in the village late in 1966, he found the Chamber of Commerce asleep. "Well, what is the government going to do for us? " they asked him. Some members felt everything was satisfactory while others despaired of being able to do anything. They mulled over a few projects, such as building a new high school or old folks home, but no action was ever taken toward making them happen. The livliest group in town was the Investors' Club, a gathering of local farmers and businessmen who contributed $10 a month towards a future industrial project for the village. They could not, however, decide on an industry to promote, and spent their time berating the government and forecasting doom for Dominion City.

Only three new buildings have been put up in Dominion City within recent memory: a bank, a post office and a co-op store. All were built by outside agents. Local merchants have done nothing to improve their establishments. Citizens in Dominion City do not attend meetings of the village council or school board, nor do they take an interest in meetings outside of their own small groups. Committees seldom have more than three to seven members, and behave like underground cells, each man afraid that the others will find out what he's thinking and expose him as a traitor. When someone finally breaks the silence and proposes a plan, everyone around the table immediately says "No." "No . . . no . . . no . . . no . . . it can't possibly work." Silence falls again. If the instigator of the scheme is bold enough to try again at every meeting, in three or four years he may succeed in boring the group into accepting it. By this time, the plan is of course obsolete. It is always the same men who do the talking at meetings; the others sit and stare at them until they are compelled to take the lead. Decisions are seldom, if ever, made at meetings. The same discussion is carried on for years, beginning and ending nowhere. Meetings continue to operate on the same principle as the one which chose Dominion City's name—boredom. The single visible achievement of the Chamber of Commerce in 1966/1967 was the decision of the cafe owner to install two new plate glass windows. Public meetings are the same. Questions have to be wrung from the audience. Everyone seems to have come to look at everyone else.

The people have a need for secrecy, for subterfuge, because their lives are so painfully public. Their refusal to say anything, their refusal to commit themselves openly, seems to be a last self-defence, an illusion of privacy. Because their private lives are made common talk through gossip and the telephone party line, they react by keeping their public selves hidden. They shut up and conceal the very ideas and information that should be discussed openly.

Bingo is the best expression of this concentrated silence. Bingo is popular in Dominion City, and is played in absolute silence, rows and rows of heads bent over the little white cards in deadly competition as the caller barks the number. The Indians sit at a separate table at the back of the hall. The feeling of comradeship is almost religious in quality—communion through silent prayer—the ecstasy of 'Bingo! '

Debt too, has left scars. People who have fought free of the storekeeper are leery of getting back in the hole again. The residents of Dominion City are conservative and penny-wise. The village was unable for years to get running water because of the widow vote. The widows live on pensions and have septic tanks, so they do not need running water or sewage and have little sympathy with the businessmen who do. The widows finally agreed to running water in 1964 but objected to sewage. Three years later they weakened. The streets have to be plowed up twice and it is costing the widows $80,000 more than if they had agreed to both water and sewer at the same time.

Conservatism, which produces poverty, is strengthened by poverty. Businesses going bankrupt or closing down—seven have closed down in the village in the last few years, and over 100 people have left—make the remaining businessmen tense and afraid to invest. Troubles recently have been intensified by poor crops due to wet soil caused by poor drainage, which in turn is caused by lack of organized action, due to conservatism, a conservatism caused by the very problems it fails to solve.

Dominion City will, if it survives, be a welfare town or, at best, a civil service town. The past is still shaping the present and the future in Dominion City. The old folks who built the town keep it alive simply by growing old and being in need of an old folks home.

An umbilical cord five miles long connects Roseau reserve and Dominion City. This road is always filled with Indians—on foot, in cars, hitching rides, in the water truck—going to and from Dominion City. To look at, the two communities, the brown and the white, are separate, segregated, unconnected. That five miles of barren prairie seems to divide them completely. Subtly and almost invisibly, however, they are as closely joined and mutually dependent as identical Siamese twins. They share similar problems, a similar outlook, similar hopes and fears. One could not live without the other.

Along the road the Indians bring money into Dominion City. All the money which Indian Affairs invests in the reserve ends up in the pockets of businessmen in Dominion City and Letellier, a total per year between $100,000 and $200,000. Indians prefer to shop in Dominion City, so the village gets between half and three-quarters of the cash.

In return, the Indians take food, clothing, wine and beer back to the reserve. During the summer they buy up old cars, and now that a farming corporation has started on the reserve, they buy farm machinery too. Roseau Indians are perfect consumers. Their sole purpose is to consume, and this they do extremely well. Everything the salesmen have to offer is devoured, everything they buy disappears instantly or soon wears out. They are always buying and make an ideal market. Trouble arises only when their attitude of total consumption extends itself to theft and drunkenness.

Roseau families are three-car and four-car families, although no one car runs. The cars last a few weeks and then are allowed to rust in the yard like multi-colored beetles on their backs. The guts are gradually removed to replace worn parts in next year's car. Cars are essential to the Roseau people. They have to travel to their employment—south to potatoes or west to sugar beets or east to pulpwood and they also have to get all their food from Dominion City. A man with a car in working order is in a position of great influence. While many people can afford the $100 or less to buy a car, they cannot afford to keep up the repairs on it or even to buy gas for it. Just as horse stealing from the enemy was a favorite game of the Indians a hundred years ago, so car stealing is today. Boys and young men steal cars from people in Dominion City and the surrounding towns, run them dry of gas or burn the engine out in a night, and abandon them. A lot of drinking takes place in the cars; often they are involved in accidents and smashed up. The people of Dominion City are not that rich, and they resent having their cars ruined.

> *"You never know if your car is going to be there when you come out of the store or a meeting. It's a long walk back to the reserve, especially in the winter and if a man's been drinking. They take cars to get home. Sometimes they're smashed up, sometimes not. One of them tried to steal my car once. I came and told him to get out. The car has one of those swing-away steering wheels and won't start unless the wheel is in position. He couldn't start it. He was so drunk he couldn't even move. He just sat there and stared up at me blearily. I tried to drag him out but he couldn't stand up, I called the police and we got him out. He just leaned against the car, couldn't walk. I wouldn't just drive away and let him fall flat."*

Dominion City woman

The Indians get as roaringly drunk in the Queen's Hotel beer parlor as they do on the reserve, and the same fights ensue. A lot of white people get drunk in that beer parlor at the same time. Women come in to find their husbands, get drunk themselves, and then start bawling their husbands out for spending all their time in the pub. People start pushing and shoving and yelling, glasses smash to the floor, other people yell at them to shut up, the women start smashing the furniture around until they are ejected on to the street. The monthly docket at Magistrate's Court in Emerson has a list of six to a dozen Roseau Indians up for being drunk and disorderly, drinking in a public place and similar charges. All plead guilty; some pay fines; most go to jail for a week or two. It is usually the same small group of people that gets picked up time after time.

> *"It's got so you can't walk down the street without being molested. People are getting beaten up. Men coming out of the beer parlor with a case of beer find themselves surrounded by Indians and get the beer stolen. They start fighting on the street—broken beer bottles and everything. They walk along at their own pace, can't be hustled or look out."*

citizen

The Justice of the Peace was beaten up by a group of Indians one night as he was coming out of the beer parlor after having made a loud derogatory comment about the Indian race. Most people felt the beating was justified and no charges were laid. Dominion City has a policeman, a thin young man who is completely unable to cope. He was pursuing a group of Indian youths one night when they turned and started to chase him, so he ran. Since that time, the Dominion City police force has not been effective. The village can only afford to pay a policeman $250 a month plus expenses. The more money they have, the more cars and beer the Indians consume and the more trouble they cause. Extra income is not spent on essentials, food and clothes for the children, but on luxuries. More money does not change the pattern of spending, but enhances the habits already there. More welfare makes the Indians drunker, and does not make the children fatter.

Crime runs in cycles around Roseau. In the winter, when people are poor and without cars, it is confined to the reserve. In spring and fall, the Indians ride forth to harry the countryside, spreading destruction 30 miles in all directions. By midsummer, they have fanned out so far almost no one is left at home to worry the Emerson R.C.M.P.—the R.C.M.P. 30 miles away has its hands full.

The Roseau Indians fight only each other but they steal from white people. It is extremely unusual to hear of a white man being attacked or a woman molested by Indians. Instead, stores, garages and homes are broken into regularly. All the excitement for the Indians seems to lie in the feat of breaking in, not in stealing because they take little of value. Even a car is not stolen for any useful purpose. This too seems to be a carry over from the tradition of "counting coup"—touching one's enemy or stealing a march on him without killing him. A man is pitted against his own strength and cunning.

"The whole proplem is drinking . . . There's the makings of a murder every Saturday night. It's just luck that it doesn't happen more often. They're not afraid to go to jail. Conditions are better in jail, especially in winter. These people have the worst crime rate per capita—a poor breed of Indian, Saulteaux . . .

"It's just the reverse of the normal pattern—when they have money, they're trouble. When they're poor, everything's ok.

"Their route runs east and west, from north of here to about fifty miles west, in the sugar beet area. They don't steal from the farmers while they're working for them but they'll go back later.

"There's no malice meant. They feel no guilt for death or injury, no remorse."

R.C.M.P. corporal

"The women come around to the door a lot, selling rugs. The rugs cost about $3.50. They come to collect rags to make the rugs with too. I usually save a lot for them. They bring flour to sell too—as low as $2 a hundred-weight—and tools and other stuff."

Dominion City woman

The Roseau Indians are peddlars. They sell what they are given by Indian Affairs to the people in the village. The flour—100 pounds a year for each man, woman and child in the band—is part of their treaty payment. It is free and delivered to the reserve. The people have no place to store this flour—they sell it in Dominion City for what they can get. The paint for the houses and tools which Indian Affairs gives them to fix up their homes goes the same way. The Indians lug the stuff from door to door in Dominion City—the paint too goes for a couple of dollars. The village people don't ask where it came from. Stolen goods are also disposed of in this way. More than one house in Dominion City has a shiny white coat of Indian Affairs paint.

"The people come to town on welfare days and bring all the kids in the car, even in winter. Sometimes it's funny and sometimes it's sad—survival of the fittest, I guess. The parents disappear into the beer parlor and leave the kids shivering in the cars. They never have any food, maybe a bag of potato chips, and they get so cold sitting out there. Their hands are nearly frozen off. We sometimes go past cars parked on the street at night; there's women sitting there wrapped in blankets or kids sleeping in the trunk. If we ask them if they need help, they shake their heads."

Mrs. Ramsey

"You guys are paying our welfare, you're the suckers."
Steve Seenie

"The Indians chase the white men off the reserve every now and then. The last bunch was some guys from a town north of here, St. Malo. A lot of white men go to the reserve at night, looking for women, carrying a case of beer under their arm. The Indians take it for a while, then they get mad. There's lotta guys won't dare go near there now."
Mr. Mc.

"They have orgies in town here that'd turn your stomach. Bootlegger here in town keeps a house. They go there to drink their wine and stay overnight—a place to congregate. There's Indian blood here in town—third generation. Pretty kids. Blood mixes well with English. French and Indian is not a good combination. The Indian gene is weaker than the white."
local resident

"In all the newspaper stories about the murders and rapes and bad things on the reserve, they always say 'Roseau Reserve is near Dominion City'. Why do they always have to drag Dominion City into everthing? The reserve is closer to Letellier, but Letellier never gets mentioned all the time in the papers!"
Mrs. B.

"A lot of Indians used to work for farmers around. Farmers never paid them in full. If you owed them something they'd come back; otherwise you'd never see them again.
"Quite a few farmers lease reserve land."
Dominion City man

"I drove an Indian back to town. Didn't want anybody to see me. What would people say, my driving an Indian? I let him off at the edge of town. Later, I saw him on the main street. He smiled and nodded at me. He came over and asked me for $2. He said he had no money to buy booze."
Mrs. G.

Before an election, a lot of liquor mysteriously shows up on the Roseau Reserve. Townspeople and farmers take it there to persuade the Indian to vote for the party of their choice. Electioneering is quite ruthless:

> *"I appointed a new man as returning officer on the reserve because the one before had been a Liberal. I gave him the ballot box and the instructions.*
>
> *"The night before the election, the Liberals had a big party and got him drunk. About 6 a.m. his wife came pounding on my door, saying her husband hadn't come home and wasn't going to be in any shape to conduct the election.*
>
> *"I drove out to the reserve and picked up the ballot box. I didn't have any choice but to take it to the man who had done it before. He was up and dressed. 'I was waiting for you,' he says. Everybody in the house was sleeping on the floor. I gave him the ballot box.*
>
> *"Well, about 8 a.m. my man shows up at home. He's sobered himself up enough to hold the election. Boy, was he ever mad when he found out his wife had told me and the ballot box had been handed over to the Opposition. He left his wife for a week over it."*
>
> Conservative Party worker

> *"A lot of the trouble started a few years ago when some boys from the reserve got into a fight with some fellows from Dominion City. They chased each other around the roads in cars one night and ended up on the reserve. The Indian guys were outnumbered but they beat the hell out of the town boys. People were pretty mad about that."*
>
> Chief John James

The Indians spend a great deal of time in Dominion City. Many village residents drink beer with them, play bingo with them, buy things from them, give them rides, hand them money. The Indians eat and drink pop in Solnes' Cafe; they shop in Sokilyk's store; they patronize Shroeder's garage. Many village people feel they *know* the Indians, they feel they are friends with them. They know them by name, can recognize them on the street, have done business with them (credit and voucher) Townspeople and reserve people have gone to school together and played baseball and hockey together.

> *"I went to school with John James in Greenridge. I've known him all his life. I know him real well. We played baseball together. Johnny Jim used to come to our place for dinner. I remember he tried growing cucumbers. Couldn't figure out why he couldn't spend his money twice. He'd buy gas to take the cucumbers to market to sell, then he'd spend the money he got for them and wouldn't pay for the gas."*
>
> Lorne Ramsey

John James is the present chief of the reserve. Lorne Ramsey is chairman of the new division school board and former chairman of the Dominion City school board, the board which kicked the Indian kids out of the Dominion City school.

Dominion City people tend to be quite affectionate towards the Indians, blaming their deplorable physical condition or bad conduct on other things—the government, welfare, youth—and the townspeople feel quite protective towards the Indians.

> *"'Everythin's lily white in Dominion City! ' I could have shot somebody after I read that."*
>
> Lorne Ramsey

> *"All we've heard for the past year has been Indians, Indians, Indians. Indians are people, just like you and I. I have to be so careful that my son doesn't pick up bad ideas. One of the university students said to me; 'What do the people here say when they see an Indian in town? There's that dirty drunken Indian.' I told him they say just what they'd say if they saw you drunk on the street—'There's a drunken slob.'"*
>
> kindergarten teacher

> *"We had no trouble with the reserve until the younger generation. They never used to steal.*
> *"They're comical, fun-loving people, quite a nuisance.*

Spend all their money. Always begging—a nuisance. The law is too lenient on them.

"They come around asking for money—we're paying for the whole thing through welfare.

"Welfare money is killing people. Do the same to any other town.

"People blame the people of Dominion City for not opening our arms to the Indians but we have reasons . . . They're not clean. Can't take a case of beer outside. They'll take it away.

"I was always friends with them.

"There's no future for them. They're just hopeless. Take many generations. As long as they're allowed to live on the reserve, they will keep to the old ways. They should changeover.

"Sterilization . . . if I advocated this I'd deserve to be chased out of the country.

"It's a headache. The government is at its wits' end. Then the do-gooders start hollerin'.

"This is a bad reserve. Any reserve close to a French settlement is always demoralized . . . lower character. There's been ten to twenty murders since 1945. It's heartbreaking. Used to be about 350 people, now up to 700. All on welfare.

"Farmer bordering the reserve sold out. Said he couldn't keep a thing—always breaking into his shed, gas tank. They blew up a store once—used a Molotov cocktail. They never show up when you need 'em the most."

Jim Waddell

"A few generations back, the Indians were not much different. They travelled in a horse and buggy—so would whites. Everybody had cookstoves and hauled water. They should have been given the right to vote from the start—never had a reserve. If they move, their treaty should be increased. Move them into town."

Garnet Kyle

There is a great deal of traffic along that road between Roseau and Dominion City but it's the Indians doing the travelling. Three people who live in Dominion City go to the reserve—the kindergarten teacher, the teacher in the red school and Pat Dunphy, the Community Development Officer. No people from Dominion City visit their Indian "friends" on the reserve. No Indians visit homes in Dominion City. Nor do they belong to the Chamber of Commerce or any other of the thirty organizations in town.

> *"When I first came here and saw Indians I never really saw them. We used to drive past the reserve. I'd say to my husband 'Why don't you take me there? ' He'd say 'Oh, I'd never take you down there.'"*
>
> farm woman

"Out There"

> *"I was at a meeting on integration once. A woman got up, a teacher, started saying how she was for integration because I was such a wonderful person and she's known me all her life and that because John James was such a fine man then the Indians should be taken into the school. Well, that made me mad. I told her, 'I don't want my personality discussed in public. It's not me that's being integrated—it's all the Indian people. I don't want them to accept just me; they've got to accept everybody—all my people.' Why should she talk about me as being so great; what about the rest of the Roseau reserve people? I'm not going to be accepted by white people if the rest of the Indian people aren't. I'm not going to leave them behind back there. It's got to be all of us. It's not right to single me out alone."*
>
> Chief John James

After the former chief, Albert Henry, was expelled from the reserve, Steve Seenie organized Roseau almost single-handedly. As welfare officer, he has what amounts to power of life or death over the people, and he is not lenient. He also takes responsibility for meeting and dealing with most of the out-siders who come to the reserve—government people, university students, reporters. He drives the children to kindergarten and sends his own daughter. He deals with problems that arise at the school and acts as unofficial janitor for the band hall. Steve is called to solve any problems which arise on the reserve.

Steve is affable and easy-going, yet able to speak his mind when necessary. He "knows everybody", as one Dominion City resident put it, and spends a lot of time in the beer parlor, drinking with the townspeople and talking. Steve acts as a buffer between the reserve and the town. No one can dislike Steve. White people can talk to him, and he helps allay their fears. In return, he protects his own people. By spending all his time in town, he makes it unnecessary for anyone from town to go to the reserve. Steve is an important connection between town and reserve, but a connection which, eventually, creates barriers and misunderstandings. By knowing and liking Steve, the Dominion City people feel they don't have to bother with the rest of the reserve population—the delinquents, the drunks, the fighters. This attitude—one could call it selective tolerance—is what Chief John James objects to so strongly.

"Indian Affairs came up with the idea of having a farm corporation—four men to take over the land and farm it together, 1700 acres altogether once we get all the leases back from the farmers. They told us to choose four men. We got the four. Indian Affairs rejected two of them. Said they had police records and therefore couldn't borrow money. We had to look around for two more. We found them, Harry Roberts and Oliver Nelson, my brother . . . Oliver's in jail now.

"I farmed for three years on my own—only broke even one year. Other two years I lost. We farmed 1200 acres last year—lost 300 and 40 per cent of the crop. Rain was heavy in July. Land isn't properly drained. We're going to have to do something about the drainage. We have to pay 25 per cent of the profit to the band. Last year we grossed $21,000. Most of it had to go to pay back the debt. At $27,000 we're breaking even—lost $6,000. It could go as high as $60,000. Average $40,000.

"If there was something here for all these people, they'd stay. Can't make a living here. We have to have an economic structure before we get a townsite. A person with no income can't keep it up—have to pay for water, fuel, sewage.

"We had a community farm in 1946-47. Just went kaput. Not well organized. No equipment, not much moeny. Employed four men. Had a manager, just like the assistant agent is now. The men had to rent combines from outside— that meant they got them after everyone was finished threshing—too late."   Stan Nelson

Indian Affairs is repeating an experiment on Roseau which failed in 1946. Except this time there is no "manager" employed by the Branch. Instead, there is an "economic consultant" who comes down from Winnipeg once a week. Indian Affairs pays his salary. All decisions made by the four (now three) farmers have to be approved by Indian Affairs through the consultant, including the selection of the men from the reserve who will be permitted to be farmers. It will be interesting to see if it works this time.

"I decided I wanted the white man's things for myself too. I went through some moments of real despair, but my attitude changed. I have a real commitment to the reserve now. I hope I can stay here and my kids will live here too."
                                                   Stan Nelson

Stan looks terrifying, but he is considered to be "the best Nelson" and one of the most progressive and responsible men on the reserve. There are dozens of Nelsons, and they are known for miles around. Stan is the oldest of them and is now in his late thirties or early forties. His father, who had a reputation for toughness, is dead, but his mother still lives in Letellier. He is not quite on the reserve—his house is the only one on the other side of the road. This isolation symbolizes his partial rejection by his own people. He ran for chief and was defeated by John James. Stan is the head of the "Nelson faction" on the reserve—a combination of physical strength, intelligence and education which frightens other Indians. The Nelsons will probably take over and dominate the reserve, if the other boys can stay out of jail. Stan has a high school education. His brother Don, 25, has his grade 12 and is trained

as an accountant. He now has a job with the Wawanesa
Insurance Company in Dominion City. Both are thoughtful,
quiet-spoken, proud men.

Two Men

Stan Nelson is the Garnet Kyle of Roseau Reserve. As the
communities are twins, so are their leaders. Both men live on
the fringe of the community—of it, but not in it. Stan lives in a
new bungalow across the highway from the reserve; Garnet Kyle
lives in his new home across the road and railway tracks from
Dominion City. Both men are within sight of the community—in fact about three minutes' drive from the centre. Their
houses are the first buildings a visitor notices as he comes into
the respective communities. They are the first citizens. Each
provides many of the ideas which feed into the community and
the bulk of the impetus for change and progress. Both are
well-educated and have strikingly similar personalities,—soft-spoken, quiet, listening. Both feel rejected by their
home community; Garnet Kyle ran for reeve of the municipality and was defeated. They are frustrated, in that they get so
little co-operation from the people they desire to serve and
help, and their ideas are frequently ignored. Stan is building a
rink and hall for the reserve; Garnet was influential in obtaining
an old folks home for Dominion City.

Kyle and Nelson are both farmers. Stan Nelson could learn
ten times as much about farming from Kyle as he ever will from
the economic consultant. Both men are anxious to learn, eager
for conversation. They are genuine leaders. Both are interested
in the Chamber of Commerce. Garnet Kyle is a past-president;
Stan Nelson has never belonged.

Garnet Kyle and Stan Nelson live five miles apart along a
straight gravel road. They have never met.

Dominion City blames everything on the school board.
They are prejudiced; *we* are not. Three of the five board
members, and the three accused of prompting the expulsion of
the Indians, are farmers. They are prosperous while Dominion

City is poor, and resents their wealth. These men are also ignoring the town and spending their money in other communities. Dominion City doesn't like that either.

Bill Kyle receives the greatest share of the blame in the expulsion, although he neither moved nor seconded the motion. Bill Kyle is the richest farmer in the area, and bought his Chrysler in Winnipeg. Revenge takes devious forms.

The expulsion did not come suddenly. Dominion City had been having school troubles. In December, 1965, the old high school, a two-storey yellow brick building built in 1916, was condemned by the fire inspector and ordered closed. It was near Christmas holidays, so rather than find new quarters for the children immediately, a watchman was stationed beside the old wood-enclosed furnace while the children studied upstairs.

A public meeting, attended by about 45 people, was held in December. At that meeting, the question of integration was raised in public for the first time and a vote was taken by show of hands. For total integration eight hands went up. For partial, gradual integration, twenty-seven hands were raised. For no integration at all, eight hands again went up. The people of Dominion City were apparently in favor of things as they were.

Integration was not working, however. It had been bought in Dominion City as it had been in The Pas and everywhere else in Canada. A "gentleman's agreement" had been made between Indian Affairs and the school board in 1962 to admit a small proportion of Indian students. The Indian pupils were not to exceed one-quarter of the total school population and would be hand-picked by Indian Affairs. The Indians themselves were never involved in the negotations, but merely gave their approval to what Indian Affairs suggested. The first year, only about a dozen pupils came, and they were barely noticed. In 1963, about 25 came into town and at that time, were scattered in all grades from one to ten, one or two in each grade. Problems began to be noticed in the third year, 1964-65, when 36 Indian pupils were coming into the town school.

Then Indian Affairs took all the students out of high school and sent them away to residential schools with "better study facilities". The board was still held to its 25 per cent Indian agreement, but now the 25 per cent was to be entirely in elementary classes. Another difficulty confronted the board. The Indian students were dropping out in grades five and six. This meant that *all* the Indian pupils would be in grades one to four. Dominion City's school would be Indian to grade five, white from grade five up.

So integration had failed long before the board took its drastic step. Dominion City would have accepted the large number of Indians in the lower grades had they been able to meet the standards. The simple fact is that the Indian children were *not* able to keep up with the white children. They *were* pulling the class behind. The white children were being "swamped."

One of the things the Indians in grade one didn't know was English. They speak Saulteaux at home a good deal of the time and their English vocabulary is often loaded with unacceptable words. They were undisciplined, unable to concentrate, missed days, and came late. Their parents took them out of school in May or early June and didn't bring them back until late September. Because the white children did not have the same difficulties, they would have to be taught separately.

The breakdowns in the integration deal began to show, as they showed also in The Pas. The school board—and the Indians—felt that they had been deceived and misled by Indian Affairs. Indian Affairs had not told them about the problems the school would face, or that the children would face. Indian Affairs had not mentioned dropouts, absenteeism, failures, poor English, poor health. The board simply dropped the pretence by rejecting the Indians. Just having Indians in the building does not mean the school is integrated, and with the Indians all in the lower years, the Dominion City school was *not* integrated.

The decision was taken with the knowledge and tacit approval of both communities. The guilt or the credit for honesty, is not the school board's alone. It is shared by both communities, Indian and white, alike. Everybody knew what the board was going to do at least a week before. Gossip spreads readily through Dominion City and filters out to the reserve via Steve Seenie. No one in Dominion objected, or, if anyone did, no delegation of irate citizens appeared at the board meeting to protest, although Lorne Ramsey tried to stop it:

"Ramsey called me aside. He said there was going to be a meeting. I could have gone. Why didn't someone from Indian Affairs go? They could have asked to meet with the band.

"We wanted to stay out of it as much as possible. The next time, the town can come to the reserve."

Steve Seenie

The board did the only honest thing it could under the circumstances, except one. It could have talked to the Indians and worked out some solution with them. That never crossed the board's mind. The deal had been made with Indian Affairs, and the Board felt it had been tricked by Indian Affairs. The Indians never really figured in the picture at all.

"The Indians didn't protest or say anything about having their kids kicked out. Couldn't have cared less, I guess."

Lorne Ramsey

But they did care.

"I think they waited until the people were out of the way in Macdonald. It came all of a sudden. They never told us about it. They called the kids names in school. They kicked the kids out.

"Every time an Indian went into the hotel in Dominion City after that, he was ready to fight the whole hotel."

Archie Accobee

Instead of talking to the Indians, the school board chose to talk to the newspaper. Feelings of bitter hatred and offence arose in both Dominion City and the reserve, as taunts and threats were exchanged in print via the *Free Press* and *Tribune*. The tenuous links which had been established between town and reserve deteriorated. Old "friends" no longer spoke or drank together. The atmosphere of benevolent tolerance had disappeared and feelings of frustration which had been hidden were made public, written on all faces. Each community, each twin, retreated into its own sense of outraged virtue.

Integration

Education was a touchy topic in Dominion City in the autumn of 1966 and was discussed in whispers. Some people accused the school board members of having ulterior motives for getting rid of the Indians, and no one would say anything in public. Relations between the village and the reserve were also delicate while fights and squabbles were liable to break out on the smallest pretext.

The residents of the village spoke nostalgically of the old days when everyone got along with the Indians. They reminisced about pow-wows on the reserve and friendly baseball games in town. The beginning of decline in the relationship was pinpointed to about 20 years before, just after the Second World War ended. Since then, things had gone from bad to worse. The falling out had coincided with an increase in government welfare to Indians and their legalized access to liquor. Liquor was, in fact, the paramount concern of both reserve and town. "What are you going to do about our liquor problem? " was the first thing the Indians asked Pat Dunphy. The villagers also admitted that many unfortunate incidents had stemmed from drunkenness. This intoxication was not confined to the Indians, and it was apparent that too much liquor was being consumed in both communities.

Each community contained articulate people, but no one was talking. Each had, like Lena Boubard, gone inside. They talked, however, to Pat Dunphy, who found himself playing diplomatic courier, shuttling between town and reserve with messages, hints, innuendoes, threats and peace proposals. As an outsider, he provided a safe, objective point of view. Many Dominion City people never realized how prejudiced they were until Pat asked them, bluntly, have you ever been to the reserve? Many were astonished that Pat would not only go there, but return unharmed. Similarly, Pat informed the Indians that stealing cars was not guaranteed to bring about a good relationship with Dominion City. As this indirect communication increased, people were amazed to discover that Indians and villagers thought alike. The Indians shared, or at least professed to share, the villagers' obsessions with press criticism, vandalism, drinking, violence, industry, beautification and re-creation. The only difference was point of view.

The reserve was totally disorganized; no chief had been chosen to replace the one chased away, and the band hall was full of flour sent free by Indian Affairs to Indians who no longer lived there. By winter, some small progress had been made. About a dozen young men had enrolled in upgrading classes, expressing, suddenly, a fervent belief in higher education while pocketing their weekly going-to-school pay. Kindergarten enrollment increased from five to eleven.

In November, the school board hinted it might consider re-integrating the Indians in the school system. Surprising things began to happen in January, when 17 Roseau men were hired by a pulp cutting plant in Ontario, the first time any of them had acquired full-time employment in years. "It seems too good to be true that all these men needed was a chance to work or go to school," commented Pat Dunphy. It was too good. The men quit, complained about wages and discrimination, threatened, went back again and quit again. But Dominion City was heartened. The Indians pestered Dunphy with their demands, expecting him to conjure up schools, money, and jobs, and berated him when their dreams didn't come true. Their impatience was encouraging.

A new chief and band council were elected in February. For the next month, they held meetings four and five times a week to make up for all the time lost over the past 20 years. Committees on housing, sanitation and finances were struck off. Stan Nelson rounded up truants (attendance at the reserve schools climbed 30 per cent) and apprehended lawbreakers. The reserve became more organized and more productive than Dominion City. The possibility of a meeting between the band council and the Dominion City Chamber of Commerce was discussed, and the Dominion City community club invited the new chief, John James, to take part in its winter carnival. In full regalia, including tomahawk, James gave an exhibition of pow-wow dancing, whoops and war chants which brought down the house. Afterwards, many people expressed the feeling that maybe Indians weren't so bad after all.

Just after the carnival, in March, Dominion City voted in a new school division. The old Dominion City school board was defunct. The division, taking in several small villages, meant that one of them would get a new consolidated high school. Competition would be fierce, and the town needed the new school in order to survive. The Indians were needed in order to get the school and Dominion City decided to get the Indians.

Negotiations began. Lorne Ramsey, chairman of the old school board and member of the new, had gone to school with John James, chief of Roseau, 25 years before. It was easy for them, after the initial meetings over the winter, to renew their acquaintance. School integration began to work—25 years late.

In April, John James and Lorne Ramsey confronted each other across a table in a cold, draughty room filled with stuffed owls in the Dominion City Queen's Hotel. The topic was integration. Agreement was total: immediate integration of Indian children into the public schools. The reserve schools would be closed. An Indian would be elected to the school board. Difficulties were discussed calmly and objectively. Everyone parted friends. Indian Affairs was not present at the meeting.

Chapter 11
The Drink-In

*"Please don't sell my Daddy no more wine, no more wine;
He may be no good but he's still mine."*

song

An Indian staggers into the pool hall in Gleichen, Alberta. He unzips his trousers and, holding out his penis, urinates on the pool table with a fine fountain-like spray. The manager, a white man, grabs him and throws him out. An Indian woman, who has been sitting on the floor against the wall, leaves a small pile of excrement when she gets up to leave. Outside, another Indian urinates against the side of a parked car. A woman lies on the snow-covered road, vomiting.

The white residents of the two dead-end little towns, Gleichen and Cluny, Alberta, are extremely upset over this behavior. The two towns, on the edge of the Blackfoot reserve, have developed a reputation for theft, muggings and fights and have become known as "Indian towns." Some businesses have been broken into so many times that their theft insurance has been cancelled. White residents feel their property is worthless, since no people will want to live in Gleichen and Cluny. The change came in the summer of 1966 when Indians in Alberta were granted the right to drink in beer parlors. The pubs in the two towns were flooded with Indians. They said it was "a good feeling" to go into a bar, raise two fingers and be served by a white man. Many Indians drank beer until they reeled from drunkenness and their money had disappeared. They would then start begging for more from passersby, or pestering for a ride back to the reserve. Since the Indians were several miles from home, there was no place for them to urinate or be sick except the main streets of Gleichen and Cluny. The bartenders threw them out as soon as their money was gone or they showed signs of passing out. Indians, men and women, would be shoved into the dirt in front of the pubs, watched by a milling crowd of Indian children, left to fend for themselves. The children, to amuse themselves, would plunder cars or throw rocks through windows. When the pubs closed at 6:30, the Indians would swarm out and into nearby businesses, desperate for a place to go to the bathroom. Proprietors found their stores being used as lavatories; they would find Indians asleep in their beds, bath tubs and chairs. Thus all the businessmen closed their shops at the same time as the pub.

In Cluny, the local firehall is a favourite hangout for the Indians' drinking parties. It is across the street from the hotel and heated. The stench from urine and excrement in the hall is overpowering. Beer bottles, dirty clothing, garbage, wine and vanilla bottles litter the floor.

The owner of the pool hall in Gleichen, Stan Bogstie, who is also the town undertaker, says "everything has gone haywire" since the Indians were granted drinking privileges in the town's beer parlor in 1966. "Drunken Indians use the town's main street and adjoining properties to indecently assault and have intercourse with Indian women," he said. "Trouble originates in beer parlors. I've seen Indians so drunk they had to be carted away."

Gleichen, a poverty-stricken white town, has 426 residents. The Blackfoot reserve, grubby and also poverty-stricken, has 2,300 residents. Seven hundred are adults. Court convictions under the Liquor Act tripled in one year. White women are terrified to walk down the street, even in daylight. "I wouldn't walk downtown in Gleichen if someone gave me $500," said the mayor's wife. The women say they are now unable to shop and visit because of fear of molestation by drunk Indians. Mr. Bogstie said that at least 10 Indians had died from alcohol and side effects in a few months. Gleichen and Cluny used to be railway and farming towns. Now they are booze towns. The main income comes from the sale of beer and wine. The hotels do the best business.

The residents of Cluny and Gleichen wrote letters and petitions to Premier Ernest Manning demanding an investigation into Indian drinking. Police are blamed for being too lax, hotel keepers are blamed for serving the Indians liquor, the Indians blame the white people for being mean to them. "There's not much else for many of my people to do except drink in town." said Adam Solway of the Blackfoot band.

The mayor of Gleichen proposed a course to educate Indians in the niceties of social drinking. "Something has got to be done! " say the people of the towns. Several are thinking of moving away. They can't sell their homes or businesses because no white person wants to live in Gleichen.

The behavior of the Indians appears to be extraordinary, primitive and inexplicable. Or is it? The Indians are having a drink-in.

Freedom rides have desegregated buses in the United States South. Sit-ins have desegregated restaurants. The Indians are experimenting to see if a drink-in will desegregate a white town. The principle is the same—mass, persistant, non-violent civil disobedience. The Indians break all the liquor laws, and break them to such an extent that the police cannot keep up with them, short of putting the whole reserve in jail. They come into the town and refuse to leave. They won't go home. They jam the beer parlors. They pollute the fire hall. They pack the grocery stores and the main street so the women can't shop. They pester and threaten the white citizens. They urinate on the pool tables. They steal from parked cars. They fight and scream and kick, crawl down the streets, leaving a trail of vomit. This is not normal drinking. It is aggressive, hostile drinking. It is war.

Drinking is a symbol of equality to the Indian. It represents his acceptance in a white town which bars him from all other forms of integrated activity. Many Indians became enfranchised for the right to drink, and it is the only form of civil rights they know. The Indian may be illiterate, poor and dominated by Indian Affairs, but he knows he can drink as well as the white man. He tries to prove he can drink more and better and becomes a champion drinker. Indians drink with more flair, with more imagination, with more dramatic ability than most white men. The more an Indian drinks, the more he proves his right to equality, his right to hold up two fingers and have a white waiter come skipping over to serve him.

Indians also know, from long experience, that excessive drinking annoys white people. It gets them upset. They pay attention to a drunk Indian; a sober Indian they never see. Drinking is an excellent way for the Indian to get Canada's attention. During 1967, the Gleichen-Cluny drink-in received extensive coverage in all the major newspapers in Canada, and was exhaustively detailed by the Edmonton *Journal*. It was also the subject of a half hour television documentary by the CBC. All this publicity did little to improve the "image" of the Indians in Canada's eyes, but it did much to harm the reputations of Gleichen and Cluny, and that served the Indians' ends as well.

Mass public drunkenness can destroy a town. Respectable people leave, businesses close, insurance is cancelled, real estate is worthless, and visitors and farmers stay away. The town becomes an "Indian town," a slum, a plague center, quarantined. Gleichen and Cluny are not the first, nor the only, small towns to be attacked by an Indian drink-in. Indians urinate on the streets in Kenora, Ontario. They jostle and molest people in Dominion City, Manitoba. They fornicate publicly in Prince Albert, Saskatchewan. They jam the bars and crowd the sidewalk on Winnipeg's Main Street, "Apache Row." They lie in the gutters in The Pas and Kamsack. They fight and quarrel among themselves. Bartenders throw them out on the streets; they stagger and crawl. They curse at passersby or beg. They steal beer from men coming out of hotels, and steal from each other as well. Wherever the Indians go in large numbers, blight follows. White people react with anger and revulsion, calling for police protection: "Send the Indians back to the reserves." "Lock 'em up." "Gas 'em." Still the Indians come, staggering, bottle in hand.

The jails fill up to overflowing. Indians fill the dockets in the courts. All their offences are liquor charges or related charges of fighting and theft. They are indifferent, resigned. They make no defence. They are unrepentant.

> *"This Indian situation is greatly affecting the financial standing of our community. Our cafes and confectionery shops have to close early because they just cannot cope with the trouble caused by the Indian population. There are cases where these people do not use washroom facilities provided but urinate on the floors of our eating establishments and food stores. In other cases, the businessman has to put money out of his own savings to pay for damage done by these people. People from surrounding towns who for years made Kamsack their shopping headquarters have taken their business elsewhere on account of the Indians. No one can tell us that the Indian leaves his money in Kamsack when it is a known fact that it is returned to the government through the purchase of beer and wine."*
>
> Letter from Citizens' Committee of
> Kamsack, Saskatchewan to
> Provincial Attorney-General, 1963

The town affected by the drink-in does not literally die, but it loses its good name, and changes character. Businesses associated with liquor thrive. Grocery stores do well. The main source of income becomes welfare and the town is populated by members of the welfare industry, police, probation officers, social workers. The chambers of commerce which complain so bitterly about their losses from Indians do not mention their profits. These towns are usually much wealthier after the Indian invasion than before, except the wealth is underground and often illicit. Like Indians who are forced to appear poor in order to acquire relief, these towns have to appear poor in order to hide the dirty money. The town ceases in effect to be a town and becomes, like The Pas, a large slum. Bootlegging is prevalent in all these communities, and some white men make a great deal of money from the drink-in. Life, in Kamsack, has become a drunken brawl: "At present, in many cases, the Indians take the initiative in getting into trouble with the white men, particularly when the latter are under the influence of liquor."

Kamsack protested originally in 1958 in a letter to the Minister of Citizenship and Immigration, pointing out that the "aimless lives" of the Indians keep them on the streets of Kamsack from early morning until late at night, and that all live off welfare money which is spent on liquor. In 1960, about 550 drunk Indians were arrested in Kamsack. Acts of violence are reported increasing.

"Women and children, yes, even men are afraid to be on the streets after dark in fear of being beaten, insulted or molested," said the 1958 letter. Kamsack's problems are the same as those of Gleichen and all the other towns. This uniformity of behavior by the Indians and of reaction by the white residents is one of the most significant aspects of the drink-in. Whether the Indians are Cree, Saulteaux or Blackfoot, they behave in exactly the same manner, loud, insulting, aggressive.

The drink-ins are spontaneous and unconscious. Although they paralyze numerous towns simultaneously and create maximum frustration and anger in the white residents, they are unplanned. No one runs around from reserve to reserve saying "O.K. fellas, we're going to have a drink-in next week." No one provides buses or the money to buy the beer. The movement has no spokesmen, no leaders, no organization, no name. I call it a drink-in because that is, to me, the most accurate word, but I have heard no one else describe the process. Drink-ins appear to be a genuine, unplanned, emotional response by thousands of Indians who speak different languages and are unaware of each other's existence. The drink-in is a totally Indian movement, there are no white people in the vanguard, and it is as spontaneous as the first Negro sit-ins and freedom rides in Alabama.

The drink-in is the only form of protest which unites Indians. Because people act from unconscious motives rather than from planned tactics does not make their protest any less effective. It makes it, in fact, more efficient. Incessant public drunkenness renders towns helpless because the residents don't understand what is happening. Indians have perfectly logical and understandable reasons to drink. There is no need to look for disguised aggression as a motive. Any group of people that is chronically poor, dependent, unemployed, badly educated and segregated will suffer the tensions and despair that lead to alcoholism. Certainly, Indians in western and northern Canada suffer from all these handicaps. They suffer also from the destruction of their old way of life by contemporary technology, from government restrictions and controls, from the scorn and opprobrium of white Canadians.

Normally, however, individuals within the group will respond differently to these strains. They will develop various kinds of neuroses, and they adapt in different ways. The extraordinary response of the Indians is that they have turned in such great numbers to alcohol. Alcoholism is almost a cult.

Bacchanalia

Wild, frenzied orgies are conducted on the main streets of many small towns and cities in Canada day and night. The Indians are having a perpetual happy party. God-fearing citizens are shocked—it's savage, primitive, pagan. The Indians' traditional religious beliefs, stamped out and repressed by the Christian churches, seem to have gone underground to emerge, disguised, as alcoholism. The Sun Dance is now a tourist attraction, but the Blackfoot, by their drinking habits, can still irritate missionaries and white intruders. They terrify them and keep them away. The Indians can put a hex on a town, in effect, by the drinking. Drinking also places a stigma on an Indian, keeps him separate from *white* culture, and thus preserves his Indian identity. Alcoholism, by casting scorn and shame on the Indians, protects them. It is a profoundly subtle defensive tactic.

Strong traditions exist for the Indians' mass adoption of excessive drinking. The Indians' religious beliefs and their whole social structure were built around visions or dreams in which man made contact with the spiritual world. A state of frenzy would be induced by various rituals including starvation, torture, exposure and the consumption of herbs. In his ecstatic condition, the Indian would become literally possessed of a spirit. Medicine men exerted their authority through their ability, real or pretended, to make contact with the spiritual world and to relay messages to the tribe.

Through drinking, Indians are able to maintain the frenzy and the oblivion in public without fear of persecution and condemnation which their real rituals would excite.

Alcoholism is not a recent development among the Indians. Liquor was originally banned from reserves at the request of chiefs who were distressed by their people's drinking. The behavior of the Blackfoot has, if anything, improved in the past 100 years. Missionaries and traders have left many accounts of violent, suicidal Indian drinking around the forts and posts. Liquor also has a social and economic tradition with the Indian, one which ties him very closely to white people. Liquor is a symbol of his equality. It is also a symbol of his working-man's status. Rum and whiskey were used as payment by fur traders for many years. Indians received liquor, not money, for their furs. Liquor occupied, therefore, the position of "salary" in their dealings with white men. The better trapper a man was, the more liquor he got and the drunker he became. Drunkenness was a sign of status among many Indians.

Although the old fur trade way of life has passed out of existence, the Indian continues to respond in these ritualized ways, drunkenness and debt. His experience with liquor was directly contrary to that of other people. Liquor was a reward for good conduct and high productivity. It was not considered evil by the traders. By the time the teetotaler missionaries arrived, the traders had already indoctrinated the Indians to see drunkenness as a commendable state. No feelings of guilt or shame were attached to it.

The R.C.M.P., then called the North-West Mounted Police, came into existence to combat Indian drinking and attendant problems of violence and robbery. This is, in western Canada, still the prime function of the R.C.M.P. Throughout the prairies, rural detachments of the R.C.M.P. spend between 80 and 90 per cent of their time dealing with Indian liquor offences. The original sore spot was Fort Whoop-Up, an American fur trade post south of the Blackfoot territory which succeeded in parting the Indians from their furs in exchange for as much liquor as they could hold. Appalling fights broke out when the Indian camp was totally drunk. Men stabbed and killed each other, tents were burned, women were raped and beaten. Screams and whoops filled the air as the Indians chased each other around until they dropped from exhaustion. The traders watched with amusement from the protection of the fort.

Many missionaries reported almost continual drunkenness in their Indian flocks. The traders and settlers who brought liquor also probably were the reason why the Indians drank it. Through the oblivion of alcohol, they could escape the fear and uncertainty inspired by the foreigners' power. Their drunkenness also coincided, in the west, with the disappearance of the buffalo. Drinking declined and almost disappeared as the Indians settled down on reserves under the wings of the government and missionaries. As long as the Indians were assured of protection and sufficient food, their demand for alcohol decreased.

Recently drinking has increased in *direct proportion* to the Indians' dependency on welfare since welfare money is spent on liquor. Drinking has shown a rapid, marked increase since the end of World War Two. Indians appear to be as deeply affected by the advent of automation as they were originally by the infiltration of the French or English. This second upsurge of drinking is also associated with the second disappearance of the Indians' way of life. The economy which he laboriously built up after the treaties—farming, trapping and fishing—is now obsolete and the Indian is, yet once more, faced with starvation and extinction.

When the Indians were established on reserves, they were forced into an economy which was even then out of date. It took them more than 50 years to learn how to settle down, glean fish, or till the land. They changed from nomads into agriculturalists. Even the Indians of the north were forced to see the game and fish as a "harvest" for sale or barter. A change which, in the normal course of time, takes hundreds and thousands of years the Indians accomplished in two generations. No sooner did they become fairly proficient at farming and fishing than the economy was revolutionized once more, and they were expected to become push-button factory workers. The Indians would have no trouble making these adjustments were they not held back and restricted by government laws. It is this friction between the Indian's own desire to adapt, his fear of change, and impositions which the government places on him that produces alcoholism.

Excessive drinking is ultimately suicidal. Not only does it rot the organs or lead to death from accident or exposure, but it also destroys the family and the society. Children, left for hours without food outside the beer parlor, are dirty, sick and neglected. A society of drunks defies existing taboos, and the norms of the orgy become social norms. A party which is held every day ceases to be a party—it is an economy. Drinking is built into the traditions of contemporary Indian culture. It provides an escape from otherwise intolerable strain. The Indians may be dirty, vulgar and promiscuous, but at least they are alive.

"I Can't Remember: I Was Drunk"

Liquor also provides an excuse for an Indian when he is trapped. In many cases, Indians will claim to be drunk when they are not. They use intoxication deliberately and consciously as a defence. Indians hauled into court on charges ranging from theft to murder parrot the identical excuse: "I was too drunk to know what I was doing. I can't remember what happened." From their stories, many Indians appear to be peculiarly subject to blackouts and amnesia when drinking.

The Indians also know that most white people tend to see them as "drunken Indians" with an innate biological intolerance for alcohol. When an Indian drinks, think the sober white people, anything can happen.

"Magistrate Isaac Rice urged that action be taken to prevent a certain 'class of people' from drinking liquor. He said there is something in their body chemistry which doesn't mix with alcohol. 'Until we can get somebody to stand behind me and stop them from drinking, anarchy will rule,' the magistrate said. . .

"He made these comments in city Magistrate's court Thursday after convicting James Robert Morrissette, 23, of 239 Pritchard Ave., of assault causing bodily harm in the knifing of Ivan "Choc" Smith, 32, of 437 Jarvis Ave."

Winnipeg Tribune,
Nov. 18, 1966

The Indians often make drunkenness their alibi, and unless a judge or magistrate is particularly astute, he will be taken in by the excuse, since it is very difficult to disprove. From transcripts of court hearings, it can be detected that often Indians are not nearly as drunk as they claim to be. A man who claims to be oblivious should also be incapable of planned action. Yet many Indians who claim to be dead drunk go through complicated motions to steal cars or break into buildings. Indian alcoholism is sometimes faked deliberately. It is also phony in other, perhaps unconscious, ways. The line between faked drunkenness and exaggerated or dramatized drunkenness is very fine.

Indians are not, according to accepted standards, alcoholics. A sociologist who spent several summers with the Saulteaux Indians of northwestern Manitoba reports:

> *"There are 'drinking problems' to be sure, especially in the larger bands . . . but there appears to be little, if any, actual alcohol addiction of the chronic phase for treaty Indians living on these reserves. Of the numerous persons interviewed, none has ever experienced surreptitious drinking, 'blackouts', a rationalization of drinking behavior, persistent remorse, the dropping of friendships, protection of alcohol supply, morning drinking, tremors, psychomotor inhibition or obsessive drinking. These are among the 39 attributes established by the Alcoholism Subcommittee of the World Health Organization."*

John Steinbring, "Culture Change Among the Northern Ojibwa," in *Transactions of the Historical and Scientific Society of Manitoba, series 111*, no. 21, 1965, p. 20

Included among the reserves which Professor Steinbring investigated was Fort Alexander, a band which has a province-wide reputation for hard, incessant drinking. "The occurrence of a chronic alcoholic would be extremely rare among the Lake Winnipeg bands," said Steinbring.

Indians do not hoard liquor, and their drinking lacks the secretive, masochistic quality of alcoholism. Drinking is seldom a day-long affair, but a social event, always associated with a party or an escapade. It seems, in fact, to be an excuse for a party. Indian drinking has the grim, black comedy of the Dance of Death. Indians go to their doom, but noisily and merrily. It is the act of drinking, the ritual, not the liquor itself, which seems to be most important. The ritualized, uniform, dramatic quality of Indian drinking indicates that it may have been absorbed as an integral part of reserve society. This is suggested by Steinbring:

"Despite the fact that there are few, if any, addicted alcoholics among these people, the institution of Alcoholics Anonymous is sweeping the country, and is being absorbed by all of the Ojibwa bands as they are connected to the road system. In a certain band, all but one of the adult males have joined AA. Few ever had severe drinking problems, and some had never used alcohol. AA is a male oriented group, which links well with native custom. Public activities have always been the province of Ojibwa men. The testimonial assumes particular importance. The verbal arts are highly developed in Ojibwa culture, and they find their best expression among the traditional persons of leadership and authority, the elder men. Young men had begun to question the authority of the elders, but AA has now formed a means to reconsolidate traditional leadership. Oratorical skill is achieved only through long experience and the ideas conveyed through it have a depth and practical currency which the young men are again beginning to accept. Because of its decentralized nature, each band can and does form its own chapter of AA (one large band has two). This permits the exclusive use of native language, a very unifying factor. There is a definite religious dimension to AA, and in some cases an ecstatic involvement has been observed. In one band the meetings are held on Sunday, and when the only 'holdout' in this community was asked why he did not join AA, he replied, 'If I joined AA, I'd only quit the church like all the others.' Ojibwa people will tell you that all of the Indian's troubles are the result of drinking. What they are doing, in effect, is to

rationalize cultural loss around alcohol. And AA (which they were able to choose without any kind of external pressure) becomes a means to renewed social strength. Among the many North American nativistic movements, its form is actually unique in only one main respect. AA serves the purpose it was intended for in Western society. And, because it does not contain magical formulae, bizarre performances, or narcotics, it should prove extremely difficult for that external world to disparage and renounce its development, as has always been the case with other revivalistic efforts. It is awful to say so, but this may even be a somewhat optimistic view. Some less secure members of Western society will probably feel 'bilked', despite the fact that the reformative character of AA has not yet been consciously expressed as a group force."

John Steinbring

The people of Little Black River, one of the reserves with this AA organization, refer to events as happening pre-AA or post-AA. The year 1963 is the *anno Domini* "when we got AA." All happenings to the band are interpreted in the light of AA. If band members are robbed or threatened by other Indians it is because "they are jealous of our AA."

Jekyll and Hyde

Indians are usually fighting drunks. Parties frequently end in fights and the fights frequently cause maiming or death. The most passive, apathetic Indians can be changed, after one bottle of cheap wine, into snarling, swearing street brawlers. Silent women suddenly exhibit a vocabulary of choice profanity shouted at the top of their lungs in the town's main street. White people do not care if the Indians drink or not, but they object to the fighting that goes with it. Incidents of Indians beating or attacking a white person are rare, and white women are, in spite of their fears, almost never assaulted. But the Indians certainly attack each other. They go after one another with knives and beer bottles in streets and alleys, they beat each other up, they poke out eyes and tear out hair.

Psychologists and sociologists explain these outbursts of violence on the ground that Indians are very inhibited people.

Traditional Indian society was decorous and severely circumscribed with rules of conduct. Politeness and respect were to be shown at all times. The society was in such a delicate state of equilibrium that anger or violence could disrupt it, and deviant people were killed, expelled or, in the case of the mentally ill or defective, often accepted as "seers" and prophets. Life was in many respects highly disciplined. The Indians had to endure solitude, hunger and anxiety. All their lives were spent with their own family groups or in tiny bands of people. Wars between rival bands were continual. Aggression was expressed by horse stealing or feats of daring against a rival tribe. Within the tribe, anger and violence were repressed or taken out through some ritualized form of self-mutilation.

When this little group of people was threatened by an overwhelming foreign force, the internal tensions became explosive, and alcohol provided a release by destroying inhibitions. It destroys, for a time, the Indian's cultural background, and makes him the same as a drunken white man. It also enables him to forget the worries associated with the disappearance of his way of life. Intoxicated, an Indian's repressed hates come to the surface and are expressed physically and verbally. He hits out at his wife, his children, his friends. This violence, like the drinking itself, is strongly suicidal, and the victims are those persons nearest to the drunk man. He is hitting, indirectly, at himself. The guilt which an Indian does not feel about drinking he will feel about the beatings he administers to his friends and family. Guilt does not, however, stop the violence.

Much of this 'drunkenness' appears to be self-induced, almost hypnotic. Indians appear to be able to get insanely drunk on a couple of bottles of cheap wine or a few beers. Even hardened drinkers, men or women who have been drinking for years, exhibit a tendency to become irresponsible and oblivious after a small quantity of liquor. Indians seldom drink hard liquor; it's either wine, beer or "moose milk" (home brew). The Indians' drunkenness has a stagey, exaggerated quality, as if they are *willing* themselves to get drunk, play-acting at being drunken Indians. Indians have told me they have seen dozens of people get roaringly drunk on moose milk which had almost no alcoholic content at all. The people convinced themselves it was potent and it was. The psychological association of magic and visions give alcohol its power; the actual alcoholic content is irrelevant.

A drunken Indian's behavior has a uniform, stereotyped quality. He acts the same whether he has had one bottle of beer or 20. Indians who drink heavily behave as if they are drunk even when they are sober, and drink is simply an excuse for self-expression. The gradations and varieties of drunkenness appear to be missing in the Indians — they are sober or dead drunk and there seems to be no inbetween.

This excessiveness, this exaggeration is essential to the success of the drink-in. In towns like Gleichen and Kamsack, the hidden aggression of drinking is directed against the white population and the clue is the fact that Indian drinking is public. Drunken Indians have a compulsion to be seen and be heard, so they yell, grab you by the arm, shove people around. They fill the street and the sidewalks and the bars. It is the fact that the Indians are drinking in the street that distresses the white people. All the private acts — the fornication, the urinating, the vomiting — are carried on in full daylight on Main Street. There is a striking difference between the behavior of Indians in the pubs and just outside the front door. Inside they are quiet, peaceful and well-behaved; out on the street, they are violent and vulgar. Drinking provides an excuse for the Indians to be rude and hostile to white people. Things they would never dare say or do when sober they can do when drunk, or when pretending to be drunk, and the humble, submissive Indian becomes suddenly bitter and antagonistic. The whole performance relies for its effect on the reaction of shock and revulsion by white people, for if the townsfolk didn't react, the Indians would probably shut up and calm down. But the townspeople must react; they can't help it. Reaction to drunkenness is built into their puritan tradition as solidly as drunkenness is built into the Indian's psychedelic tradition. That's why the Indians have a drink-in. The drink-in is a classic example of non-violent protest. "Shit on you," the Indian is saying.

Chapter 12
Underground

Preservation

"Some North American Indian cultures have 'gone underground'. In order to preserve their way of life, they have become quite secretive about forms of behavior and belief. They practise the strictest form of this secrecy toward persons they identify with external pressures toward change. This is why many official persons feel that Indians have already become essentially Westernized. It is hard to imagine that a man who drives a car, owns a transistor radio, operates a chain saw, and attends Alcoholics Anonymous meetings is a 'blood letter' and may have experienced supernatural visitations.

"Magic and sorcery remain important in the thoughts of Northern Ojibwa people living on the road system. Even in presumably Westernized individuals, a belief in the cannibalistic monster, Windigo, is prevalent. Many persons would prefer to take a mentally ill child to a shaman for treatment rather than to a psychiatrist in the city. People still get very ill thinking that some evil person is using 'bad medicine' against them. Some have been known to die. A good example of a covert institution is the very Western looking 'birthday party'. Despite the birthday cake, the candles, the food, the family gathering, and the dancing, this event is steeped in magico-religious beliefs. It is felt to be essential to sustaining

the life of a certain child, say, who had been preceded by several miscarriages or infant deaths. It is firmly believed that the child will die if the 'party' is not held continuously for fifteen years. Even the poorest families save diligently all year for this event . . . Dreams play a significant and fundamental role in the life of Ojibwa people. One's name may be ultimately derived from an old man's dream, or one can learn of his (or her) guardian spirit or animal protector through a dream. Bad dreams often haunt Ojibwa people, a fact acknowledged by psychiatrists who have worked with them. Certain tasks cannot be undertaken because of premonitions contained in dreams. Some forms of 'magic' are still occasionally practised. These seem to fall mainly into the areas of hunting and love. A hunter or trapper may offer tobacco to the spirits before setting out. In some families an incredible amount of tobacco is purchased each month for this and other ritual uses. Love magic requires 'professional help'. One must secure a magical concoction which is said to excite responses from the right girl or boy. Either sex may use these potions."

John Steinbring, "Recent
Studies Among the Northern
Ojibwa" *Manitoba
Archaeological Newsletters,*
Vol. 1, no. 4, 1964

It has become very clear within the last 10 years that Indians are still Indians. The aggressive "convert and civilize" approach taken by both the government and the missionaries has produced precisely the opposite response, and has caused the Indians, in self-defence, to withdraw from contact and to preserve, however they could, the important elements of their own traditions. Indian society today is comprised of two main forces which have become intermeshed. The first is a positive attempt to retain traditional cultural patterns: the second is a defence against European concepts and standards. Therefore, antagonism and withdrawal from Canadian society are built into the contemporary Indian's self-image. To be an Indian, he has to hate the white man.

The conservative, defensive reaction by the Indians is not

unique. Any culture reacts in an identical pattern when threatened. The UNESCO report, *Cultural Patterns and Technical Change,* defines five types of defensive reaction:

A return is made to old forms of behavior which are now inadequate. This response includes a great deal of hostility towards the intruding culture. The hostility increases if the people have tried new techniques and failed. They will then attack them rather than try again.

Behavior becomes more childish, emotional. Feelings of dependency and helplessness arise.

Aggressive acts occur, an undirected lashing out which may not touch the source of anger at all.

People withdraw into apathy. Apathy also includes physical and mental illness, alcoholism, drug addiction and nativistic cults, in which the former life, now seen as a golden age, is acted out symbolically. Adolescents who, in the former way of life would have remained energetic and highly motivated, suddenly cease to be able to learn and so give rise to myths about the inability of peoples newly exposed to modern technology to learn the necessary new knowledge.

Unpleasant encounters or situations are avoided. The unresolved tensions find expression in diverse and often unrelated ways, such as chronic fatigue, preoccupation with health, compulsive ritual, new activities which are socially approved, assigning blame for the situation to others, retreat into endless thinking about the situation without any attempt to check the thinking with reality.

All these traits certainly describe Indian reactions, and they also describe the reactions of many white Canadians, certainly in small towns like Kenora and Dominion City and The Pas. Indians are not the only people who don't behave according to enlightened principles. The peasants and working-class people of small Canadian towns react with precisely the same rigidity and conservatism when faced with a new and threatening situation. Universally, their tendency is to take refuge in pointless rituals and to return to old forms of behavior like committees, police control, and moral outrage. These white people are as frightened of change and of government intervention as are the Indians. The Dominion City people exhibited the same silence and the same withdrawal as Roseau reserve.

Their most important act — banning the Indians from the school — was irresponsible. When the Dominion City people let the School Board do that, they showed the same willingness as the Indians to have the government run their lives for them. And the farmers of the Dominion City area, who represent a threatened peasant culture, are as desperate to preserve their values as the Indians are to maintain their own.

The discriminatory reserve system has made it easy for each of these groups to blame the other for all its problems. Until that discrimination is removed, there is little chance that the mutual hatred will decrease, and Indians and farmers both will strongly resist its removal because then they will be forced to find other scapegoats.

In The Beginning . . .

The Indian world view before the conquest, bore, it appears, an extraordinary resemblance to that of the New England Puritans. The society was a theocracy in which religious principles dominated all aspects of life; the world was controlled by benevolent and demonaic spirits, and society was ruled by religious leaders. Social relations were dominated by fear of sorcery and death, and fear of disease acted as the prime means of social control within Indian society just as fear of sin filled this role in the Puritan world. Both societies believed in the power of certain 'witches' or magical people to hex others and cause death. This spiritual power was exercised through the infliction of illness. Illness was regarded by the Indians as a sign of wrong-doing and punishment, similar to our idea of being possessed with a devil. One man could take revenge on another by causing him to fall ill and die.

"It is strange," said Father Le Jeune, one of the first Jesuit priests to come to Canada, "to see how these people agree so well outwardly and how they hate each other within. They do not often get angry and fight with one another but in the depths of their hearts they intend a great deal of harm."

Sharing of food and hospitality among the Indians was not, as it is often suggested, a sign of communal living, but a means of self-defence against the magic powers of the guest, an effort to obtain his good will. If a man did not share, he would be assumed to be hostile and would be attacked by sorcery. Life, to the Indian as to the Puritan, was beset with unknown threats and anxieties. Both experienced persecution. It is possible the Indians' disease-based social ethic grew up after their contact with smallpox and tuberculosis, introduced very early by the traders and missionaries. The idea of disease being an indication of wrong-doing might have been an attempt to explain sudden inexplicable and incurable illness.

Indian society was characterized by extreme self-discipline and restraint. No move could be made which could be interpreted as aggression. Anger, not permitted to be expressed in legitimate ways, came out in subtle, devious ways. Gossip and ridicule, especially behind a person's back and often taking the form of 'jokes,' were common. The effect was devastating because a system of public confession during illness made everyone's private life public.

Anger, bitterness, hate and even love were repressed and internalized. Advice was given in a friendly, casual, rational tone and no one was allowed to give orders. This permissiveness was extended also to children, who were allowed to do as they pleased, with the hope that they would adopt adult functions at a very early age.

In addition to the obvious religious and sexual sanctions, the community was ruled by slander and gossip and by personal 'influence' through magic power. Aggression was conducted on a sophisticated psychological plane, a duel by sorcery. Body and soul were seen as unified and an attack on a man's mind would be reflected in his body as a symptom of disease. Life itself was a hidden power struggle involving all levels of existence and all eras in time. Standards of conduct and intellectual conceptions were not, therefore, absolute or rigid. This lack of definition, this total fluidity, probably militated against the evolution of writing because writing fixes and kills things. Each day was accepted on its own merits, as was each individual—with nothing autonomous, and everything relative.

Indian society was the exact antithesis of communal. It could be described as 'atomistic'—each person on his own. It was without formal laws or institutions, and the main social ties were family ties. An atmosphere of anxiety and disapproval about certain modes of conduct and the fear of sorcery were the only modes of social control, while individualism was the supreme value because the hunting way of life depended on the skill of the hunter alone.

Indians reacted to white men exactly as they reacted to each other. The white man was possessed of a superior power, and was, therefore, to be conciliated and never angered. He could, however, be slandered, cheated and attacked by sorcery. The white men, moreover, soon identified themselves as malevolent powers (the Indian's world, like ours, divides into God and Devil.) The missionaries alienated themselves by treating the Indians as savages, children and pagans. All the Indians' manitous were identified with the Devil and condemned. The Indians' rituals were scorned and, in the case of the Sun Dance and potlatch (gift-giving ceremonies of the west coast Indians) banned. In addition, the missionaries presented an over-simplified Sunday School version of Christianity which was virtually meaningless and certainly less powerful than the Indians' own beliefs. The missionaries made little or no effort to understand the people they were teaching, and preached a rigid dogma which the Indians could take as presented or ignore. Frequently, baptism did not involve any teaching of religion whatsoever, but the priest or clergyman simply sprinkled some water on an Indian's head and rang up another score for Christ. Those missionaries who did attempt some teaching soon found themselves outflanked by less scrupulous clergy who soon had sprinkled all their flock in a rival faith. Many Indians found themselves members of two or three denominations. Once, of course, they had been baptized, they saw no further reason to understand Christianity since they were already saved.

The missionaries were frustrated by evident antagonism or indifference on the part of the Indians, who did not want to be Christianized. Frequently the missionaries could get no one to convert so they adopted subtle tactics and often would sneak up and sprinkle water on small children when their parents were away. The easiest way was to baptize Indians as they were dying. (Most Indians became Christianized during the smallpox and TB plagues.) The Indian was flat on his back and helpless, the relatives were grief-stricken, and the missionary was saved the trouble of trying to communicate Christian doctrine. The missionaries became, unknown to themselves, Angels of Death in the Indians' minds. The clergy had arrived before the small-pox and had, with the traders, brought the germs. Because they were always talking about death and became firmly associated with death in their religious observances, the Indians perceived them as causing death.

Today, the churches have nearly abandoned Indians. The old people cling to their manitous and the young are as agnostic as most young Canadians. On Musqueam reserve in the heart of Vancouver the Indians continue to observe the torture-fasting rituals of their ancestors although now some of the young men call in the R.C.M.P. for protection when their turn has come to be put through the ceremony by the older men.

The Indians reacted to attempted innovations of farming, cattle-raising and education with the same passivity with which they greeted Christianity. They agreed readily to anything the government or missionary proposed. Farms and schools were set up, churches were built, and the Indians began to settle down and till the land. They showed friendliness and co-operation. This initial burst of enthusiasm lasted for about a year or two but slowly dwindled. Cattle were eaten and the men returned to the hunt at the height of the harvesting season. Machinery was broken and no one made an effort to repair it. Schools were built but could get no pupils to attend regularly. The Indians built little houses but lived in them as if they were tents, and initial attempts at making furniture soon failed. Many 'model' communities sprang up on Indian reserves across Canada, complete with clapboard churches with flying buttresses and row housing, but they soon became slums or ghost towns. Through passive resistance to all forms of change, the Indians managed to scuttle every attempt to make them into white men. They refused to speak clearly or articulately to white men; no one could communicate with them. They appeared stupid. Teachers gave up trying to educate them. They adapted white customs and drew a protective screen behind which they could hide their real identity.

The Indians' entire social structure was built around the ritual of hunting; farming was meaningless. The Indians played at farming while they continued to hunt, even when the game had disappeared. They are still hunting. Indians construct a fictional world which they attempt to reproduce. It is successful as long as white society can be kept at a distance and the old way of hunting can be preserved, at least in facsimile. The Indians will borrow the white man's food they like, strawberry jam and liquor, and will play with his gadgets, outboard motors and record players, but they will not undergo any significant change in cultural pattern.

As the world is remade in the white man's patterns, and hunting disappears, the Indian finds himself under great stress to find something 'Indian' to put in its place. The Indians become caricatures, playing at being Indian, and all their responses, once so full of social and supernatural significance, are meaningless gestures, even to themselves. They adopt the white man's view of the world and are conditioned by it.

The strain of attempting to exist in this limbo causes many Indians to regress to an artificial primitivism, and responses become irrational, childish. Indians become emotionally excited, easily frustrated, and they drink. Physical gratification replaces the vanished moral code, so that violence comes to the surface when the old inhibitions are no longer working. The tension breeds apathy and mental exhaustion, and the Indian has only the strawberry jam of Western culture to sustain him. He is, in addition, indigent and dependent.

Even when the Indian lives in the Western world and, ostensibly, accepts its values, he is taught to be hostile to it, to preserve an Indian culture which exists only in the memories of the old. Young Indian children learn resistance even without understanding why, but the passivity becomes much more hostile. Not only do the children learn to value and repeat the primitive, impulsive, promiscuous and violent behavior of their reserve society, but they define themselves as 'not-white men.' Once the Indian value tradition has been destroyed, they have no choice but to do this. To preserve itself, Indian society will evolve customs deliberately at variance with, or opposite to, dominant white customs. Indian society becomes delinquent society. If they adopt Western techniques, they do so in order to further their own way of life. The more moral the white people, the more immoral the Indians. The vices of the white man are the virtues of the Indian. His reason for existing came to be to plague the white man.

Delinquent Society

From the counterpart of a Plymouth Puritan, the Indian has become a typical slum dweller. His values are the values of the lower class throughout North America. His fear, his rigid responses, his poor education, his apparent stupidity, his unemployability, his immorality, drunkenness and his scavenging, feast-and-famine attitude to life is that of many slum-dwellers. He hates the government, avoids social workers, depends on doctors and evades the police no more than other poor people do.

Cultures, like people and communities, grow. One evolves slowly out of another. Slum society evolved out of Indian society. It appears that a delinquent, aggressive society is now evolving out of the slum society. The lower class still belongs within the social framework, even if at the bottom. A delinquent class, however, is outside the social system, and antagonistic to it. Although the definitions of lower class, poverty, ill health, mental illness, poor education, fit the present Indian society, the definitions of delinquency do also.

The passive, submissive forms of withdrawal which Indians adopted to protect themselves left no room for the expression of anger other than through self-abuse. Much of this anger was expressed within the community. Anger at humiliation still takes the form of wife-beating, drunken brawls with friends, vandalism, theft.

Children are born and grow up in this upside-down culture. They come to see it as normal and adjust their behavior to it. Young Indian delinquents are described as being typical of their race and culture. They are not really delinquent; they are Indian. They share the values of their society, and they only get into trouble when they come in contact with the white man's law. Coming into contact with the police seems to be, from the growing number of Indians in jail and foster homes, an essential part of Indian culture.

The conventional term for these antagonistic Indians is 'sociopath.' It describes violent anti-social behavior which does not seem to be a product of mental illness, but of social environment. A sociopath, viewed in the terms of the society to which he is antagonistic, is described as showing emotional immaturity, compulsive behavior and a need for immediate gratification of impulses. He has a belief in his own immunity to social customs and laws and he is an outsider. The sociopath lacks a conscience or a sense of guilt and anxiety about his behavior and doesn't care about consequences, or enjoys misbehaving. He defends himself by escape, running away, lying, concealment, and his life is governed by no rules, no moral concepts. This behavior is totally pleasure-seeking. Passions are intense and are expressed in extreme physical ways — crime, destruction, fights, lies, cheating — and destructive acts will be repeated again and again.

As evidence of sociopath behavior, resulting from tensions in the home and tensions in relation to the outside world, the conduct of Indian delinquents makes perfect sense.

The language of criminology describes a slum-delinquent culture such as the Indian-Metis culture as a 'subterranean' culture or a 'contra-culture.' It is closely similar to the tight-knit ghettos which develop in large cities, sub-communities in which everyone is, in some way, criminal. So universal is the 'crime', ranging from prostitution to murder, in these areas that the police tend to ignore most of the anti-social behavior and deal with only those offences which are directed at the 'outside,' respectable world. Within a delinquent sub-world, only a tiny fraction of the anti-social behavior is directed outside. Most of it is directed at other residents within the community, who steal from each other, fight each other, drink with each other and sleep with each other's wives and daughters. A child growing up in such a community soon learns his values from the adults, and he too becomes a primitive in order to survive in a violent, emotional, physical world where everyone is concentrating exclusively on staying alive. Children become more dexterous than their parents, better at stealing, fighting and lying. Not working, living on welfare, hating the police, taking advantage of one's neighbour, drinking, and promiscuity become positive values, shared by the entire community.

Thus, as the "underground" characteristics of the white man come to the surface in the Indian stereotype, the underground of respectable white society, hidden from public view, becomes obvious and dominant within Indian society. Indian youths do not form organized gangs—they don't have to. Their whole reserve community is a "gang." They are protected by their parents and the other Indians, since adults also reinforce the standards of delinquent behavior. In Indian and Metis communities, the adults, many with criminal records and most with anti-social behavior, are the gang leaders. Although they do not take direct parts in car thefts or break-ins, they encourage such behavior and set the pattern for it. Young Indian delinquents follow in their father's footsteps. As they grow older, the nature of their offences changes from theft to drinking and fighting.

There is a considerable difference between this kind of anti-society, which now exists on reserves like Roseau River in Manitoba and the Blackfoot in Alberta, and simple cultural disintegration. Many outsiders mistakenly see the ritualized drinking and aggression as evidence of disorganization, but it is not. Such behavior is subtly organized and reinforced. A reserve community is forced to exist as it does because it is a legal entity and because the Indians do not feel welcome elsewhere, and the people therefore adapt to the situation as best they can. Where there is nothing to do getting welfare and stealing cars become employment, and the people become quite happy and content with their lives.

> *"It is necessary to distinquish between the confused, anxiety-ridden, anomic state characteristic of the individual personalities of many marginal men and a much more complex social-cultural phenomenon: the emergence of new, group-reinforced, cultural forms that are nurtured by the frustration, anger and hostility which often follow closely on the heels of . . . bewilderment about 'self' induced by discrimination, rejection and other forms of threat . . . The first produces . . . our Marjorie Morningstars and Sammy Glicks; the second produces our Black Muslims and the night riders of our perennial Ku Klux Klan."*
>
> Martin and Fitzpatrick, *Delinquent Behavior*, New York, Random House, 1964, p. 54

As this observation suggests, this form of delinquency is often closely associated with race. Cultural or national pride is transformed into racial pride, and society splits into groups of mutually hostile factions. With Indians and Metis, hostility is directed against the "white man," or, at least, the white man is used as an excuse for hostility. Because it is the "white man's" police, police are to be evaded, to be called only in extreme emergency. No one co-operates with them, and conflicting information or none at all is provided. The police are forced to ignore the community, leaving themselves open to charges by the Indians that they are remiss in their duty and that crime is their fault, or they have to use various means of intimidation to get information. Then they are accused of pushing the people around. The R.C.M.P. has received a widespread reputation for discriminating against Indians and for being rough and unfair but if anything, the reverse is true. The Indians are prepared to accuse the police no matter what happens.

Government, similarly, is "white man" government and has no relation at all to the Indians who see it as irrevocably opposed to themselves. Government is responsible for making the treaties and for breaking them. Because the government guaranteed hunting rights over Crown land, the Indians assumed that the government also guaranteed the game would remain in the woods and the fish in the lakes. When game disappeared or became insufficient to support the population, the government had "broken its promise". No treaty could provide against the inroads of white settlers or trappers, yet the Indians saw it as a total guarantee of their old way of life. By suggesting that the Indians would be able to hunt and fish as long as the sun shines, the government made an impossible promise. The sun went out some time ago.

Churches are "white" churches which segregate Indians. Schools are "white man's schools." Children are allowed to go in order to learn to read and write. Once they have achieved this much, parental pressure is strong on them to drop out. Parents fear their children will "go white".

Indian children who are issued eyeglasses will break them so they cannot see properly. They do not do homework. They lose their books and papers. They sit in class like bumps on a log. Not only are they handicapped and deprived, they are hostile and frightened. They cannot learn and they *will not* learn. Many students who with great effort progress in residential school to reach grade 10 or 11, will suddenly be summoned home at Christmas to help the family, never to return, and many years later, they are still on the reserve, functionally illiterate and bitter. Similarly, those who venture out to work will frequently return for no apparent reason even when they have been reasonably successful.

The traditional ethic of non-interference, which once fostered strong individualism and self-reliance, now functions to maintain the delinquent society. No one will tell another to his face that he is doing wrong, or interfere to stop a crime or to straighten out a deteriorating social condition. The tribe or band continues to be ruled by subtle anxiety, fear of sorcery and social pressure, but now this pressure is in the direction of gangsterism. An "ethic of recreation" comes into play. When work is no longer meaningful, play is made important, sex is recreation, drinking is partying, theft is an adventure, fights and beatings are entertainment.

The people will not acknowledge their hostility. Parents promise faithfully to make their children attend school or stay out of trouble, but they do not do so. Strong disapproval of drinking is expressed but nothing is done to stop it. When children are burned in a fire after a brawl, everyone is upset but no steps are taken to prevent it happening again. All evil comes from the white man; the Indians are virtuous.

So important is it to hate the white man that women will prostitute themselves to tourists and farmers deliberately as a kind of retaliatory masochism. They are then able to accuse the men of being lecherous. Frequently, white men are invited on to Indian reserves to parties, provided they bring liquor, and the Indians who invite them offer their own wives and daughters to the white men. After a time, the Indians will gang up and chase the white men away or beat them up. The Indians get an even more intense reputation for viciousness and, in the eyes of the Indians, the white men are snivelling cowards. As an excuse for the beating, the white men are accused of corrupting the Indian women.

Indian communities which have developed into criminal undergrounds have managed, with extraordinary ability, to recreate the old hunting life of the past. The society is fluid and unorganized. Social status depends on feats of prowess, although that prowess may now be sexual or alcoholic. Each man tries to outdo the others in vice, and the heroes are the men with the longest criminal records. A reserve like Roseau River has reached this ideal state of being a warlike Indian encampment in the middle of a peaceful, settled peasant farming region. Southern Manitoba is a picture-book: picture-book medieval towns and picture-book Indians. The Indians, like knights of old, gallop out in their old jalopies to pillage and burn the sleeping peasant countryside. The farmers translated their past into the New World and so have the Indians. No peasantry can exist in a feudal system without the knights. The Indians are necessary to the whole structure. Change them and the system would fall apart. The peasants would have nothing to fear; they would no longer be peasants. As long as the Indian braves thunder around striking fear into the people's hearts, everyone is happy.

Chapter 13
Mirror, Mirror . . .

"Who are you? " said the Caterpillar

When the men from Hay Lake, Alberta, carried their crude handmade placards through the streets of Edmonton, few Edmonton citizens noticed. "We're People First, Not Just Indian's." If the watchers saw it and read it, they laughed to themselves at the mis-spelling. The curious turned away, relieved, satisfied, secure. A march down Jasper Ave. was a disturbing, unprecedented thing, but these silent men were only overgrown children, as we always knew they were. Perhaps some people wondered why these men came, what they wanted.

What do they want? The sign answers the question. Occasionally, in the history of a country or a people, a single event, symbol or phrase will sum up, to express in an oblique and startling way the collective desires of that country or that people. It is never an intellectualism, but an act or a word which is crude, unexpected, embarrassing in its open display of emotion. "We're People First, Not Just Indian's" is one of those magic phrases, just as that march on the Alberta Legislature in Edmonton was one of the classic acts in the history of the Indian people of Canada. That childish, mis-spelled, vulgarly obvious slogan is the key.

The cancerous filth, hunger, disease, violence and perversity of Canada's Indian reserves become meaningful when looked at in the light of this phrase, as through a pair of special eyeglasses. The garble of complaints and grievances, of whining, bitter denunciations, of rhetorical fantasies and delusions which erupts periodically from Canada's Indian spokesmen begins, from this perspective, to make sense.

It has been obvious for some time that Canada's Indians are in trouble, but just what the trouble is no one is sure, not even the Indians. "The trouble with the Indian is . . ." has been a very familiar phrase in Canada for one hundred years. Everyone has his diagnosis and his cure. Solutions have varied in popularity, according to the changing fancy of what Canadians estimate as their highest values. The trouble with the Indian has been interpreted in the light of one Canadian myth after another.

At first it was simple heathenism. One could expect little from a savage. However, a few drops of water sprinkled on the savage's head failed to bring about the expected transformation. He would have to be civilized as well as Christianized, and civilization, at the turn of the century, meant farming. The trouble with the Indian was that he had a "natural antipathy" to farming, so farming was not the solution. The trouble with the Indian was ignorance. He was too backward and illiterate to be able to learn farming and he couldn't write or read instructions from the Indian agent or do simple arithmetic. The new answer was educate the Indian just enough for him to make a decent living on the reserve, a little of the three R's and lots of manual training like knitting and raising chickens.

This new emphasis on general learning rather than practical farming came at the end of the depression when almost every Indian, as well as a great proportion of the Canadian population, was living on relief and it was clear from the Saskatchewan dust bowl that farming was not the answer for every Canadian, Ukrainian, Scotsman or Indian. But education has not been the cure. The trouble with the Indian today is poverty. Poverty has been popular since war was declared on it in 1965. Poverty, for the Indian, is believed to result from education, or the lack of it, or the wrong kind. The Indian cannot, or will not, hold a steady job, so that his income falls to subsistence level and he goes on welfare. The solution for this current Indian problem has not been found yet, although thousands of bureaucrats, social workers and politicians are working on it. Soon the solution will be discovered, and soon it too will fail.

All these solutions are based on the premise that Indians are not people.

Of course this is denied by everyone. Bureaucrats and social workers will throw up their hands, aghast. 'No, no, that's not true. Of course Indians are people. We love them. Why, it's anti-democratic, it's un-Canadian to say that! '

Why that strident cry in big black capital letters, carried through the streets by the people of Hay Lake? It is absurd for walking, talking, thinking human beings to feel it necessary, indeed desperately imperative, to affirm, in public, to all the world, that they are, in fact, people. Whoever said they weren't? Indian Affairs? The Church? If the assumption of inhumanity were not there, the Indians would feel no need to affirm their humanity, to begin their campaign with the statement merely of the crude fact of their physical existence, but that's where, apparently, they have to begin — in the humiliation which produced those words: "Not Just Indians."

People who sound as if they know will tell you that the people of Hay Lake are a very poor type of Indian, a very inferior breed, a low-class race, the worst of all Canada's Indians. Perhaps, the implication is, there are real grounds for them to have doubts about their humanity. But, the experts say, take the Mohawk, the Blackfoot, the Blood—that's a different story. These people are advanced, civilized. They don't think the same way.

But they do. In every Indian and Metis community in Canada the same phrase is repeated over and over, perhaps not in the identical words of Hay Lake but similar: "Why don't they treat us like human beings? " "I may be an Indian but I'm just as good as any white man."

I sit on a battered wooden kitchen chair in a gloomy shack that reeks of smoke, stale cooked lard, and urine, listening to the crunch of bones and raw flesh as a cat devours some whitefish from a bucket in the corner. I try not to be frightened or sick as I continue in some aimless, circuitous conversation with which everyone is bored but too polite to say so, staring at the unkempt, round-shouldered, calloused men lounging around the room and wondering how the devil I got there. A bleary-eyed, aged man with broken fingernails, hunched over in the chair beside me turns, puts his face close to mine and, staring at me out of red-rimmed eyes, his hands clenched and his body tensed to shaking like some Old Testament prophet clutching lightning bolts, says, hoarsely: "We are human too."

The word "human" is almost whispered—a word that has to be forced and may bring unforeseeable consequences. There is no anger, no hate, no bitterness, sadness or despair in the words. They are spoken in a flat, monotonous voice with a slight quizzical inflection, a half-question mark, as if generations of tribal wise men had pondered the question of their humanity and had decided, after much heated debate, in the affirmative, but were still not absolutely certain.

The old man—he could be 40 or 70—looks at me wide-eyed with an expectation of argument or contradiction, as if he had opened up a fertile field for conversation. I am dumb. There is just silence and the mutter of the wood in the stove. I am expected to say something, to assure this man that he is a person, but how do I do it?

Do I pat him on the head and say "Why, of course you're a person, my good man." This seems to be what is wanted, but I can't do it. Whatever I said, he wouldn't believe me anyway; he'd still doubt. I smile and say nothing. It's impossible. Unfair. I am angry. I'd like to hit him, or cry. There is no word, no gesture, no right response. Only one word is needed—yes, or no. We look at each other with meaningless significance, characters in a melodrama. He turns away. The white man has failed again.

Canada's Indians are, in the eyes of other Canadians, non-people by the mere fact of being Indian. A great and growing number of other Canadians are non-people too. They don't realize it yet, or, if they realize it, they haven't accepted it. A great many people I have met in the past year would like to walk in the streets carrying black-lettered signs saying "We're People First, Not Just White Men," or "We're People Too, Not Just Teenagers" or "We're People, Not Civil Servants." So far they haven't done it, I suppose because, unlike the people of Hay Lakes, starvation is not the alternative yet.

Starvation, or some other form of extermination, is the alternative for non-people as soon as they become unproductive, as the scrap heap is for used cars or the garbage dump for discolored lettuce leaves. When we speak of people being "used" in a derogatory sense, we seldom take it to its logical conclusion: people, like things, are discarded when their utility has ended, when society finds them too expensive. When a society strips down for a war, even if it is a war on poverty, the luxury items—such as the poor—are the first to go, as the Jews in Nazi Germany were the first, followed by the intellectuals of rival countries.

People used as tools are less efficient than automatic machinery. In an efficient society, as ours is, non-people have become inefficient and therefore expendable. The rising cost of living is making tame pets, such as Indians, difficult to keep.

The solution is obvious, easy, and cheap. It is to build up great garbage dumps, slag heaps and cesspools of useless, non-functioning, waste humans who are hemmed in, kept down, disinfected, shut up, boxed in and ignored until the effort required to keep the lid on the box is too great for the society and it breaks open.

The Indians, rats in psychologists' wire cages, have been our subjects for between 100 and 350 years. They have been on the receiving end of almost every bureaucratic program, religious crusade and psychological gimmick conceived by the Canadian mind. They have been poked, prodded, berated, praised, analyzed, frightened, studied and theorized about. They have been treated like guinea pigs and supermen, like children and saints. They have been ignored, brainwashed, flattered and ridiculed. Each new wave of crusaders which has surged over the reservations, only to stagnate in sloughs and ditches, has been convinced that it was going to succeed, that it was going to turn these savages, these barbarians into civilized human beings, into citizens who would be an integrated and productive part of Canada. Something has always gone wrong. The wells have been poisoned; the wave has turned into slimy backwaters breeding infection. Every day more disinfectant is needed, the walls have to be built higher, the lid is harder to keep on.